SUPPORTING PEOPLE
WITH DEMENTIA AT HOME

Related Titles
in Association with PSSRU

Series Editors:
Professor David Challis, University of Manchester
Professor Martin Knapp, LSE
Professor Ann Netten, University of Kent

Performance Indicators in Social Care for Older People
David Challis, Paul Clarkson and Raymond Warburton
ISBN 978 0 7546 4744 7

Long-Term Care: Matching Resources and Needs
Edited by Martin Knapp, David Challis, José-Luis Fernández and Ann Netten
ISBN 978 0 7546 4341 8

Towards Quality Care
Outcomes for Older People in Care Homes
Caroline Mozley, Caroline Sutcliffe, Heather Bagley,
Lis Cordingley, David Challis, Peter Huxley and Alistair Burns
ISBN 978 0 7546 3172 9

Care Management in Social and Primary Health Care
The Gateshead Community Care Scheme
David Challis, John Chesterman, Rosemary Luckett, Karen Stewart
and Rosemary Chessum
ISBN 978 1 85742 206 1

Equity and Efficiency Policy in Community Care
Needs, Service Productivities, Efficiencies and Their Implications
Bleddyn Davies and José-Luis Fernández
ISBN 978 0 7546 1281 0

Caring for Older People
An Assessment of Community Care in the 1990s
Linda Bauld, John Chesterman, Bleddyn Davies,
Ken Judge and Roshni Mangalore
ISBN 978 0 7546 1280 3

The Personal Social Services Research Unit is based at three branches, at the University of Kent, the London School of Economics and the University of Manchester. The Unit undertakes social and health care research, supported mainly by the Department of Health, and focusing particularly on policy research and analysis of equity and efficiency in community care, long-term care and related areas – including services for elderly people, people with mental health problems and children in care.

The PSSRU website is at www.pssru.ac.uk.

Supporting People
with Dementia at Home
Challenges and Opportunities for the 21st Century

DAVID CHALLIS
CAROLINE SUTCLIFFE
JANE HUGHES
University of Manchester, UK

RICHARD VON ABENDORFF
PAMELA BROWN
JOHN CHESTERMAN
formerly PSSRU, University of Kent, UK

at the University of Kent,
the London School of Economics
and the University of Manchester

ASHGATE

This work was undertaken by the PSSRU, which receives support from the Department of Health; the views expressed in this publication are those of the authors and not necessarily those of the Department of Health.

Published by
Ashgate Publishing Limited   Ashgate Publishing Company
Wey Court East   Suite 420
Union Road   101 Cherry Street
Farnham   Burlington
Surrey, GU9 7PT   VT 05401-4405
England   USA

www.ashgate.com

British Library Cataloguing in Publication Data
Supporting people with dementia at home : challenges and
  opportunities for the 21st century.
  1. Dementia--Patients--Home care. 2. Dementia--Patients--
  Services for--Evaluation.
  I. Challis, David, 1948- II. University of Kent at
  Canterbury. Personal Social Services Research Unit.
  362.1'9683-dc22

Library of Congress Cataloging-in-Publication Data
Supporting people with dementia at home : challenges and opportunities for the 21st
century / by David Challis ... [et al.].
    p. cm. -- (In association with PSSRU)
  Includes bibliographical references and index.
  ISBN 978-0-7546-7479-5 (hardback) -- ISBN 978-0-7546-9872-2 (ebook)
  1. Dementia--Patients--Home care. I. Challis, David, 1948-
  RC521.S86 2009
  616.8'3--dc22

                                                          2009024258

ISBN: 978-0-7546-7479-5 (hbk)
ISBN: 978-0-7546-9872-2 (ebk)

10/15/10

Contents

List of Figures and Boxes

Figures

Boxes

List of Tables

List of Abbreviations

ACT	Assertive Community Treatment
AdHOC	Aged in Home Care Project
ADL	Activities of daily living
AT	Assistive Technology
BRS	Behaviour Rating Scale
CAPE	Clifton Assessment Procedures for the Elderly
CAPRE	Case Planning and Review form
CARE	Comprehensive Assessment and Referral Evaluation
CMHN	Community Mental Health Nurse
CMHT	Community Mental Health Team
CPA	Care Programme Approach
CSIP	Care Services Improvement Partnership
CSSIW	Care and Social Services Inspectorate Wales
DHSS	Department of Health and Social Security
DSM-III-R	Diagnostic and Statistical Manual of Mental Disorders, Third Edition, Revised
GP	General Practitioner
HM Government	Her Majesty's Government
HSC	Health Service Circular
ICM	Intensive Case Management
LAC	Local Authority Circular
LCMS	Lewisham Case Management Scheme
MHOA	Lewisham Mental Health of Older Adults
NHS	National Health Service
NICE	National Institute for Clinical Excellence
NSFOP	National Service Framework for Older People
NVQ	National Vocational Qualification
OBS	Organic Brain Score
PSI	Psychosocial Intervention
POW	Production of Welfare
PSSRU	Personal Social Services Research Unit
RC/AL	Residential Care/Assisted Living Facilities
SAP	Single Assessment Procedure
SCIE	Social Care Institute for Excellence
SSD	Social Services Department
SSI	Social Services Inspectorate
SW	Social Work

SWSG	Social Work Services Group
UK	United Kingdom
USA	United States of America

Foreword

There are issues of which it might be written that *'plus ça change, plus ç'est la même chose'*. Too few are evaluated in depth – indeed, in the USA, the number of full and rigorous evaluations of systemic changes seems actually to have diminished. This book illustrates the benefits of the kind of research programme which emerges when such a *plus ça change* issue is first formulated in contemporary terms, whose longevity matches the duration of the issue, whose foci and content adapt to changing contexts and ideas, and which make broad evaluations of models whose logics are highly explicit. Its depth, perspective and chiaroscuro illustrate how earlier programme argument has been deepened and broadened, how ideas and hypotheses from earlier generations have been developed and tested, and also how continuities in argument, collection designs, measurement devices and other features of the PSSRU framework, the Production of Welfare approach, have contributed to one another to allow more precise and illuminating analysis.

Readers will be interested in different themes to which the book contributes. Two particularly caught my eye.

One is matching care management inputs of all kinds to user and system circumstances and values, what during the early nineties the Department of Health christened *'differentiation'*. This is perhaps the key theme of the study as it is a key theme in the history of care management discussion in this country and abroad. Early experiments showed that for some users, improving the performance of care management tasks could allow more benefit to be produced from the resources. From then on, one of the most important intellectual challenges became to construct a body of knowledge and logic to help achieve requisite matching, and as part of doing so, to secure systems with the requisite variety in care management (and service) policy. The authors and collaborators of this publication have long been among those collecting and collating evidence from leading countries both in the UK and further afield. This text illustrates how greatly the Lewisham Case Management Scheme and related projects contributed to the theoretical development.

In this study, like other PSSRU experiments, matching the content of the main service inputs to the user was tackled by internalising their management within the team, not by creating a complete purchaser-provider split at this level. The analysis reported here strongly suggests that for this key subgroup, as for subjects of previous PSSRU research, the early purely brokerage model of case management was unlikely to be the best approach, although its logic clearly appeared tempting to policy-makers and managers.

Related is the *intensity* of care management inputs in time, expertise and other resources. The book further develops an important argument that post-community care reform outcomes are worse for many highly prioritised users because those who would benefit most from them have too rarely had access to care management of the intensity and user-bespoke arrangements designed into almost all of the PSSRU experiments, including the Lewisham study. Thus, a local care system is imbalanced and is inefficient unless first, it provides a variety of care management with respect to intensity (and other characteristics); and second, provides the processes that create a good match between user circumstances and care management model.

The text does indeed demonstrate the benefits created by the service's intensity and other characteristics and 'arrangements', and so suggests potential benefits of similar development elsewhere for local policy-makers. It shows how essentials of the original project were absorbed into a wider service system for older people with dementia to provide the highest of the three 'levels' of care management which policy makers recommended and considered to be developing more generally by the late nineties, but with the important difference that at this level, what the service provides is likely to be atypically intensive, specialised and effective. That so many elements of the original scheme have survived to the present is itself evidence of the strength of the model. In this respect it complements earlier PSSRU work, particularly that undertaken in Gateshead.

A second contribution to catch my eye is the discussion of *integrating resources hitherto provided in different policy silos.* The Lewisham experience is particularly informative about the integration of health and social care resources. It confirms that the task is to balance differing objectives of various health and social care paradigms. Moreover, it confirms that it is naïve to imagine that simply merging social care into the national health service will suffice, or indeed, greatly improve the balance for most users, despite the interdependence of inputs and outcomes across health and social care.

The results illustrate how service users in different circumstances and with different values and wishes are best managed with arrangements built around different degrees and nature of partnership or integration, job-re-engineering, and the like. Had well-conceived and fully evaluated experimental programmes (*inter alia* measuring all the costs and outcomes for users and others) preceded policy action, there might have been much more grounded logic to guide the design of attempts to improve outcomes during the late 1990s by inter-silo integration of some kind. We must be grateful that the 2005 Green Paper, *Independence, Well-being and Choice*, and more recently the *National Dementia Strategy* illustrate how central government continues to accept responsibility for key features of the success of the system. Furthermore, we look forward to the evolution of a policy which achieves a balance that truly reflects the wishes, needs and interests of users and carers, particularly if over the next few decades, the balance between demands and resources worsens.

This book provides evidence and argument important for tackling some of the long-standing challenges of care for older people with dementia now and during the challenging period we are now entering.

Bleddyn Davies
Emeritus Professor of Social Policy,
The London School of Economics and the University of Kent
Director of PSSRU at the University of Kent from 1974–1999

Acknowledgements

The publication of a National Dementia Strategy in 2009 makes the contents of this book particularly timely. It has been in the gestation period for some time and many people have assisted both in the conduct of the research and in the preparation of the manuscript. Unfortunately not all can be mentioned personally here.

We are particularly grateful to the older people and their carers who allowed themselves to be interviewed at length on a number of occasions. After much thought, we decided to use the term 'client' in this book, to describe the older people with dementia who were the subjects of the study, and the term 'carer' to describe relatives, friends and neighbours who provided informal and unpaid care to the clients. To some extent, the choice of terminology was arbitrary and in no way diminishes the important contribution made by these individuals.

Our collaboration with colleagues in what is now known as the Mental Health for Older Adults service within the South London and Maudsley NHS Foundation Trust, covering the borough of Lewisham, is longstanding. Professors Elaine Murphy and Alastair Macdonald facilitated the development of the research study together with Amanda Edwards on behalf of the local authority. More recently, Carolyn Richardson arranged for us to meet members of the current service. Lis Hunter, formerly case manager in the initial study, provided an interesting historical perspective when the book was being drafted.

Colleagues in the Personal Social Services Research Unit have provided assistance in the drafting of this manuscript. Glenys Harrison and Sue Martin have provided secretarial support. Paul Clarkson provided us with valuable comments as did former colleagues Reba Bhaduri and Karen Stewart.

Finally we should like to thank the Department of Health which funds the Personal Social Services Research Unit and The Gatsby Charitable Foundation who provided initial funding for this research.

David Challis, Caroline Sutcliffe,
Jane Hughes, Richard von Abendorff,
Pamela Brown and John Chesterman

Chapter 1
Older People with Dementia:
The Development of Community Care

Introduction

Providing integrated and co-ordinated community-based care for older people with dementia has gained prominence against a background of an ageing population and greater financial restraints in many countries. In the UK the number of people with dementia is growing rapidly, and is forecast to rise by 38 per cent between 2006 and 2021, with the greatest increase among those over 80 years of age (Knapp et al., 2007). Indeed, this age group, which is more likely to need nursing, residential or home care, is expected to increase from 2.6 million in 2004 to 5 million by 2031 (Government Actuary's Department, 2006). Moreover, the numbers of older people with cognitive impairment are projected to increase at a faster rate than those with functional disability alone (Melzer et al., 1997; Comas-Herrara et al., 2007).

Increasingly, government policies are focusing upon meeting the needs of frail older people in their own homes. However, a significant proportion of those requiring community care services are likely to be the very old and those with cognitive impairment (Melzer et al., 1999). Additionally, in view of a continual downward trend in care home provision (Department of Health, 2001a; 2002a; Social Services Inspectorate (SSI), 2003; National Statistics, 2007), a larger number of older people with dementia will require support in the community. Care management remains the mechanism for assessment and providing for needs, with an emphasis on a transparent process for the allocation of resources and increased flexibility in their provision (Committee of Public Accounts, 2008; Department of Health, 2008a; 2009a). For older people with complex needs including those with dementia it is likely that this care will continue to be co-ordinated by a care manager (Cm 6499, 2005; Cm 6737, 2006).

In the last two decades of the twentieth century there was increasing recognition of the importance of the contribution of carers to the care of vulnerable adults on a day-to-day basis (Cm 849, 1989; Cm 4169, 1998) and also in respect of older people with dementia (Levin et al., 1989; Myers and MacDonald, 1996). The White Papers *Caring for People* (Cm 849, 1989) and *Modernising Social Services* (Cm 4169, 1998) began to make explicit the crucial contribution of carers to the support of vulnerable adults. The latter allowed more potential for carers to exert influence over service provision, particularly with the extension of direct payments to this group of people (Department of Health, 2003a). However, despite this focus upon greater flexibility and choice for carers, it is apparent that, due partly to the rising age of the caring population, the availability of informal care may be outstripped by increases in the care needs of older people (Wanless, 2006; Pickard et al., 2007), leading to greater demand for formal care services.

The Lewisham Case Management Scheme (LCMS) described in detail in this book, was designed to provide an appropriate community-based approach to the long-term care of older people with a diagnosis of dementia, identified as having unmet needs and likely to be at risk of entry to a care home, despite input from statutory services. The scheme was located in an existing service setting, a specialist multidisciplinary community mental health team for older people. Its importance lies not only in being one of a family of care management projects designed to provide effective community-based long-term care for older people that spanned the health and social service divide (Challis and Davies, 1986; Challis et al., 1995; 2002a), but also because it was distinctive in its target population. Its subsequent evolution into mainstream service provision reflects its relevance to current developments in the care of older people with mental health problems. The research component of the scheme played an integral role in the management, planning, and ongoing development of the scheme, and therefore programme fidelity (Bond and McGrew, 1995; Teague et al., 1998) until it became a mainstream service within the multidisciplinary team. The research study compared individuals in one community mental health team for older people receiving case management, to those in a similar community mental health setting without a case management service. Older people were recruited to each arm of the study by applying similar referral criteria and were interviewed at uptake and again at six and twelve months, as were their carers. Service utilisation and cost information, which was collected on a comprehensive basis, was tracked through time over a twelve-month period.

The scheme at the heart of this book encompasses many of the principles and practices central to the programme of reforms embodied in the National Service Framework for Older People (NSFOP) (Department of Health, 2001b). It also demonstrates the importance of the link between specialist health care and social care in the care of older people with dementia (Philp and Appleby, 2005) and the personalisation of care with its emphasis on the flexible use of resources to meet assessed need (Department of Health, 2008a; 2009a). As a prelude to this description, the first two chapters of the book provide a historical review of the policy context in which care management arrangements have evolved together with the processes intrinsic to it and the organisational context in which it is undertaken. Thus, this chapter reviews a range of policy initiatives central to the evolution of community care, particularly in the context of the development of services for older people with dementia, and for their carers and provides an introduction to the book as a whole.

The Development of Community-based Services for Older People

Arrangements for the care of vulnerable older people, including those with mental health problems, have changed in many ways since the advent of the Welfare State in the late 1940s. However, there have been few developments specific to the needs of older people with mental health problems and particularly for those with dementia. The review of policy initiatives in the post war era detailed in Box 1.1 highlights this. Indeed many of the developments were not specific to older people but intended to benefit all vulnerable adults, particularly in the context of home-based care. However, early in this period there were three particularly relevant to the care of older people with dementia.

First, as described by Means and Smith (1998), most of the care that was provided by the state was institution based and of poor quality, and it was recognised that this state of affairs could not continue. In 1946, the Nuffield Provincial Hospitals Trust in *The Hospital Surveys: The Domesday Book of the Hospital Services* reported problems with the care of older people and poor conditions in public assistance institutions. The following year the Seebohm Rowntree Committee (1947) survey of old people's homes also described poor conditions in institutions housing over 1000 people, and recommended changes to both the structure and organisation of the establishments. More than a decade later it appeared that little had changed despite the creation of a health service that was free at the point of use and the requirement placed on local authorities to provide residential care to those in need irrespective of age. Townsend (1957; 1962) described the 'warehousing' of older people in former workhouses that had become residential care homes. Concurrently he reported the scarcity of support services for older people who were not placed in institutional care (Townsend, 1962). Robb (1967) detailed poor standards of care, including allegations of ill-treatment within hospital provision for elderly mentally infirm patients. However, it was almost a decade later that the extent to which older people with mental health problems were being admitted to and assessed in mental hospitals became clear. To counter this, the White Paper *Better Services for the Mentally Ill* (Cmnd 6233, 1975) recommended that their needs should be assessed at home or in out-patient clinics where possible.

This reflects the second theme relevant to the care of older people with dementia: the fragmented and uneven development of community-based services for vulnerable adults. Many community-based services for older people were provided by voluntary organisations until the 1970s and these were neither regular nor extensive in coverage. Whilst the first official mention of 'community care' has been attributed to the 1957 Report of the Royal Commission on Mental Illness and Mental Deficiency (Cmnd 169, 1957) which preceded the 1959 Mental Health Act, there was little evidence of its systematic development in respect of any user group between 1945 and the publication of the White Paper *Growing Older* in 1981 (Cmnd 8173, 1981). This advocated that older people should remain at home rather than be admitted to long-term care, and also emphasised that the principal role of the state was to meet basic care needs. However, it was not until 1977

Box 1.1   Community care: policy developments 1942–1996

Date	Policy initiative	Key points
1942	Inter-Departmental Committee on Social Insurance and Allied Services (Cmnd 6404) Beveridge Report	Recommended the reform and extension of the social security system and the creation of a National Health Service.
1946	National Health Service Act	Established free health care at the point of use and marked the decline of the old system of public assistance institutions under the Poor Law.
1948	National Assistance Act	Placed a duty on local authorities to provide residential care for those in need of care due to age or other circumstances.
1959	Mental Health Act	Reoriented mental health services away from institutional care towards care in the community.
1962	National Assistance (Amendment) Act	Permitted local authorities to provide meals on wheels.
1963	Health and Welfare: the Development of Community Care (Cmnd 1973)	Reaffirmed government commitment to de-institutionalisation and promotion of community alternatives. Highlighted wide variation in home help provision across the country and staff shortage.
1968	Health Services and Public Health Act	Local authorities given responsibility for overall welfare of older people and encouraged development of home care for older people.
1970	The Chronically Sick and Disabled Persons Act	Strengthened the duty on local authorities in relation to assessment.
1970	Local Authority Social Services Act	Created new local authority departments to unite previously fragmented social work functions and provided a single point of entry for all.
1973	NHS Reorganisation Act	Responsibility for social care services provided in hospital transferred to local authorities.
1975	Better Services for the Mentally Ill (Cmnd 6233)	Recommended assessment of elderly patients' needs should take place at home or in out-patient clinics.
1977	National Health Service Act	Placed a duty on local authorities to provide home care.
1981	Growing Older (Cmnd 8173)	Advocated the concept of the 'enabling authority' providing a framework of services to complement existing assistance from family networks and the notion of care by the community.
1989	Caring for People: Community Care in the Next Decade and Beyond (Cm 849)	Objectives included the development of community services to allow people to receive care at home and the introduction of assessment and care management to achieve these goals with choice and independence as the underlying themes.
1990	NHS and Community Care Act	Established local authorities as the lead agency in community care requiring the development of care management systems, introduced a complaints system, a new inspection system and a new funding structure for residential and nursing home care.

that the provision of domiciliary (home) care, of which older people were the main beneficiaries, became mandatory. Moreover, whilst the reforms of the 1970s were designed to create a more co-ordinated approach to the provision of care at home for vulnerable adults, one of the consequences of the changes was that the division of responsibilities between providers of health and social care became more apparent.

A third theme is the extent to which developments in the community care policies for older people focused upon the provision of community-based services as an alternative to long-term residential, nursing and hospital care. Two reports by the Audit Commission in the mid-1980s were critical of the effectiveness of government community care policy in a number of areas (Audit Commission, 1985; 1986). The availability of payments to those entering private care homes without any assessment of their needs, created 'perverse incentives' to enter residential care rather than have care at home. The failure to transfer the balance of care from hospitals and other residential institutions to community-based care was highlighted, and also a lack of clarity and cost-effectiveness of existing targeting policies on those with the greatest needs was noted (Gostick et al., 1997). In response, the White Paper *Caring for People* (Cm 849, 1989) set out the government's commitments to encourage older people with physical or mental health problems to live independently in their own homes or within 'homely settings in the community', correcting what was described as a 'built-in bias towards residential and nursing home care' (para 1.1). A number of objectives were proposed, of which two were central to the provision of community care of older people: making needs assessment and case management a cornerstone of care; and promoting domiciliary care, day care and respite care to enable older people to remain in their own homes where possible. This commitment to promote independent living and also provide tailored services to suit individual needs was further endorsed in the White Paper *Modernising Social Services* (Cm 4169, 1998) by the incoming Labour administration of 1997.

Policy developments in the twenty-first century in England have emphasised the importance of addressing both the health and social care needs of older people in a co-ordinated manner, as illustrated in Box 1.2. A recurrent theme in many policy documents since 1997 has been the provision of integrated health and social care. This is apparent in two guises. The first is in the range of services available for specific conditions, such as mental health problems in older people and second, the organisational structures through which they are delivered. Both have important implications for the development of services for older people with dementia.

With respect to specific conditions, the NSFOP (Department of Health, 2001b) described a 'programme of action and reform' (foreword, ii), regarding the provision of health and social care for vulnerable older people. This comprised targets for reform and development of particular services relevant to conditions more common amongst this group including one to promote good mental health in older people and improve the treatment and support of older people with dementia and

Box 1.2   Community care: policy developments 1997–2007

Date	Policy initiative	Key points
1998	Modernising Social Services (Cm 4169)	Proposed services to help adults to live independently. Created more consistent service provision to ensure that services met individual needs. Also proposed improved joint working, more integrated health and social care and high standards of care. Permitted direct payments for people aged 65 and over.
1999	Health Act	Created new flexibilities for the NHS and social care to work together to provide better integrated services which focused on individual needs.
2000	Care Standards Act	Revised consolidating legislation which included a regulatory framework for care homes and introduced regulation into domiciliary care.
2000	The NHS Plan: A plan for investment. A plan for reform (Cm 4818-I)	Proposed the establishment of a new multi-purpose organisation to commission and be responsible for health and social care. Introduced Intermediate Care as a new tier of services to allow people to remain at home immediately after or through a period of acute illness. Made a commitment to care by a registered nurse free for all regardless of the setting in which it was provided.
2001	National Service Framework for Older People (Department of Health, 2001b)	Designed to raise quality and decrease variations in service provision by specifying standards and service models, identifying strategies to support their implementation and specifying milestones to monitor progress. The mental health of older people was identified as a discrete area of enquiry.
2001	Health and Social Care Act	Established Care Trusts to commission and/or provide integrated health and social care with the aim of improving the co-ordination of assistance to vulnerable users.
2005	Independence, Well-being and Choice (Cm 6499)	Developed a strategic commissioning framework across all agencies to ensure a balance between prevention, meeting low level needs and providing intensive care for those with complex needs. Confirmed the role of care managers in co-ordination of care for older people with complex needs.
2006	Our health, our care, our say: a new direction for community services (Cm 6737)	Aimed to improve prevention services; give people more choice in social and primary care services; address inequalities and improve access to community services; and increase support to people with long-term needs. Provided older people with greater control by the extension of self-assessment and the introduction of individual budgets.
2006	A new ambition for old age – Next steps in implementing the NSFOP (Department of Health, 2006)	Set out priorities for the second half of the ten-year NSFOP programme. Established a Department of Health board to respond to the challenges in developing older adult mental health services. Aimed to secure comprehensive specialist mental health services for older adults, particularly community mental health teams, memory clinics, and liaison services.
2007	Putting People First – A shared vision and commitment to the transformation of Adult Social Care (HM Government, 2007)	Set out a programme of change for Adult Social Care, developing personalised services. Emphasised a common assessment process, person-centred planning and personal budgets.

depression. It specified that the latter should be achieved by the early recognition and management of mental health problems and by facilitating access to specialist care. Although it has been recognised within these policy developments that the particular characteristics of older people with mental health problems are distinct from those of other groups, and appropriate service arrangements relating to health and social care have been specified in response to this, few initiatives were particular to older people with dementia. In contrast, it is noteworthy that in Ireland, plans were set out specifically for the care of this group of people. An objective in the Health Strategy *Quality and Fairness: A Health System for You* (Department of Health and Children, 2001) was to implement a seven to ten year rolling action plan for dementia, following recommendations of the Irish National Council on Ageing and Older People (O'Reilly and O'Shea, 1999; Quill, 2002). The latter advocated a model of good practice for dementia care for older people and their carers in Ireland by focusing on the development of an infrastructure of health and social care services in the community specific to the needs of older people with dementia and their carers. It has facilitated the expansion and integration of community and hospital-based old age psychiatry services, and the establishment of new units for treating older people with dementia (Department of Health and Children, 2005).

In England, policy initiatives have included those designed to promote more integrated organisational structures for the delivery of health and social care, although these have not been disease or condition specific as, for example, in Ireland. Of particular importance in this context was the Health and Social Care Act of 2001 which enabled, for example, integrated Care Trusts to provide a range of services to meet the health and social care needs of a defined target group. This proposed integrated care with the NHS and other services in order to improve service delivery and facilitate the development of organisations to achieve this goal (Cm 4169, 1998; Cm 4818-I, 2000). Interestingly, this incorporates some of the features of vertical integration, a term traditionally associated with the literature of economics (Johnston and Lawrence, 1991) but also applied to organisational theory and the developing phenomenon of partnerships (Challis et al., 1998a; Hudson and Hardy, 2002). In the context of the joint provision of health and social care, vertical integration has been described as the bringing together of different processes or stages that are sequentially related to the same outcome for an identified group requiring care (Challis, 1998). An example of this as suggested by Hudson and colleagues (2002) is a Care Trust, which provides both secondary health care and community-based services incorporating health and social care. This partnership is a concept which is regarded as an important mechanism for promoting the delivery of integrated health and social care for vulnerable adults, including older people with dementia, and, as such, is central to the government's modernisation agenda for health and social care (Cm 4169, 1998; Cm 4818-I, 2000; Cm 6737, 2006). Moreover, Challis (1998) has argued that this organisational construct is consistent with an agenda of targeting, continuity of provision and long-term care for vulnerable people, which are key features of intensive care management (Challis et al., 1998a).

Another theme in service development during this period has been the creation of fairer and more consistent services across the UK – with due regard to the Human Rights Act of 1998, as reflected in subsequent guidance (Cm 4169, 1998; Department of Health, 2002b,c). In addition, the necessity for appropriate support for ethnic minority groups has also been highlighted within the care management process (Cm 4169, 1998; SSI, 1998a) as required by the 1976 Race Relations Act and the 2000 Race Relations (Amendment) Act. Furthermore, principles and practice must reflect the Equality Standard for Local Government introduced in 2001 as a tool to mainstream the principle of equality in service provision and employment and to combat discrimination associated with race, gender and disability (Cm 4169, 1998; Improvement and Development Agency, 2007). In respect of older people with dementia, service developments need to evolve in ways that promote good equality practice, demonstrating that they meet both the needs and expectations of all service users. In pursuit of the principle of equity, it is further envisaged that all individuals eligible for publicly funded care will have a personal budget. This will permit transparency in the process of allocating resources and will be separate from the identification of the means by which a care package is devised (Department of Health, 2008a; 2009a). This is also relevant to the provision of community-based care for older people with dementia. Moreover the provision of greater resources and the importance of accessible and suitable community care for this group of vulnerable older people remain of paramount importance in view of the projected increase in their number (Knapp et al., 2007). More recently the transformation of social care (HM Government, 2007) was produced, giving a further focus upon common assessment, self assessment, person-centred planning, and personal budgets and reinforcing a number of other features of the 2006 White Paper (Cm 6737, 2006). Most recently, the Dementia Strategy highlighted improved community-based services for older people (Department of Health, 2009b, 47–50).

The Contribution of Carers

The policy of maintaining vulnerable older people in the community has placed increasing reliance on their informal carers for support and care. Family carers of older people, who comprise around three-quarters of all carers (Pickard, 2004), have been the main source of this support (Twigg, 1998; Pickard, 1999). The importance of their support has become greater due to the projected rise in the numbers of people aged 85 and over (Wanless, 2006) who will need more care (Wittenberg et al., 2001). Historically, community care services were provided for older people living at home with little support (Pickard, 1999), although carers have benefited from specific carer services such as support groups and breaks from caring, or from services directed at the cared for person, for example day care or respite care (Twigg, 1992; Pickard, 2004).

Twigg and Atkin (1994) have provided a widely quoted conceptual framework comprising four models to describe the response of service agencies to carers. In the first model, carers are regarded as 'taken for granted' resources, and in the second, agencies work alongside carers as co-workers, integrating their work with the support provided by carers. This takes account of carers' interests and well-being, yet the person requiring support remains the priority. In the third model, carers are viewed as co-clients in need of assistance in their own right, with services designed to relieve their situation and improve well-being, in some cases at the expense of the older person. For example, the older person may receive respite care away from their own home, primarily to provide relief for the carer. The fourth model assumes that the role of the carer is superseded and their care input is no longer required, maximising independence for both client and carer and its focus is more upon the relationship between younger disabled adults and their carers. Subsequently, the concept of carers as experts was coined (Nolan et al., 1996). This describes those who demonstrate skills and expertise in caring which have developed over time (Nolan and Keady, 2001). The use of two elements of Twigg and Atkin's conceptual framework, carers as a resource and carers as co-clients in their own right, are particularly relevant to this scheme both in the emergent policy context and the research study at the heart of this book.

A number of policy initiatives following the community care reforms in relation to the carers of older people are illustrated in Box 1.3. In advance of these, the Griffiths Report (1988) acknowledged that the majority of informal care was provided by family, friends and neighbours, and the role of public services was by definition, to 'fill the gap' or provide care where informal care had broken down. It placed carers firmly in the role of a resource in its recommendation that care packages to individuals should build on the 'available contribution of informal carers and neighbourhood support' (para 1.3.3). One of the goals of community care was therefore, to give support and relief to carers coping with the stress of caring for a dependent person. Although the White Paper *Caring for People* (Cm 849, 1989) took further many of the principal themes of the Griffiths Report, ensuring that service providers made practical support for carers a high priority, and 'taking account' of carer needs, neither recognised carers as service users in their own right.

It can be argued that the concept of carers as co-clients was demonstrated in the 1995 Carers (Recognition and Services) Act and strengthened by the 2000 Carers and Disabled Children Act. These were designed to provide a framework for greater rights for carers and to ensure that their needs were recognised and assessed. However the extent to which this has been achieved is unclear, particularly in respect of the carers of older people with dementia, since evidence to date is scarce. It has been suggested that carers were unaware that they had received an assessment and that their needs were often overlooked by service providers (Clarke, 1999; Wood, 1999; Moriarty and Webb, 2000). Subsequently it has been acknowledged that carers are 'expert partners' in care, who should

Box 1.3   Community care: policy developments for carers 1988–2008

Date	Policy initiative	Key points
1989	Caring for People. Community Care in the Next Decade and Beyond (Cm 849)	Objectives included the provision of practical support and advice for carers, and tailoring care packages to meet both client and carer needs by supporting the carer in their role.
1995	Carers (Recognition and Services) Act (Department of Health 1996a)	Formalised the right to people providing 'substantial' care on a 'regular' basis to ill, elderly or disabled friends or relatives to ask for a separate assessment. Required local authorities to take their views and results of their assessment into account when deciding on services for those they cared for.
1999	Caring About Carers. A national strategy for carers (Department of Health, 1999a)	Recognised need for carers to have their own health needs more appropriately addressed, and have a voice in the planning and provision of services. It also gave powers to local authorities to provide services for carers.
1999	Better Care, Higher Standards. A charter for long term care (Dept of Health/Dept of Environment, Transport and Regions, 1999)	Provided guidance for local housing, health and social services in six areas, two of which related to helping users and carers specifically.
2000	Carers and Disabled Children Act	Allowed carers to be assessed even if the person they cared for had refused an assessment or service. Required local authorities to provide direct payments to carers for services to assist in their caring role and introduced a voucher system to facilitate flexible use of respite care.
2004	Carers (Equal Opportunities) Act	Placed a duty upon councils to inform carers of their rights to an assessment of their needs. They were obliged to consider how service provision may impact upon carers' lives, in relation to work, education or training, and leisure activities.
2006	Our health, our care, our say: a new direction for community services (Cm 6737)	Aimed to establish a dedicated helpline for carers and ensure that every council has home-based respite care for those in crisis. Allocation of funding for an Expert Carer Programme to provide training for informal carers.
2008	Carers at the heart of 21st century families and communities (HM Government, 2008)	Identified a number of short and long-term priorities for a 10 year programme of support for carers. Areas included information and advice, carer breaks, emotional and physical health of carers, financial benefits and employment. Has advocated investment in assistive technology and telecare to improve support offered to the carer and cared-for person.

be permitted a more central role in care processes with access to integrated and personalised resources (HM Government, 2008). The implications of this are yet to be determined. The importance of implementing this for people with dementia is highlighted in the Dementia Strategy (Department of Health, 2009b, 49–50).

The Structure of the Book

The remainder of this book explores care management arrangements in the context of care of the older person with dementia, the model of case management, the research design, and how the scheme evolved during the life of the research study. It describes the development of a paid helper service, outcomes for the older people with dementia and their carers, variations in costs and finally the subsequent evolution of the scheme into mainstream service provision. The study addresses the objectives of the Dementia Strategy (Department of Health, 2009b), particularly those of improved community support services and the carers' strategy for dementia.

Chapter 2 explores issues in the development of care management arrangements for older people with dementia. Following this, Chapter 3 describes the model of case management for older people with dementia as undertaken in Lewisham, and outlines the unique features of its service setting at the inception of this research. In Chapter 4, the research methodology is outlined including the choice and types of measures used, case selection and components of case matching. The procedures used for interviewing clients and carers, and for evaluation of costs and outcomes, service provision and practice, are also explained. Chapter 5 examines and evaluates case management practice within the scheme as it evolved during the research study. It describes the processes of case finding and screening, assessment of need, care planning, monitoring and case review, case closure and discusses the role of advocacy in respect of older people with dementia. Chapter 6 describes the development, management and evolution of the paid helper service, a specialist domiciliary service for older people with dementia and outlines the main characteristics of the paid helpers, their recruitment, and the management and organisation of the service. Chapters 7 and 8 describe the outcomes for the older people and carers in the experimental and control groups. The former examines the success of the scheme in terms of the older people's needs and its effect on their quality of life. The latter describes the extent to which carers were relieved of the tasks of caring, and examines the influence of the scheme on carers' quality of life and level of strain. In Chapter 9 the effectiveness of the scheme in terms of costs to agencies, carers and aggregated costs to society for the experimental and control groups is explored. Chapter 10 describes the factors associated with variations in cost for the older people in both groups and examines differences in cost for a variety of older person and carer characteristics. Lastly, Chapter 11 examines the subsequent evolution of the scheme within the local network of health and social care for older people with mental health problems and reviews the relevance of the research findings in the context of the current policy framework.

Chapter 2

Care Management for Older People
with Dementia

Introduction

It has been suggested that six characteristics distinguish care management from other service-related activities (Challis et al., 1995). These are shown in Box 2.1. As noted in the previous chapter the enduring relevance of care management in the context of community-based care for older people with dementia has been highlighted (Cm 6499, 2005; Committee of Public Accounts, 2008), and defines it as a model of long-term care (Challis et al., 1990), in contrast to short-term task-centred interventions (Reid and Shyne, 1969; Goldberg et al., 1985; Burns et al., 2005). However, specialist care management for older people with dementia remains an area of practice in which there is much scope for innovation and development.

Prior to reviewing the development of care management arrangements for older people with mental health problems and particularly those with dementia, it is relevant to reflect on the definitions and terminologies used. The Griffiths Report referred to a 'care manager' (Griffiths, 1988, para 6.6), whose purpose

Box 2.1   Characteristics of care management

Functions	Co-ordination and linkage of care services
Goals	Providing continuity and integrated care; increased opportunity for home-based care; promote client wellbeing; making better use of resources
Core tasks	Case-finding and screening; assessment; care planning; monitoring and review; case closure
Characteristics of recipients	Long-term care needs; multiple service need
Main features	Intensity of involvement; breadth of services spanned; lengthy duration of involvement
Multi-level response	Linking practice-level activities with broader resource and agency-level activities

Source: Challis et al. (1995)

was to oversee the functions of assessment and re-assessment; however, the subsequent White Paper '*Caring for People*' (Cm 849, 1989 para 3.1.3) used the term 'case manager' to describe the same role. Following this, Department of Health guidelines demonstrated a preference for the term 'care management'. These terms have been interchangeable in many jurisdictions in North America. In Northern Ireland both terms were initially used with an explicit distinction made between them (Department of Health and Social Services, 1991) although this is no longer the case (Department of Health, Social Services and Public Safety, 2006). Both English and Welsh guidance for local authorities and health services (National Assembly for Wales, 2002; Department of Health, 2005a) suggested 'case management' as an alternative term for 'care management'. However, it has been suggested that the debate about terminology demonstrates the importance of the clarity of the meaning attached to the process rather than the precise terms used (Challis et al., 1995). On the basis of this, both are used in this chapter in reference to work cited, and attention is paid to defining the components of the process. Subsequent chapters use the terms 'case management' or 'case manager', reflecting the title given to the research study at its inception, and to the role adopted by members of the team performing this task.

Thus the aim of this chapter is to explore the multiplicity of factors which have influenced the development of care management for older people with dementia thereby providing contextual information for the description and analysis of the Lewisham Case Management Scheme in the remainder of the book. The studies reviewed provide information about the development of care management arrangements to co-ordinate community-based care for older people with mental health problems and in particular those with dementia. Critical factors in the evolution of the concept of community care as an alternative to placement in a care home are thereby highlighted. Much of the literature is derived from the UK and England in particular, but some overseas references are also included. In many instances these refer to research conducted over a significant period of time, a feature not often replicated in the UK literature. Overall, this chapter explores a diverse literature including policy initiatives and pilot projects and provides a mix of qualitative and quantitative data relating to care management. However, one of its important deficits is the absence, with certain significant exceptions, of robust economic evaluation of the effectiveness of care management arrangements, a feature of the study at the core of this book.

Early Influences

Care management has its origins in North America (Davies and Challis, 1986; Beardshaw and Towell, 1990; Fisher, 1990–91). It developed as part of the move in the balance of care away from institutional to community-based provision (Huxley et al., 1990; Challis, 1992a,b, 1994a,b). Of particular significance in this context was the family of 'Channeling Projects' commissioned by the federal government of the United States in the 1980s. 'Channeling' was described as the process required to link those who need long-term community care to the appropriate services (Department of Health Education and Welfare, 1980). Thus, these projects sought to link older people with long-term care needs to appropriate community-based services and promote a cost-effective use of scarce resources (Davies and Challis, 1986). The development of care management for older people is therefore inextricably linked to these factors and with the development of community care. In the UK this initiative was replicated in the 28 Care in the Community projects designed to help long-stay hospital residents move to community settings, initiated by central government in 1983 (Knapp et al., 1992). These pilot projects covered all client groups, although seven projects provided community care for elderly people and of these, three were specifically for 'mentally infirm' older people.

In England, three pilot projects relating to case management for older people influenced the White Paper *Caring for People* (Cm 849, 1989, para. 3.3.3) which preceded the community care reforms in 1993. These were undertaken in Kent, Gateshead and Darlington (Challis and Davies, 1986; Challis et al., 1990; 1995; 2002a), the last of which was part of the Care in the Community initiative referred to above. The purpose of the Kent Community Care Project (Challis and Davies, 1986) was to provide long-term care at home for frail older people living in the community at risk of admission to a care home. It involved decentralisation of resources by transferring these to frontline fieldwork staff with their own caseloads in a social services department, to encourage a more flexible response to needs. The Kent Scheme compared two similar groups of frail older people; one received case-managed community care whilst the other received standard services. Within the Gateshead scheme there were two distinct stages. The first was the social care scheme, designed as a social services initiative to prevent unnecessary admissions to care homes (Challis et al., 1990). Subsequently, the project developed close links with primary care thereby facilitating the contribution of health colleagues to the care management process. Both initiatives targeted older people at risk of admission to a care home and those receiving care management were compared with similarly matched groups of older people receiving the usual range of services (Challis et al., 2002a).

The Darlington Community Care Project (Challis et al., 1995), the third of these pilot projects, was designed to provide a community-based alternative to long-stay hospital care for physically frail older people. It sought to extend the case management approach of the Kent and Gateshead studies using the same methodology. However, in Darlington the approach was developed in a multi-agency setting, aiming to discharge people from hospital rather than prevent their admission to long-stay care, with the service deploying its own home care assistants. The project was designed to examine how appropriate this model of community care was for older people with varying degrees of physical and mental frailty and their carers; to compare the relative costs of care at home and in long-stay hospital care; and to examine whether health and social services may be successfully integrated at the client level. Interestingly, these projects demonstrated that it was possible to provide care for clients with cognitive impairment in their own homes (Challis and Davies, 1986; Challis et al., 1995; 2002a). Moreover, a hallmark of all these case management pilot projects was that each addressed issues relating to the effectiveness of services. This was achieved by examining the relative costs and benefits incurred by the older people and their carers following the introduction of the schemes, including those to different agencies and to society as a whole.

Overall, the pilot projects had three specific features, which were particularly relevant to the subsequent development of care management in the UK. First, they focused on a single client group, and procedures and protocols were developed which reflected this. Second, within this broad group the services were targeted on a small subset that was defined as having complex health and social care needs. Third, clients were identified by the use of case-finding and screening processes, as appropriate. In this context the purpose of case-finding is to increase the possibility that those who require the service receive it, and that of screening to ensure that those defined as inappropriate for the service do not receive it (Challis and Davies, 1986). The Gateshead and Darlington pilot projects also highlighted another key feature, namely close links with providers of health care in either a primary or secondary health care setting (Challis et al., 1995; 2002a). Other studies have explored links between care management and the provision of health care targeted on older people at risk of placement in care homes. Dant and colleagues (1989) evaluated a health authority initiative which employed care co-ordinators based in primary health care teams. Bland and colleagues (1992) evaluated a multidisciplinary team based in a hospital social work department. These studies, albeit in different ways, highlighted the importance of links between health and social care in the provision of care management. This has subsequently been recognised to be an important component of community-based care (Challis et al., 2006a), and for older people with dementia, the importance of this link is clear and, as noted above, has been formally recognised (Committee of Public Accounts, 2008).

In the USA, Eggert and colleagues (1990) reviewed three models of intensive case management, also incorporating a health dimension; a 'Centralized Individual' model; a 'Neighborhood Team' model, and a 'Home Health Care Team' model. These differed in terms of their functions of client assessment and reassessment, direct service and crisis intervention. Analysis revealed that people suffering from dementia experienced a greater reduction in their use of health care and had lower costs under the 'Neighborhood Team' model. In this approach, case managers had much smaller caseloads; made more home visits; referred clients to other services more frequently; and operated within a defined geographical area thereby gaining knowledge of local resources. More generally, the importance of identifying the appropriate level of case management intensity initially, and appropriate adjustment by means of effective monitoring was noted. This illustrates the importance of a differential approach to the assessment of need; the appropriate targeting of case management on clients for whom it is likely to be both beneficial in terms of outcome, and if at all possible cost-effective; and the importance of monitoring within the process. The latter, by implication, emphasises that care management is a model of long-term and not short-term care, a characteristic feature, as noted in Box 2.1. The research of Eggert referred to above is important in terms of the focus of this chapter, and indeed this book, because it also provides early evidence of the potential of case management to enable older people with mental health problems given sufficient and appropriate care, to remain in their own homes.

Further research undertaken by Eggert and colleagues (1991) related to case management in a multidisciplinary setting. It was based on the Kent Community Care Project (Challis and Davies, 1986; Davies and Challis, 1986) and compared just two types of case management for patients living at home requiring skilled nursing care: the 'Centralized Individual' model and the 'Neighborhood Team' model. The 'Centralized Individual' model had social workers and nurses as case managers but they had larger caseloads than those in the 'Neighborhood Team' model. The former rarely made home visits, and provided little continuity of care, with reassessments often done by different nurse assessors. The 'Neighborhood Team' model was designed to promote a multidisciplinary case management approach with nurses and social workers acting as case managers. While both groups had high health service costs, these were lower in the 'Neighborhood Team' due to reductions in days spent in hospital and in the receipt of home care. The authors concluded that the reduction in hospital days was achieved by a combination of enhancing the chances of earlier discharge through transfer to nursing home placement (resulting in a substitution of nursing home days for hospital days) and providing better organised home support and care. This highlights the opportunity for service substitution to provide more appropriate care at a lower cost, by virtue of regular monitoring and small caseloads.

In summary, the Gateshead and Darlington pilot projects in the UK identified factors relevant to the development of case management for older people, including those with cognitive impairment in a multidisciplinary setting prior to the introduction of the community care reforms in 1993. The research reported by Eggert and colleagues in the USA also illustrated this and revealed the variable impact of case management and therefore the importance of targeting the service, recognising the opportunity for service substitution and reviewing service inputs in relation to changed circumstances. The key features of these case management projects are illustrated in Box 2.2. It is notable that the research described in this book incorporated the features of these early projects.

Organisational Influences

Two years prior to the implementation of the community care reforms and the introduction of care management arrangements, the Care Programme Approach (CPA) offered a means to co-ordinate care at home for older people with mental health problems (Department of Health, 1990a). It was designed to ensure that the continuing health and social care needs of patients were assessed before discharge

Box 2.2   Features of case management projects: UK and North America

• Specialism by client group
• Targeting care management on people with complex needs
• Multidisciplinary assessment rather than mono-disciplinary assessment
• Close links between health and social care
• Small caseloads
• Cost-effective care requires effective targeting
• Regular review of service inputs
• Opportunities for service substitution through regular review

from hospital; that services were in place to meet these needs; and that a named person ensured their provision. Although primarily associated with younger adults, a criterion for inclusion within it included a history of self-neglect, which can be a feature of mental health problems in old age. However, the extent of its use in respect of older people with dementia is not known (Philpot and Banerjee, 1997). Perhaps more important in this context, significant areas of overlap between care management and the CPA as well as marked differences have been found in respect of older people with mental health problems (Hughes et al., 2001). Indeed the CPA was described as a specialist variant of care management for people with mental health problems (Department of Health, 1995). Together these two directives provided the policy framework within which services developed in the last decade of the twentieth century for older people with mental health problems, and the relationship between the two was not clarified until the introduction of the Single Assessment Process (SAP). For older people with dementia, it specified that care management arrangements were the most appropriate means to co-ordinate home-based care (Department of Health, 2002b).

Earlier policy guidance that accompanied implementation of the community care reforms in 1993 outlined three stages of a care management system: assessment of the circumstances of the client and carers; negotiation of a care package with clients, carers and relevant agencies, and implementation and monitoring of the agreed package, together with a review of outcomes (Department of Health, 1990b). Subsequently, seven tasks in the care management process: publishing information, determining level of assessment, assessing need, care planning, implementing the care plan, monitoring, and review (SSI/SWSG, 1991a,b) were identified. The degree of local authority discretion in the development of care management arrangements resulted in considerable variation in patterns of provision between local authorities (Weiner et al., 2002). Moreover, it was suggested that the emphasis placed on the adherence to the seven tasks in the care management process resulted in local authorities focusing on these as discrete entities during the early stages of implementation, rather than developing arrangements more in keeping with the concept of care management as a model of long-term care (Gostick et al., 1997). Within this context, specialist care management arrangements for older people with dementia have struggled and continue to struggle to emerge. It can be surmised that this state of affairs will continue with proposals to transform social care and, particularly, those to ensure individuals eligible for publicly-funded adult social care have a transparent allocation of funding to meet assessed need (Cm 6737, 2006; Department of Health, 2008a; 2009a).

In the remainder of this section, organisational factors central to the development of care management in the UK are reviewed under three broad headings: arrangements for the commissioning of services designed to support vulnerable older people in their own homes; financial arrangements; and the development of single discipline and multidisciplinary specialist teams both within local government and spanning health and social care. These issues are described in general terms although, wherever possible, illustrations are specific to care management in the context of services for older people with dementia.

Commissioning Services

The separation of the purchaser and provider functions within social services departments was a requirement placed on local authorities by central government as part of the implementation programme for the introduction of the community care legislation. It was introduced as one of the means of promoting the development of the enabling role of the local authority in the context of social care provision (Cm 849, 1989). Over half of English local authorities had introduced this division of function prior to or during 1993 (Challis et al., 1999) and an early study noted a rigid interpretation of the split (Challis, 1994c). On the other hand, subsequent research suggested that the development of a purchaser/provider split was a slow, evolutionary process (Wistow et al., 1994; Gostick et al., 1997; Lewis et al., 1997). Since the care of vulnerable older people, including those with dementia, continues to constitute the largest component of work undertaken by local authorities, the introduction of this separation has arguably had a significant impact on the delivery of services for this user group. The policy guidance accompanying the White Paper *Caring for People* (Cm 849, 1989) stressed that the development of the enabling role of the authority should be apparent at two levels in the organisation: at the 'micro level', in respect of the provision of services in response to individual need and at the 'macro level', involving plans to meet strategic objectives (Department of Health, 1990b). In retrospect it can be argued that this separation of the commissioning and providing arms of service provision within local authorities has delayed the development of specialist care management arrangements for older people with dementia at both levels.

At the 'micro level', whilst in advance of the introduction of the community care reforms, it was noted that a needs-led approach 'pre-supposes a progressive separation of assessment from provision' (Department of Health, 1990b, 25), although guidance did not include a requirement for budgetary devolution to front-line workers, with appropriate systems for financial management and monitoring. The absence of this was significant in the development of care management arrangements for older people with dementia and intensive care management more generally for two reasons. First, it has long been understood that devolved budgets can provide a more flexible response to needs within a complex package of care (Audit Commission, 1996), typically required by older people with dementia. Second and closely allied to the first point, devolved budgets are a feature common to many demonstration programmes of intensive care management in England (Challis et al., 1995; 2002a). More generally it should be noted that the separation of the purchaser and provider functions is in contrast to practice within these pilot projects of care management for older people that influenced the White Paper *Caring for People* (Cm 849, 1989, para 3.3.3). Here, a close relationship between care managers and those providing practical care was a significant component of the service delivery system (Challis et al., 1995; 2002a). This illustrated the inadequacy of a rigid purchaser/provider split, one of the most important organisational aspects of care management arrangements within the UK, at its inception in the 1990s. In terms of future arrangements for the care of older people with dementia at home, it is relevant to note that proposals for the personalisation of social care encompass the development of more flexible responses to need as a central plank of the proposed changes (Department of Health, 2008a; 2009a).

At the 'macro level', the commissioning role of social services authorities in respect of community care has developed following the introduction of the community care reforms. As noted above, one of the objectives of the White Paper *Caring for People* (Cm 849, 1989) was that social services authorities should be 'enabling' agencies securing the delivery of services, not simply by acting as direct providers, but by developing their purchasing and contracting role. It was envisaged that this change would increase the use of independent sector providers and consequently widen the range of options and consumer choice. However, in the period following the introduction of the community reforms in 1993, two factors initially impeded the development of commissioning services in response to the special needs of older people with dementia. First, since social services departments often delivered services for these people in ways which did not separate them out from other services for older people, it was difficult to get accurate data on the numbers of people with dementia receiving a service, and the money being spent on such services. Hence, there was no reliable data available to inform the commissioning process. Second, there was difficulty in developing integrated commissioning arrangements for older people with dementia at a local level between health and social services authorities. This was not simply due to personnel changes but because responsibility for this group of people was initially vested in different service divisions – in services for older people within social services departments, and in mental health services within the NHS (Department of Health, 1997a). Moreover, as the Audit Commission (2002) subsequently noted, clear goals were and still are required, including the intended balance between home-based, day, outpatient, residential and hospital services, yet these essential building blocks were often not in place.

Arguably, one of these goals should have related to the development of specialist domiciliary care services for older people with dementia. In 1998, the White Paper *Modernising Social Services* (Cm 4169, 1998) outlined measures to improve service commissioning processes in the areas of needs analysis, strategic planning, contract setting, market management and contract monitoring to help ensure that services met specific needs. Subsequently, government guidance (Department of Health, 2002c) confirmed the duty placed on councils to have services in place to meet eligible needs, with the caveat that specialist services for groups of service users should be developed where there is justification for such. Most recently, this finds expression in guidance which required local authorities to provide intensive care and support for adults with 'high-level' complex needs (Department of Health, 2009a). Although there is no specific reference made to older people with dementia, these initiatives provide a framework for the development of specialist resources for them. Interestingly, such an initiative was integral to the LCMS and its development as described in Chapter 5. More recently there has been renewed emphasis on commissioning, joint commissioning between health and social care agencies and locally agreed performance measures (Cm 6737, 2006). These developments, combined with the recent emphasis on partnership working and the requirement to develop a joint strategic needs assessment, provide a mechanism to promote a co-ordinated response in respect of commissioning services for older people with mental health problems and particularly those with dementia (National Audit Office, 2007). This has the potential to increase the range of services available in a locality to support older people in the community.

Financial Arrangements

The financial arrangements consequent on the introduction of care management arrangements in 1993 also have found expression at both the 'macro' and 'micro' level in the sense that they have influenced the provision of care at an individual level and the overall context in which this service is provided. At the 'micro level', i.e. the provision of services to individual users, two aspects of practice were integral to effective financial management within the pilot projects. These were: devolved budgeting to case managers; and clear expenditure limits with explicit unit costs for purchased services. The importance of the first of these was discussed in the previous section. It has long been accepted wisdom that explicit unit costs permit care managers with service users and carers to make informed choices of the likely costs and benefits of alternative courses of action: for example, between five hours home care or attendance at a day centre (Challis and Davies, 1986). However, research indicated it was unlikely that significant components of care packages were costed in the period following the introduction of the community care reforms (Challis et al., 1999).

More recently, attention has been focused on the equitable division of resources and the opportunity for service users to receive a sum of money and take responsibility for their own care (Department of Health, 2008a; 2009a). The latter initially found expression in the introduction of direct payments which local authorities are required to offer to individuals assessed as eligible for assistance and equipment to enable them to make their own decisions about how care and equipment is purchased and provided (Department of Health, 2000a). Early research on their use by older people indicated limited take-up (Fernández et al., 2007) suggesting that for older people with dementia, the challenge of tailoring services to individual need will continue to be the preserve of the care manager. Subsequently, proposals for the introduction of personal budgets were designed to foster a more transparent allocation of resources, and allow people to create their own packages of care. However, it is also recognised that some older people will prefer that this is undertaken by a care manager (Cm 6499, 2005; Department of Health, 2008a; 2009a; Glendinning et al., 2008) and again it can be surmised that this group will include older people with dementia. In this context, a crucial indicator of success will be the capacity of care managers to extend the range of service provision beyond that of home care and day care, the hitherto typical service response (Department of Health, 1997a; Moriarty and Webb, 2000). To achieve this will require both an explicit personal allocation of resources to individuals and costs attached to each service. It has been suggested that costed care plans for older people with complex problems will not become a reality until all aspects of both health and social care are routinely costed (Challis et al., 2007), a prospect of particular relevance for those with dementia.

At the macro level, legislation was introduced at the end of the 1990s to allow changes to be made in the financial arrangements underpinning joint working between providers of health and social care, as noted in Chapter 1. In terms of the provision of integrated care to older people with mental health problems, and particularly those with dementia, changes consequent on the implementation of the Health Act (1999) are arguably of particular significance. Whilst the legislation incorporates a new statutory duty for NHS Trusts to work in partnership with other NHS organisations, and local authorities 'for the common good', it has been suggested that the distinguishing feature of this legislation compared with that before in this field was the subsequent introduction of 'flexibilities' which created new opportunities to remove barriers to joint working (Henwood and Wistow, 1999). These variously allow for pooled budgets, delegated commissioning, or integration between services. However, an early monitoring exercise found very limited uptake in terms of services for older people with mental health problems (Hudson et al., 2002). Subsequently the NHS Act (2006) has reaffirmed the centrality of these mechanisms in pursuit of the development of more integrated services. As Box 2.3 demonstrates, each brings benefits of particular relevance to the development of care management arrangements for older people with dementia: more flexible packages of care; improved arrangements for the commissioning of services; and greater continuity of care. The Dementia Strategy (Department of Health, 2009b) reinforced this with recommendations for improved home care, short breaks, and a joint commissioning strategy for dementia. These are further addressed in this book, and indeed they are at the centre of the LCMS, whose

Box 2.3   NHS Act 2006: Section 75 flexibilities and services for older people with dementia

Type of flexibility	Description	Possible gains for specialist services for older people with dementia
Pooled budgets.	Health and local authorities pool finance, enabling staff to develop care packages irrespective of source of funding.	Development of more flexible and idiosyncratic packages of care.
Lead commissioning: Service commissioning for a target population is the most frequently cited example.	Primary Care Trusts and local authorities delegate functions to one another. Benefits identified as reduced costs and more informed service commissioning.	Improved service commissioning at a local level thereby rectifying a long-standing weakness in service provision (discussed in previous section).
Integrated provision: Provision of health and local authority services from a single managed provider.	Single organisation providing health and social care.	Greater continuity of care achieved by a single organisation providing both community nursing and domiciliary care.

evaluation demonstrates their importance in the provision of care at home for older people with dementia.

Specialist Teams

The aim of this section is to explore the composition of teams with responsibility for providing care management for older people with dementia. This encapsulates both the emergence of specialism by client/user group within local authorities and the development of teams comprising both health and social care staff. First, the development of specialism by user group within local authority social services departments is summarised. The debate regarding 'generic' and 'specialist' approaches to social care began with the introduction of the Seebohm Report (Cmnd 3703, 1968). Following the creation of social services departments in 1971, there was concern about the need for developing specialist skills required to meet the needs of particular client groups (Central Council for Education and Training in Social Work, 1975) and the development of specialism by client group within social services departments was noted. In the mid-eighties, Challis and Ferlie (1987) noted a trend away from patterns of generic working common in the days after the Seebohm reorganisation (Cmnd 3703, 1968) towards client group specialisation at both team level and in the caseloads of individual workers. The enactment of the 1989 Children Act and the 1990 National Health Service and Community Care

Act provided a stimulus to this process (Means and Smith, 1998) and this trend towards specialisation on the basis of user groups was noted in the period after the implementation of the community care reforms (Challis, 1994c; Lewis and Glennerster, 1996; Challis et al., 2006a). Increasingly, therefore, local authorities provide assistance to vulnerable adults through specialist teams. Furthermore, the caseload of older people's teams comprises a substantial proportion of service users with memory problems although they have not necessarily been diagnosed with dementia (Sutcliffe et al., 2008).

Care management for older people with dementia may also be provided through specialist services spanning health and social care. However, a national study of care management arrangements noted that less than half of the local authorities provided a specialist dementia service in conjunction with health care providers (Hughes et al., 2001). Nevertheless, where specialist teams for older people with dementia did exist they were more likely than other teams specialising in the care of older people to have NHS staff, usually community psychiatric and district nurses, acting as care managers (Weiner et al., 2003). Indeed, a national survey of old age psychiatry services revealed that almost a quarter of old age services had specialist dementia services with designated members of staff from different disciplines (Challis et al., 2002b).

On balance, it is now more likely that older people with dementia will receive support via the care management process from an old age mental health team. Nevertheless, at the turn of the century an audit of mental health services for older people in England and Wales found that specialist multidisciplinary teams for older people with mental health problems were only fully available in less than half the areas sampled (Audit Commission, 2002). Furthermore, a review of services for older people with dementia found that the size and availability of specialist Community Mental Health Teams (CMHTs) continued to be variable and only half were fully integrated across health and social care (National Audit Office, 2007). Whilst social workers, traditionally the main but not sole professional group undertaking care management, are recognised as core members of multidisciplinary teams (Department of Health, 2001b) this is not always the case (Challis et al., 2002b; Tucker et al., 2007; National Audit Office, 2007). Moreover, the debate about the professional background and job title – key-worker or dementia care adviser – of the person within CMHTs responsible for co-ordination of community-based care for older people with dementia continues (Care Services Improvement Partnership, 2005; Department of Health, 2008b). This degree of variation in both the composition of teams providing care for older people with dementia and the lack of specificity in terms of responsibility for co-ordinating care for this group of people provides an uncertain framework for the development of care management arrangements, emphasising the influence of organisational features on practice.

These findings are particularly significant in the context of the development of community-based services as an alternative to residential and nursing home care for older people with mental health problems and particularly those with dementia.

As described earlier in this chapter, the UK pilot projects demonstrated that specialism by client group is an important factor in the development of effective care management practice. Furthermore, it has been suggested, for example, that the provision of care management through specialist teams for older people is one of the necessary conditions for the development of intensive care management (Challis et al., 2001a), a prerequisite for organising complex packages of care to enable older people with dementia to continue to live in their own homes. The evidence described above suggests that this requirement may have at least in part been fulfilled. However, it has also relevant to note that whilst there are some multidisciplinary teams providing care management for older people with dementia, the provision is not comprehensive either in terms of availability or, if in situ, staff mix.

Practice Development

In many countries, government policies concerned with meeting the needs of frail older people at home are provided within an increasingly tight financial budget. As a consequence, policy and service development has taken increasingly similar forms (Kraan et al., 1991; Challis, 1994a,b; Delaney et al., 2001). In England it has been acknowledged that the community care agenda is a long-term one and thus the development of home-based care for older people is a long-term programme (SSI, 1998b; Department of Health, 2000b), and more recently this has found expression in the transformation agenda (Department of Health, 2008a). As part of this process a number of official documents have been and continue to be published in relation to developments in care management arrangements, including those for older people with dementia. These provide information and guidance and key findings selected from an expansive volume of publications and are summarised in Box 2.4. Much of this information has been drawn from the work of the Social Services Inspectorate, in particular its inspections of services, special studies and annual reviews relating to various aspects of care management as well as reports published by the Audit Commission, with a wider focus including the financial aspects of care management. Whilst these do not provide an overarching review of all official sources of documentation relating to care management for older people following the introduction of the community care reforms, they reflect particular areas of interest in the development and process of care management for older people including those with dementia. Many are derived from the period immediately after the introduction of the community care reforms. Overall, the principal themes emerging from this diverse literature relating to the development of care management arrangements are: the importance of a differentiated approach to care management; targeting of assistance on those with complex needs; the need to improve approaches to assessment; and the comparative neglect of the monitoring and review aspect of care management arrangements. Each of these

Box 2.4   A review of the implementation of care management arrangements for older people

Date	Document	Main findings
1993	Department of Health, *Monitoring and Development: Assessment special study*	New arrangements introduced by community care legislation complex and time consuming. Problems regarding assessment in terms of documentation and skills of assessors in completing the process.
1993	Audit Commission, *Taking Care: Progress with Care in the Community*	Advocated streamlining and refining assessment procedures and provision of greater choice for clients by increasing service options.
1994a	Department of Health, *Monitoring and Development: Care Management Special Study*	Observed that care management being applied to all service users rather than targeted on more complex cases. Concerns regarding lack of continuity of staff involved in tasks of care management.
1994b	Department of Health, *Inspection of Assessment and Care Management Arrangements in Social Services Departments, Oct. 1993–March 1994*	Care plans service-driven rather than needs-led. Financial systems gradually being developed with devolved budgets, more work required to reach potential clients and carers. Arrangements for monitoring care plans not well developed; reviews operate mainly on residential care placements.
1995	SSI, *Partners in Caring-Fourth Annual Report of the Chief Inspector SSI 1994/95*	Insufficient attention paid to tailoring services to identified need. Tendency to close less complex cases after implementation of care plan militated against continuity of care and provision of social work assistance, e.g. counselling.
1996b	Department of Health, *Caring for People at Home-Part II*	Improvements in provision of home care in terms of tasks and elements of personal care provided, although considerable variation nationally.
1997b	Department of Health, *The Cornerstone of Care: Inspection of Care Planning for Older People, Overview Report*	Importance of making services responsive to the varied needs of older people and carers. Flexible services required to meet a range of circumstances. Unnecessary duplication of assessment processes to be avoided. Arrangements for monitoring and delivering care plans required review to ensure needs were met and resources used effectively.
1997	Audit Commission, *The Coming of Age: Improving Care Services for Older People*	Importance of development of information systems to support process of case management with respect to financial management. More efficient and effective monitoring of services required to reduce the risk to vulnerable older people.

Box 2.4   Continued

2000 2002	Audit Commission, *Forget Me Not: Mental Health Services for Older People* and *Forget Me Not 2002: Developing Mental Health Services for Older People in England*	Older people with mental health problems require a comprehensive assessment of needs. Provision of care needs balancing in favour of home-based services. Agencies should collaborate to provide specialist multidisciplinary teams including recommended core team members.
2002b	Department of Health, *The Single Assessment Process. Key Implications, Guidance for Local Implementation* (HSC2002/001; LAC (2002)1)	Older people to be involved in and receive an accurate and timely assessment proportionate to their needs and to be informed of and give consent to information being collected and shared. Multidisciplinary assessments to be undertaken preceding substantial care packages and care home admission for older people with complex needs.
2002d	Department of Health, *Improving Older People's Services* (CI(2002)14)	Care plans found to be service-led and tasks of monitoring and review neglected. Service users and carers more involved in service planning and development.
2008a	Department of Health, *Transforming Social Care* (LAC(DH)(2008)1)	All who receive social care to be given choice and control over how support is delivered. Use of personal budgets to provide a flexible and transparent allocation of resources tailored to the individual.

themes is explored in more detail because they are of particular importance to the community care of older people with dementia.

Differentiation within Care Management Arrangements

A differentiated approach to the mode of assessment and care management is one in which a distinction is made between service users with complex needs often requiring a multi-service response and those with less complex needs which are often met by a single service response provided by one agency. Older people with dementia and their carers typically have complex health and social care needs and it is important that agencies have in place procedures and protocols within care management arrangements which facilitate an appropriate response – a feature more likely to be associated with a differentiated approach to care management with procedures specific to those with complex needs. Historically, different parts of the UK have adopted different approaches to this, although as Box 2.1 indicates, this is one of the defining features of care management arrangements.

In Northern Ireland, in contrast to other parts of the UK, proposals for improving the management and delivery of community care attempted to adopt a more differentiated approach to care management at the outset (Department of

Health and Social Services, 1991). The initial guidance specified a distinction between people with complex health and social care needs and those who required a prompt response to an immediate practical need. Care management was defined as embracing the functions of assessing need, care planning, and managing, co-ordinating and reviewing services. Within this overarching concept, 'case management' was used to identify the activity of acting as an advocate and co-ordinator of services restricted to the individual client with complex needs who required this support. In this, the role of case manager as a broker for the client between relevant agencies, monitoring the progress of the client, planning care programmes and maintaining a supportive relationship was explicitly recognised (Department of Health and Social Services, 1991). More recently this approach has been replaced with a single definition of care management. This focuses on people with complex or rapidly changing needs; has at its centre assessing and tailoring services; and is to be undertaken by qualified health or social care workers (Department of Health, Social Services and Public Safety, 2006).

Conversely, the guidance introduced at the inception of the community care reforms in England, implied that the principles of care management should be applied to all service recipients (Challis, 1994c). Unsurprisingly, research indicated that little progress was made in the development of a differentiated approach to care management immediately after the introduction of the community care reforms (Challis et al., 1999; 2001a; Weiner et al., 2002). Furthermore, it was suggested that the difficulties experienced by local authorities in coping with the volume of work was in part attributable to a failure to differentiate between levels of intervention (SSI, 1997a; Department of Health, 2001b). The introduction of the SAP (Department of Health, 2002b) which specified four types of assessment: contact assessment including basic personal information; overview assessment; specialist assessment, and comprehensive assessment has been consistent with the development of a differentiated approach to care management. This initiative can be seen as particularly important in developing care management arrangements which are responsive to the needs of older people with dementia. At the outset, as indicated in Box 2.4, it was anticipated that comprehensive assessment would be the most appropriate for this group of people since it was specified as a prerequisite for residential and nursing home placements and intensive community support, where substantial packages of care at home were required. However, early evidence of its influence on the assessment of older people with cognitive impairment is inconclusive (Sutcliffe et al., 2008). By inference this suggests that the process of identifying older people with dementia who require care management may have changed little since the introduction of the SAP.

In Scotland, following a review of community care in the decade after its introduction, a differentiated approach to care management was proposed in a way different in content to that of the introduction of the SAP in England but with the same goal – to provide an appropriate level of support to service users with complex needs. Policy guidance recommended that care management be redefined as intensive care management specifically for people with complex or frequently changing needs (Scottish Office, 1998; Scottish Executive, 2000). It used one of the pilot projects referred to earlier, the Kent community care project (Challis and Davies, 1986), as a model of good practice thereby making explicit their support of a differentiated approach to the process of care management. For older people with more complex needs, intensive care management was identified as the means to co-ordinate and deliver services in a way tailored to meet their requirements. Three services necessary to maintaining older people at home were also identified; intensive support and care schemes; more flexible and comprehensive short break services, and a shopping/domestic/household maintenance service. Additionally, care managers were to receive training in intensive care management and only those who had undertaken such training should carry it out, further differentiating the development of care management from that in England. In effect, this provided a framework for the development of intensive care management which all the early pilot projects in the UK demonstrated can support frail older people, including those with some level of cognitive impairment, in the community (Challis and Davies, 1986; Challis et al., 1990; 1995; 2002a). However, research demonstrated only limited initial progress in this respect with intensive care management most clearly identified by staff mix with qualified social workers responsible for complex cases (Stalker and Campbell, 2002). Consequently revised guidance was issued requiring care management to be re-focused on those with complex or changing needs (Scottish Executive Joint Future Unit, 2004).

Targeting

Targeting within care management arrangements may be defined as the process by which vulnerable adults with complex needs, such as those with dementia, receive the care package they require. The process and resultant package should therefore differ both in content and intensity to that received by others with less complex needs. The process of targeting resources occurs at two points in the care management process: on entry into the service and within initial assessment. In practice there was a wide variation in approaches to the screening of individuals prior to assessment (Department of Health, 1998), which is likely to mean considerable variation in targeting. This was demonstrated in a study undertaken with social services departments across England which examined the eligibility criteria of their services for older people (Challis and Hughes, 2002). It showed that there was marked variability between departments in terms of methods of eligibility determination in relation to community and residential settings and in the amount of detail gathered in order to decide eligibility for assessment and service provision, particularly with regard to the identification of mental health problems in older people. Subsequent guidance for social services departments has attempted to improve this situation by providing the basis for a national framework for setting eligibility criteria (Department of Health, 2002c).

At the outset, the White Paper *Caring for People* (Cm 849, 1989) implied that care management should be applied to everybody requiring community care and, following implementation of the community care legislation, it was observed that care management was becoming a process provided to all clients rather than being targeted on complex cases (Department of Health, 1994a), and research has confirmed this observation (Challis et al., 2001b). This is despite the fact that in England, as in other countries, care management services have, it has been argued, been intended for those people at risk of admission to long-term care, such as older people with dementia, reflecting the policy of 'downward substitution' by the provision of more appropriate and cost-effective community-based alternatives (Cm 849, 1989). It is therefore not surprising that the targeting of services on frail older people in greatest need and in particular older people with dementia has been a recurrent theme in the evolution of care management arrangements in the first decade after the implementation of the community care reforms (Department of Health, 1997a; SSI, 1997b). Subsequent research in England has concluded that there is little evidence of targeting within care management arrangements for older people in general (Stewart et al., 2003) but if it is present it is likely that the presence of short-term memory problems and level of cognitive skills would influence the type of care management (Challis et al., 2007).

Assessment

Assessment was identified as one of the cornerstones in the implementation of community care policy in England (Cm 849, 1989). However, as summarised in Box 2.4, and demonstrated elsewhere, studies of assessment procedures carried out shortly after implementation of the community care legislation (Caldock, 1993; 1994; Department of Health, 1993; Lewis and Glennerster, 1996) found that procedures and pro-formas were overly complex, and that generic documentation was ill-suited to identifying the needs of specific user groups. Indeed, research reported a good deal of variability in assessment tools and that the capacity to generate standardised information was found to be low (Stewart et al., 1999). The NSFOP (Department of Health, 2001b) sought to address these issues with the introduction of the SAP for vulnerable older people (Department of Health, 2002b) by offering guidance in two areas particularly relevant to older people with mental health problems: greater specificity about the areas to be addressed in an assessment; and multidisciplinary contributions to a complex assessment.

In an attempt to achieve greater standardisation in terms of the content of an assessment, the SAP guidance as previously noted, included nine domains, and a further 34 sub-domains. However, it was less clear about three domains explicitly referred to in the Welsh guidance on the Unified Assessment Process namely: activities of daily living; instrumental activities of daily living; and the carer's perspective and their need for assessment (National Assembly for Wales, 2002). With regard to the first two domains, research conducted with strategic and operational staff involved in the use of unified assessments has found a preference to consolidate these (Seddon et al., 2008). The third is particularly important in assessing the needs of older people with mental health problems and the burdens experienced by their carers. Moriarty and Webb (2000) suggested that, in order to support such carers, assessment documentation should include a range of needs faced by carers, such as social and leisure needs, in addition to practical care needs incorporating assessments of activities of daily living and instrumental activities of daily living.

The SAP guidance was less prescriptive in terms of assessment tools and processes and advocated local experimentation, although an accreditation process was introduced to allow the design of off-the-shelf assessment tools (Department of Health, 2003b). Consequently, following its introduction, a national survey found that two thirds of authorities were using locally developed assessment tools and only two accredited assessment tools appeared to have achieved national penetration (Abendstern et al., 2007). Interestingly, this approach was not replicated by the Welsh guidance and research noted above revealed that the process of devising assessment documentation had yet to be agreed resulting in variability in the content of information collected (Seddon et al., 2008), a similar scenario to that occurring in England prior to the implementation of the SAP (Stewart et al., 1999). Furthermore, the English SAP guidance suggested that geriatricians and old age psychiatrists play a leading role in the selection of appropriate assessment tools, ensuring that training in their use was available, and undertaking research into assessment procedures (Department of Health, 2002b). However, in a survey of geriatricians and old age psychiatrists, a minority reported that the introduction of the SAP had altered their assessment practice, and very few perceived it as involving the introduction of detection or screening tools (Tucker et al., 2009). It is also of note that old age psychiatry services in England and Northern Ireland were found to use at least three different standardised assessment scales, and a total of 62 individual instruments were identified (Reilly et al., 2004). Overall, this suggests that there is considerable scope for the development of a more standardised approach to the tools and scales used in the assessment of older people with mental health problems.

Concurrently, policy and practice guidance has increasingly emphasised the importance of multidisciplinary assessment (Department of Health and Social Services, 1991; SSI/SWSG, 1991a,b; Department of Health, 1997c; 2001b; 2002b; Scottish Executive, 2000). Research has also endorsed this. A randomised controlled study has, for example, considered the potential benefits of additional medical assessment compared with usual social services assessment procedures with a group of older people at the point of a critical care transition (Challis et al., 2004; Venables et al., 2006). The assessments were valued highly by care managers and specialist clinicians. A range of conditions previously not diagnosed, in particular cognitive impairment, were identified by the medical assessment. This could be of major benefit for care managers, carers, and ultimately service users themselves in terms of planning and provision of future care (Department of Health, 2009b). The study therefore demonstrated the value of specialist clinicians in the decision-making process regarding long-term care of frail older people, and particularly those with mental health problems. Overall, therefore, it would appear that in England recent policy initiatives in respect of the content of an assessment – standardisation, consistency, and a multidisciplinary approach – offer the potential of more accurate and inclusive approaches to identification of need, particularly in respect of older people with dementia, but as yet this is unrealised on a national scale. However, there are undoubtedly local examples of good practice in relation to all three of these aspects of assessment. Indeed the LCMS, described in detail in subsequent chapters, is one such example.

Monitoring and Review

Monitoring and review within case management have been described as the means by which changes in health status and circumstances are recorded and the components of the care plan adjusted as required (Hughes et al., 2005). They constitute one of the hallmarks of intensive care management, namely the co-ordination of a variety of related functions over time (Challis et al., 1995). Immediately after the introduction of the community care reforms, much of the time spent on case management practice in the UK focused on the initial stages of screening and assessment (SSI, 1993; Department of Health, 1993; Challis, 1994c). However, it was recognised that the time and resources focused on the monitoring and review components of the care management process in England were insufficient (Department of Health, 1993; 1994a). For example, a study of care management arrangements in seven local authorities found that all of them struggled both with methods of monitoring and review and with issues of volume. Those authorities which struggled most were those without a differentiated approach to care management (Department of Health, 1998). Furthermore, research has revealed that the monitoring and review activities were underdeveloped and highly variable both between and within authorities (Hardy et al., 1999; Weiner et al., 2002; Department of Health, 2002d).

   Similarly, a small study of local authorities revealed that many users and carers were unaware of having been reviewed and were unhappy with the process being undertaken by different individuals to those doing assessments. The authors suggested that reviews should be seen as a continuous process rather than as isolated events (Ware et al., 2003). The importance of regular systems of review has also been recognised in policy development (Cm 4169, 1998; Department of Health, 2002c; NICE-SCIE, 2006), particularly in respect of older people with dementia due to their vulnerability and their impaired ability to report any sudden changes in their circumstances (Department of Health, 1997a). Interestingly, the proposal for prompt and regular reviews has also been recommended in the equivalent guidance for local authorities and health services in Wales (National Assembly for Wales, 2002), which also explicitly acknowledged the importance of monitoring the well-being and circumstances of users within the care management process. It recommended using nominated care co-ordinators, particularly for vulnerable older people with complex needs, thereby emphasising the long-term nature of care for this group. However, as in England, reports raised concerns in respect of inconsistencies in reviews and problems in conducting these promptly (CSSIW, 2008a,b). Both monitoring and review functions within care management are important in providing effective home-based care to older people with dementia. In view of the likely deterioration in their health status over time (Moriarty and Webb, 2000), research to date suggests that this aspect remains poorly developed although it is central to the provision of community-based care for older people with dementia, as illustrated in the description of case management in Chapter 5.

Summary

This chapter has outlined key issues in the development of care management arrangements in respect of older people with mental health problems, particularly older people with dementia. The origins of the terms have been described, together with the early care (case) management projects which influenced the White Paper, *Caring for People* (Cm 849, 1989) and the guidance which accompanied the enactment of the community care reforms. Additionally, issues which arose during the initial phase of the implementation of these reforms, particularly the arrangements for the commissioning and delivery of services, financial arrangements underpinning the introduction of care management, and the emergence of specialist older people's teams, have been explored. Together, these themes are covered by a disparate literature, illustrating both the scale of the reforms enshrined in the community care legislation and the dearth of information relating to the impact of these reforms throughout the country. The development of case management practice following the implementation of the community care reforms has also been described, particularly in terms of four themes: differentiation within care management arrangements; targeting; assessment; and monitoring and review. Areas of concern within each of these themes have been highlighted using research studies and reviews of policy documentation.

The pilot projects cited in the White Paper, *Caring for People* (Cm 849, 1989), provide the components of a particular model of care management for older people. They demonstrated, in the context of intensive care management, the importance of continuity of care through the process; the significance of the combination of health and social care inputs; and the necessity of a differentiated approach in order to target the service appropriately. In developing models of care management for older people, it is necessary to determine the relative importance of these features in order both to meet identified needs appropriately and to develop strategies to manage the volume of work. Only in the second decade after the introduction of the community care reforms was guidance developed on how to address these important issues. To date, there is little documented evidence of progress towards these goals crucial to the development of a model of care management for vulnerable older people within a specialist multidisciplinary framework spanning health and social care.

The LCMS described in this book has these components and as such, this description of case management in practice contributes to the evolution of a model of care management for older people with mental health problems, particularly those with dementia. The scheme, which spanned the health and social service divide, was integrated into an existing service system within an established community mental health team for older people. It was provided to vulnerable older people with complex health and social care needs; co-ordinated by a care manager based in a specialist multidisciplinary mental health team, and with close links between the care manager, the multidisciplinary team and the services that provide care to clients on a daily basis. Most importantly, it provided long-term care to clients, with regular monitoring and review of service inputs as its hallmarks. As such it makes a significant and timely contribution to the debate about the essential components of a model of care management for older people with dementia. In terms of the SAP guidance on assessment (Department of Health, 2002b), the research study evaluates practice which provides comprehensive assessment as a prelude to the provision of a substantial package of care to allow an older person with dementia to continue to live at home. More generally, it can be surmised that the research findings will also inform the development of knowledge relating to intensive care management for older people, a specialist variant of care management still under development in a UK context.

Chapter 3
Service Setting

Introduction

The Lewisham Case Management Scheme was designed as one of a family of case management studies which, within the framework of an overall model, offered variation in the settings in which the service was provided (Challis and Davies, 1986; Challis et al., 1995, 2002a). In each of these studies, case managers had relatively small targeted caseloads and controlled resources within an overall cost framework, so as to permit the arrangement of more flexible and individualised packages of care. The aim of the LCMS was to develop a similar model to the earlier schemes, in a multidisciplinary team whose target population was older people with a diagnosis of dementia, identified as having unmet needs and likely to be at risk of entry to institutional care, despite input from statutory services. It was designed for people living at home, either on their own or living with carers, thus supporting two different but important groups, which, as discussed earlier, remain at the centre of national policy initiatives (Committee of Public Accounts, 2008; Department of Health, 2008b).

This chapter first describes the function and role of the community mental health team for older people within which the scheme was based, and second, case management and domiciliary care arrangements for the scheme. Included in this for illustrative purposes are views on the services from the perspectives of members of the community mental health team for older people and social workers on their capacity to cater for older people with a diagnosis of dementia. These provide an insight into the setting in which the scheme was located at that time.

The Community Mental Health Team for Older People

Whilst many community teams for older people with mental health problems have been noted to have similar features, historically, differences in their operation have also been observed. In a study of old age psychiatry in the UK, Dening (1992) reported that some community teams catered for the needs of both hospital inpatients as well as clients living in the community. Teams varied in the way referrals were made to them, with some operating an 'open referral' system and others only accepting referrals from general practitioners. They also differed with respect to who carried out the initial assessment, the types of assessment schedules used and therapies on offer. Other factors which affected how a community team operated, included managerial style, and methods of prioritisation of the workload (Lindesay, 1991). Since then, there has been a steady increase in the number of psychiatric services available specifically for older people, due in part to a number of national initiatives (Department of Health, 2001b; National Audit Office, 2007), and in particular by those providing community-based services within multidisciplinary teams (Philpot and Banerjee, 1997; Challis et al., 2002a; Banerjee and Chan, 2008).

During the second half of the last century in London, as in other parts of the country, there was an introduction of specialist services to provide care for older people with mental illness, rather than remaining within general adult psychiatry. This was led in the most part by a desire to bring dementia care into the remit of services for older people and to reduce what was described as age-related prejudice (Murphy and Banerjee, 1993). Strategies to expand the use of case management and develop multidisciplinary teams were implemented (Philpot and Banerjee, 1997) and subsequently a service was introduced offering early identification and intervention in dementia within mainstream services (Banerjee et al., 2007). However, despite the move away from traditional services during this time, national surveys of arrangements for old-age psychiatry and community teams for older people with dementia found considerable variation in the provision of fully integrated multidisciplinary teams, suggesting that there is still room for improved collaboration between old age psychiatry services and social care services (Challis et al., 2002b; Abendstern et al., 2006).

Historically, a number of research studies have been undertaken in the community mental health teams for older people in Lewisham both with regard to access to the service and arrangements for the initial assessment of patients. Coles and colleagues (1991) reported that a community mental health team for older people received more referrals than a traditional hospital-orientated service over a similar time period. The authors concluded that this could have been an effect of it being a new service, or a result of its open access referral system. Interestingly, the major difference between the two services was that the community mental health team for older people recognised the need for providing carer support. The effect of the open access policy to the community mental health teams for older people was studied by Macdonald and colleagues (1994), who looked at the source of new referrals to the service over five years. They found little evidence of inappropriate referrals being generated by an open access policy to the multidisciplinary teams. They also noted that some older people with mental health problems might never have been referred and some would have had a delay in their referral had they come to the service via the 'traditional' route through a general practitioner. Other research into targeted services based upon a more traditional psychogeriatric service model found that many cases were referred too near the point of placement in long-term care, with the result that placement could not realistically be prevented (Askham and Thompson, 1990). With regard to initial assessment, Collighan and colleagues (1993) found very high concordance between staff in multidisciplinary teams and independent research psychiatrists of over 90 per cent in diagnostic decisions of newly referred cases, with accuracy of diagnosis associated with length of experience of team working rather than type of qualification. Similarly, Lindesay and colleagues (1996) found satisfactory agreement between the teams and the researchers with regard to psychiatric treatments recommended following diagnosis. Although both were small scale evaluations, they provided some evidence that a variety of staff in multidisciplinary teams undertaking assessments and acting as key workers, were neither misdiagnosing referrals nor offering inappropriate psychiatric treatments.

Prior to the inception of the LCMS, members of the community mental health team for older people identified a number of problems related to the specific needs and difficulties of people with dementia, as compared to other types of client with more treatable acute mental conditions such as depression. These views would appear to be supported by research within the service which investigated the care pathways of caseloads held by the community mental health team for older people, analysed by psychiatric diagnosis. This study found a marked difference in both the amount of contact and its pattern between cases diagnosed as suffering from an organic disorder such as dementia, compared with other conditions (Brown et al., 1996). Whereas half of those with a schizophrenic illness and 27 per cent with an affective disorder (mainly depression) were on the team's caseload continuously for the eighteen months studied, for those with a diagnosis of dementia the figure was eight per cent. A typical episode of care was significantly shorter for those with dementia, averaging 36 weeks open on the caseload, compared with 90 weeks for those with depression. This is illustrated in Figure 3.1. Indeed, other research has found that older people with dementia came low on the clinical priorities of a multidisciplinary service for the elderly mentally ill (Philpot, 1990; Philpot and Banerjee, 1997), and the attitude of medical staff may negatively affect their prioritization for treatment (Ryynänen et al., 2000). Similarly, in the past, if not now, groups such as politicians and the general public have placed older people and dementia patients as lower priorities for health care (Myllykangas et al., 2003).

The service setting and roles of members of the community mental health team for older people, within which the LCMS was located, are summarised in Box 3.1. The teams were multidisciplinary, comprising psychiatrists, occupational therapists, community psychiatric nurses, social workers and a psychologist. They operated an open-access policy and offered a variety of services from a '9 to 5' duty service, assessment, short-term interventions, and occasional long-term support and had close links with general practitioners and other specialist services. Psychiatrists and other team members provided services to acute wards and long-stay facilities, including specialist nursing homes, and to the social service day centre for people with dementia, as well as more generic care services. They generally focused on clients living in the community, although an analysis of the team in which the research study was based, found that 20 per cent of its caseload were resident in care homes (Brown et al., 1996). This approach allowed for a large number of clients to be seen in their home environment at various stages of their illness. The team offered psychiatric diagnosis as well as differential diagnosis for physical and other psychiatric disorders and provided a holistic assessment of mental health problems, social situation and physical environment. One of its most

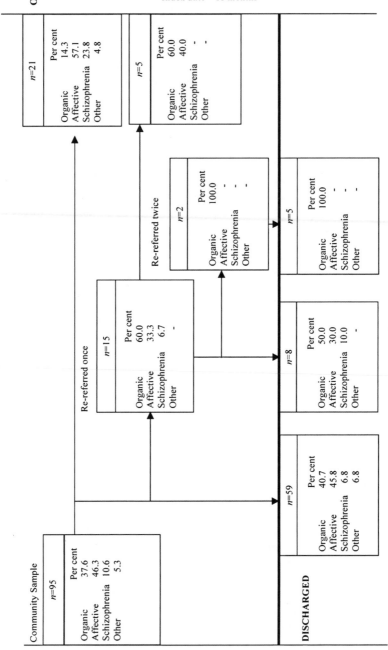

Figure 3.1   Client contact pathways: community sample follow-up
Source: Brown et al. (1996)

important characteristics was the key worker role, drawing on the specialist skills of team members, thus moving towards a 'transdisciplinary model' (Raiff and Shore, 1993) which allowed for professional skill sharing and continuity of care linked to one person known to the client. As a result of the research study, case management became a part of the community mental health team for older people. Under the auspices of case management, the service employed a differentiated approach. The hallmarks of this approach were: provision by a specialist team: variability in response to need in terms of staff level and resources; some staff with small caseloads; presence of intensive care management; and the provision of care management to a wider group of clients (Challis et al., 1998b; Hughes et al., 2005).

The service in which the scheme was based had three elements: assessment, advice and support, and referral to other services. First, a comprehensive assessment, focusing on the diagnosis of mental health problems, was provided followed by the application of a problem-solving approach for the difficulties reported by people with dementia, and their paid or family carers. In the case of new referrals in particular, this entailed close liaison with general practitioners and discussing detailed assessments at case review meetings. Second, clients and their carers were given information and advice based on the assessments, to enhance carer understanding of the diagnosis and to provide them with information about appropriate support arrangements. Team members offered short-term support which included adjustment to the diagnosis, counselling or encouraging carers to use other support such as relatives' groups and day care. The third element of intervention was referral to appropriate services, for example domiciliary care or day care, or advice on how to access benefits. This was particularly relevant to those who had no previous contact with statutory services. In addition to care focused on the individual and their carer, some team members undertook group work, such as a family therapy service and a group for men in the early

Box 3.1   The Lewisham Case Management Scheme: setting and roles

Shorter term
Key workers
Community mental health team for older people
(psychiatrists, community psychiatric nurses, psychologist,
occupational therapists, social workers)
+
Long term
Case managers
(social workers with budget for patients with dementia)
Case management

Adapted from Challis et al. (1997a)

stages of dementia. Others provided general education and training for those caring for people with dementia in both community and institutional settings. For example, team members offered training packages to staff in residential homes and in specialist facilities for older people with mental health problems. This was designed to improve staff understanding of mental health problems in the elderly and enhance recognition of their needs and rights in these settings, identified as an important area of activity in policy guidance and health care reviews (Audit Commission, 2006; Wanless, 2006; Commission for Social Care Inspection, 2008; Department of Health, 2008b). The introduction of case management into the service complemented these activities and enhanced its capacity to support older people with dementia in their own homes.

Case Management Arrangements

The introduction of professionally qualified social workers acting as case managers brought to the team a focus on the individual needs of clients and their carers in relation to long-term care at home, establishing a different approach to the prevailing ethos and orientation of the team at the inception of the study. Characteristics of the case management model, established during the period of the research, are summarised in Box 3.2.

As noted earlier in the chapter, the team operated an open access service which provided a diagnosis and assessment of the needs of older people with mental health problems. Furthermore, the location of the case management service within a community mental health team for older people meant that greater emphasis was placed on case screening rather than case finding. Typically, people with a high level of need who could benefit from this aspect of the old age mental health service were referred to the scheme, as summarised in Box 3.3. It has been demonstrated elsewhere that the effectiveness of an intervention involving people with dementia can be critically affected by the stage of the disease (Zarit and Leitsch, 2001). Hence, the selection of cases for the LCMS at the appropriate point in the disease and care pathways was important. Although carers were informed that they could refer a client directly to the community mental health team for older people without referral from their general practitioner, team members were aware that often referrals came to the service far too late for community care to be a feasible long-term option. This was observed in another study where it was noted that carers were unwilling to ask for help until they were in crisis (Levin et al., 1989). Team members also noted the difficulty of encouraging carers of older people with dementia to utilise the support services available. This reluctance was due in part to difficulties some carers had in accepting the diagnosis of dementia. Similar findings have been reported and discussed elsewhere (Gilleard, 1992; Zarit et al., 1999; Zarit and Zarit, 2006). In this setting the task for case managers was to identify those with a diagnosis of

Box 3.2   Characteristics of case management in the Lewisham Case Management Scheme

---

Target group: older people with a diagnosis of dementia, and at risk of admission to residential or nursing home care

Location: within a multidisciplinary community mental health team for older people

Style: clinical in terms of practice, incorporating assessment and planning with carers and colleagues; focusing on intervention and crisis management strategies and monitoring

Operational features:

Role specificity – social workers designated as full-time case managers

Balance of work between assessment and review – initial diagnostic assessment normally preceded referral to case managers and their long-term involvement with clients and carers

Staff mix – qualified social workers

Case-load size – small, 20 -25 cases per manager

Degree of continuity of involvement – longer-term responsibility: case managers responsible for assessment, implementing the care plan, and monitoring and review

Documentation processes – the Case Planning and Review form (CAPRE) focusing on assessment, care planning and review

Degree of influence upon service providers – own budget: development of specialist paid helper service for clients receiving case management. Use of local authority home care service although perceived as not sufficiently responsive to the needs of these clients. Some purchase of private domiciliary care to fill gaps in service provision

Management: standards and quality – case managers received peer support from the multi-disciplinary team but line management arrangements were within the social services department

Logical coherence of arrangements – integrated service model for high need group with easy access to multidisciplinary team for specialist assessment and advice, and a blurring of roles between assessor and provider viz domiciliary care in terms of the paid helper service

---

Adapted from Challis (1994c) and Challis et al. (1998b)

Box 3.3   Characteristics and circumstances of clients and carers referred to the Lewisham Case Management Scheme

Client characteristics	Carer characteristics	Circumstances
Diagnosis of dementia	Ill-health	At risk in the community
Disturbed behaviour	Distress at burden of	Awaiting discharge from
Physical frailty	caring	hospital
		Withdrawal of support by carer
		Absence of carer

dementia who could benefit from the particular approach available within the case management service.

Older people with dementia referred to case managers within the scheme were initially assessed by members of the community mental health team for older people. As a consequence, they received a composite clinical mental health assessment prior to entering the LCMS. This enabled case managers in their assessment to focus on establishing a relationship with the client and their carers and to undertake a full appraisal of their needs and behaviours and the contribution of their existing care network, involving family, friends, and paid carers. Thus, the two assessment processes were different in both form and content. The assessment undertaken by the community mental health team for older people was normally completed by one or two members within a relatively short period of time using standard documentation, the contents of which were subsequently reviewed by other members of the clinical team. In contrast, assessments undertaken by case managers were broader, encompassing information relating to carers and the clients' life histories and were completed over a longer period of time, often a number of weeks. In essence, case managers were providing a secondary assessment as part of support planning and long-term care. Assessment and case management were a continuous process, with case managers facilitating participation and negotiation in the care process (Smale et al., 1993). A unique feature of the LCMS was the development a proforma known as the Case Planning and Review form (CAPRE), devised to meet both operational and research requirements, which was undertaken by case managers at both the initial and subsequent reviews.

To understand the challenges inherent in the implementation of case management for older people with dementia, it is important to set it in the context of local service developments in relation to domiciliary care which was the most extensively used community service for older people with dementia. Nationally, it had been reported that there was much variability in domiciliary care and complex charging policies across the authorities studied, noting a tendency to maximise 'cover' rather than increase 'intensity' of the service resulting in the service being spread thinly rather than targeting those with greatest need (SSI, 1987). The domiciliary care service in Lewisham during the course of the study reflected this picture. Prior to the introduction of the LCMS, community mental health team members had also commented that services offering domiciliary care, respite day care, and residential care for people at home were insufficient in quality and quantity. Furthermore, attempts to employ local voluntary sector services to provide social support had been time-consuming and often unsuccessful. More fundamental changes in the nature of the domiciliary care service attempted to address these problems both before the introduction of the LCMS and subsequently.

Nevertheless, as the LCMS developed, both staff in the social services department and members of the community mental health team for older people continued to report difficulties in supporting people with dementia in their own homes. They identified a number of gaps in services which could not adequately meet the particular needs of these clients. For example, the domiciliary care service could not provide multiple visits throughout the day or through the night, nor was there flexibility in the time of visits. Concurrently, delays in the placements of older people in residential and nursing care resulting in them remaining at home with a high level of dependency, and very frail older people being discharged from hospital to their own homes were features of the LCMS referrals. Thus, the domiciliary care service began to focus to a greater extent on personal care rather than domestic tasks. The service was a source of referrals to the scheme, particularly in its pilot stage, and a significant part of the care network used. In respect of the evaluation of the scheme, domiciliary care workers were important informants as to the functioning of older people with dementia and, in some cases, provided the only independent information of their needs.

Studies of staff activities provide an interesting insight into the locus of work for case managers. Members of the team in which the LCMS was located took part in a diary keeping exercise carried out to investigate and discriminate between patterns of activities and time use within the multidisciplinary team (von Abendorff et al., 1994). Their working day was coded into categories; client-related work; service-related work, for example meetings or research; and other activities. About three-quarters of staff time was found to be spent in 'client-related' activities, a proportion similar to that of other studies which have found between 64 per cent and 78 per cent of case managers' time spent in direct or indirect client-related case-work (Wright et al., 1987; Fein and Staff, 1991; Tibbitt and Martin, 1991; Weinberg et al., 2003). In contrast, subsequent research has found that case managers spent significantly less time in direct contact with clients and carers in authorities using a targeted approach to the care of frail older people in comparison to authorities with specialist older people's teams (Challis et al., 2007). Two other studies of case managers' use of time provide findings relevant to the LCMS. First, clients who were totally dependent required less intensive management than those with dementia or mental illness, and paradoxically had fewer impairments in activities of daily living (Diwan, 1999). Second, a case management study which explored the relationship between the content of case managers' work and client outcomes revealed that more time spent on indirect services related to the client was associated with positive outcomes with regard to mental health and social networks, indicating that particular components of the case management process have an impact upon outcome (Bjorkman and Hansson, 2000).

Summary

The LCMS was introduced at a time when there was considerable change within the service network in which it was located, particularly with regard to the provision of domiciliary care. Furthermore, the approach of the community mental health team for older people, while valued by recipients, resulted in short term interventions which left many of the particular needs of older people with dementia unmet. Team members acknowledged that gaps in services and a lack of long-term support made it particularly difficult to provide individualised support to older people with dementia and their carers. On the other hand, the old age psychiatry services locally were well-developed and the commitment to research of senior members within the service meant that practice was both progressive and open to scrutiny. Indeed, the mental health services for older people available at that time were in advance of those in other parts of the UK benefiting as they were from comprehensive and multidisciplinary team working and continuity of care.

Case managers were, therefore, located within a community mental health team for older people, a specialist secondary health care setting which provided primarily a treatment-orientated model of care, with a focus on improvement, stabilisation and discharge. They were employed by the social services department, and were thus able to access all relevant health and social services resources for older people with dementia and their carers. It is in this context that evaluation of the case management service and its contribution and different style of work needs to be viewed.

Chapter 4
Research Methodology

Context and Design

The Lewisham Case Management Scheme was, in many ways, ahead of the policy agenda of the time in that it examined the benefits and costs of intensive care management, focused upon a specific high-risk target group and linked with a specialist secondary health care service. The focus of the research study was broad, examining the development of the case management scheme within the local service context as well as its impact and practice. It sought to address the costs and benefits experienced by older people with dementia and their carers, the operation of the new service and the identification of any care practices which improve service provision to a vulnerable client group.

The methodology was a quasi-experimental design in which the case management service received by older people with dementia and their carers, the experimental group, was compared to that offered in a similar community team setting without this innovative service, the control group. It is of note that both service settings were located within a network of services for older people with mental health problems with resources probably more extensive and more joint than were available in other parts of the country at the time (Challis et al., 2002b). Consequently, such a context was one that was, if anything, likely to reduce the kind of gain associated with the intervention so there could potentially be a conservative bias to the findings. As part of the quasi-experimental design, equivalent cases were identified in both the experimental group and control group by applying similar referral criteria, namely, those with a diagnosis of dementia, significant unmet needs and thus at risk of admission to long-term care. Subsequently, individuals were paired on a number of variables likely to be associated with outcome to create matched groups.

One potential problem with this particular research design can occur where the existence of a new service option changes referral behaviour (Challis and Darton, 1990). An example is when cases allocated to the control group are placed in long-term care before they can be included into the study since the incentive to support them at home is less than in the context of a new service present in the experimental area. This can introduce a bias against identifying a discernible reduction in the placement rate in the experimental group, as noted in other quasi-experimental studies (Challis and Davies, 1986; Challis et al., 2002a). It has also been noted that the progressive nature of Alzheimer's disease and other types of dementia creates a trajectory of care during which time there is a limited optimal period for undertaking intervention programmes (Zarit and Leitsch, 2001). Thus the very nature of the disease, and the stage of this at which individuals are included into the experimental or comparison group, can influence the outcome of the research (Challis and Darton, 1990).

Four research questions informed this study. First, were two questions regarding the outcomes for older people with dementia and their carers, and the cost of care. The second set of questions were concerned with the care processes that evolved, namely how care managers supported people with dementia and their carers in the context of a specialist mental health team for older people. These are detailed in Box 4.1. A close connection between research and service development is one that has been encouraged by researchers evaluating services (Zarit et al., 1999; Droes et al., 2000; Davey et al., 2005). The close working relationship between the researchers and the case managers and, indeed, all members of the multidisciplinary team gave a unique chance to investigate some of the key processes in the development and evolution of the case management scheme. From the outset, service development was expected to be an integral part of the work of case managers and tangible recognition of this was seen in the establishment of the specialist paid helper service as described in Chapter 6, to provide care to people with dementia in their own homes.

Box 4.1   Research questions

Research domain	Research questions
Cost and outcome	What are the outcomes for older people with dementia and their carers of a new intensive care management service? What are the costs of care in an intensive care management service compared with the usual modes of care?
Care process	What kinds of practice interventions and strategies do care managers develop for people with dementia? What forms of service developments do care managers initiate to meet need?

Interviews: Schedules and Process

Several factors influenced decisions on the choice and design of measures. Interviews and questionnaires were designed to be user-friendly. A variety of interview schedules were designed to cater for different levels of involvement and availability of carers. The mode of data collection varied between interviews and self-completion of questionnaires. Both standardised scales and those developed specifically for the study were used. The use of well-validated and reliable standardised instruments allowed for comparison with other studies, whilst measures devised specifically for the study were sometimes more suitable and briefer than standard self-completion measures. Indeed, it has been argued that the inclusion of established measures alongside new scales can help determine the validity of the latter (Zarit and Leitsch, 2001). Some items were used particularly for their question and wording style (Bebbington et al., 1986; Levin et al., 1989; 1994; Davies et al., 1990). In common with other studies (Mozley et al., 2004), occasionally small changes were made in the interview schedule in order to overcome problems of older people's low expectations and to highlight their dissatisfaction or problems.

Four different interview schedules were designed for the study encompassing a wide range of questions and measures. These included background data on the older person with dementia and their carer, information on the care packages offered, and client and carer outcomes. These were colour coded for ease of recognition and flexible use, and are summarised in Box 4.2. Each schedule was piloted, and incorporated items and approaches used by other researchers for similar client groups (for example Flynn 1986; Flynn and Saleem, 1986; Levin et al., 1989; 1994).

In this study, the definition of a principal carer was that they had to be actively involved in the care of the older person with dementia at least seven hours per week. Other carers were also interviewed, even if they were visiting only on a once a month basis. If there was a principal carer, the comprehensive carer schedule was completed with the carer as main informant. Where there was no carer, the informant schedule coupled with the brief carer schedule, were completed

Box 4.2   Interview schedules

Schedule	Main source of information	Median duration of interview
Client	Older person with dementia	Half an hour (range 25–45 minutes)
Principal carer (comprehensive)	Carer living with or in contact with client seven or more hours per week	Two and a half hours (range 1½–3 hours)
Carer (brief)	Other carer not meeting criteria above (or principal carer with no time to complete the longer version)	Three-quarters of an hour (range ½ –1¼ hours)
Informant	Also postal questionnaire version Home help or other paid carer	1 hour (range ¾–1½ hours)

wherever possible by a paid carer. The latter was also used for carers who met the criteria for a comprehensive interview schedule but who did not have time to complete a lengthy interview. In the case of carers living a significant distance away or with little time for interview, a postal version of the questionnaire was used. The schedules used for the follow-up interviews at six and twelve months for carers and informants omitted the introductory background information but included some questions about perceived change. In addition to the questionnaires noted in Box 4.2, a separate short questionnaire was used with the carers of older people who had either been admitted to residential care or had died following referral, to investigate processes around placement in long-term care and the role of services.

Since the design of this study, there have been many developments in method and practice with respect to gaining the views of people with cognitive impairment (Goldsmith, 1996; Barnett, 1997; Moriarty and Webb, 1997a; Hancock et al., 2003; Care Services Improvement Partnership, 2007). Nevertheless, in this study there was an emphasis placed on identifying aspects of client perceptions of need which has been increasingly recognised as an essential component of any service evaluation (Kirkhart and Ruffolo, 1993; Slade, 1994; Care Services Improvement Partnership, 2005). The measures used in the interview schedules, including their origin, brief description, and whose perception was sought for each domain of outcome, are described in Appendix 1. These were grouped into eight domains, detailed in Box 4.3. They include: 'descriptive' measures for example, level of physical functioning; 'evaluative' measures for example, quality of life or care; measures of 'perceived need' for example, changes in need over time; and 'intermediate' outcomes measuring processes of care, for example perceived support.

The researchers, experienced in mental health services for older people, carried out the assessments and were, of course, not blind to the intervention group. A multidimensional approach was used in order to recognise the many different possible outcomes and perspectives in this kind of service (Cantley and Smith, 2001). For example the assessment of the older person's quality of life drew on

Box 4.3   Interview schedules: domains of enquiry

Client	Carer
Functioning and ill-being	Support to client
Perspectives	Burden
Quality of life	Malaise
Quality of care	
Client and carer Overall need and related outcomes	

their perspective, that of the carer, paid carer, as well as the researcher. After each interview, researchers recorded case summaries to capture key features of the care received by older people with dementia.

The research was approved by the then Ethical Committee of Lewisham and North Southwark Health Authority and supported by senior management within the local authority social services department, and clear ethical guidelines were drawn up. A central tenet of these were, that both the older people with dementia and their carers had equal and independent rights to confidentiality, including consent to participation. Ethical guidelines specified that interviews were strictly confidential and information obtained from a carer, client or care provider would not be exchanged except in exceptional circumstances. For example, researchers would contact services in response to a carer's distressed state only at their request. Following an initial contact by letter, whenever possible the carer was asked to be present when the researcher was introduced to the older person in their own home. The interview with the client was facilitated by information previously provided by the carer, allowing the researcher to prompt responses from the older person about their life. Although carers were often present at the home, older people and carers were interviewed separately where possible and both initial and follow-up interviews were completed at similar times of day and location. As noted earlier, in circumstances where a carer was involved for less than seven hours a week, or was unable to spare the time for an in-depth interview, this was completed by a paid carer. Where two clients lived together and had the same main carer, carer data were included only once in the carer analyses.

All older people with dementia and any involved carers were interviewed immediately on entry to the case management scheme by the researchers and again at six and twelve months. A similar practice was adopted for those in the control group when identified as potentially suitable. In total 215 interviews with clients and 262 interviews with family carers were undertaken. The latter acted both as a source of detailed information on the functioning of the older person with dementia as well as providing important independent 'consumer' views about service quality and effectiveness. Occasionally, a paid carer was interviewed to provide details about the client's functioning and their perception of the client's needs. Altogether 132 interviews were carried out with paid carers, mainly home care and related staff, and exceptionally wardens of sheltered accommodation and paid helpers who were recruited as part of the intervention. With regard to family carers, the majority were female, caring either for parents or partners. Over two-thirds were in contact more than three days a week providing care for seven hours or more per week. This is akin to groups identified in other similar specialist interventions (Askham and Thompson, 1990; Moriarty and Webb, 2000). There were no differences between the carers in the experimental and control groups with regard to age, working status, and days per week in contact. Around half of carers lived either in the same household or next door (47 per cent in the experimental group, 53 per cent in the control group).

Interviews were completed with a significant proportion of older people with dementia, despite their level of cognitive impairment, although more detailed attempts to gain insights into, or use observational assessment of quality of care were not feasible given the resources available and the setting. However, when an interview was attempted, on average more than eight out of ten respondents were able to give a clear and coherent picture to the researcher, with 89 per cent of clients in the experimental group and 84 per cent in the control group completing a full or partial interview. This supports the findings of Mozley and colleagues (1999), which showed that many people with quite severe cognitive impairment were able to reliably comment on aspects of their satisfaction with life. A significant proportion of clients enjoyed the interview and many were able to express their feelings about the importance of their home and social network. Where the older person and carer were seen interacting together, this often gave a powerful insight into the nature of their relationship. The refusal by a number of older people with dementia to be interviewed was indicative of the difficulties in providing help for this group, despite their clear expressed wish to remain at home and requirement for services. Overall, interviews with the older people with dementia were a rewarding and memorable part of the research experience. These interviews contributed significantly to understanding their situation and their care networks as well as identifying the need for services. The researchers often developed positive relationships with respondents, particularly carers, which contributed to the collection of high quality data.

Case Selection

A multidimensional approach was used in the selection of older people for inclusion in the study. As noted previously, the service provided by the scheme focused primarily on people with dementia and related mental health problems. At the outset of the research study, it was envisaged that individuals assessed by the team would meet widely used criteria but that there might be exceptional clients selected by the team for support. First, cases for the experimental group were selected using information from their case notes and the assessments of key workers in the team (Collighan et al., 1993). Second, they were assessed using the OBS (Organic Brain Score) of the Comprehensive Assessment and Referral Evaluation (CARE) interview schedule, (Gurland et al., 1977) using the accepted diagnostic cut-off of three or more used in previous research to indicate the likely presence of dementia (Lindesay et al., 1989; Lindesay and Murphy 1989; Macdonald et al., 1982). The latter was derived from data collected in the first interview with the client. Third, based on the interview with the carer and client, the researcher examined to what extent the DSM-III-R (American Psychiatric Association, 1987) criteria for dementia were met. Although clients did not always meet the criteria of all three approaches, they all met the criteria of at least one definition of eligibility. No clients were excluded from either group on the basis of the particular form of their diagnosis of dementia. As Table 4.1 indicates, it was evident that these cases individually presented a cross-section of the dementia-related problems encountered in community care and to which this service was targeted. With regard to the control group, the researchers simulated as far as possible the screening of referrals as described above, in the team from which cases for this group were recruited.

An objective computer-based matching procedure was used to generate matched groups. As noted in Table 4.2, six controls and three cases in the experimental group were placed in long-term care in the month after the initial research assessment commenced and they were thus excluded from the research study. This tendency for placement in long-term care to occur before inclusion in the research more frequently for control group cases has been discussed earlier in this chapter. Other differences between the initially recruited experimental and control groups became apparent. The presence of a husband or wife with dementia and a caring partner who was physically but not mentally frail, or couples who were both confused were noted in the experimental group, but no suitable equivalent complexity was found in the control group. This suggests that certain more complex cases were

Table 4.1   Selection criteria: diagnosis of dementia

Diagnostic grouping	Experimental	Control
A. Alzheimer's disease (and no other accompanying diagnosis)	25 (56%)	28 (56%)
B. Other dementias and concurrent diagnoses	20 (44%)	22 (44%)
Total	45	50
B. Other dementias and concurrent diagnoses:		
Multi-infarct dementia (and no other diagnosis)	11 (24%)	8 (16%)
Frontal lobe dementia	1	2
Dementia with recent history of depression and/or paranoia	1	3
Sub cortical-type dementias (including multiple sclerosis, supra-nuclear palsy, and temporal arteritis)	2	2
Cognitive impairment additional to longstanding psychiatric history or learning disability	4	5
Mild cognitive impairment, often accompanying a recent acute confusional state	1	2

Table 4.2   Client selection

	Experimental	Control
Included:	45	50
Excluded:		
Moved out of area	0	1
Placed within one month of discussion	3	6
Refused to participate in research	0	9
Excluded after assessment	5	0
Total	53	66

specially referred to the team from which the experimental group was derived for possible inclusion in the study. Another difference was the higher rate of refusal to participate of married caring partners of clients in the control group compared to the experimental group.

To produce two similar groups for some of the comparative analysis, cases were then individually matched on a set of variables which have been shown to influence the outcome of community-based care, particularly predicting placement in long-term care. A researcher with no knowledge of the individual cases and who was blind to their outcomes carried out the process in order to minimise the probability of prior knowledge of cases influencing and thereby contaminating the groups selected for this stage. This initial computer matching was carried out on the basis of variables selected from six domains as shown in Box 4.4. Three of the domains related to the personal characteristics of the older person with dementia – their cognitive and physical functioning and the extent of disturbed or 'trying' behaviours (Levin et al., 1989). In addition, two components of their social situation were included – whether or not they lived alone and the stress experienced by their carer – together with details of the length of their current contact with specialist mental health services. In four of the domains it was possible to select a clinically significant cut-off point for each scale, which was based on the known properties of the scale or epidemiological data derived from use of the scale, taking into account the actual distribution of the scores of the sample.

The matching procedure of cases in the experimental and control group followed four sequential steps and this process is summarised in Table 4.3. Computer-based matching by specific variables was followed by 'clinical matching' of individual cases at each of the first three stages of matching in the instances where more than one case could be matched to one other. In these circumstances, four additional variables were considered; gender of the older person; gender of the carer; age of the client and relationship of the carer with the older person. These are detailed in Box 4.4. First, it was possible to match 20 cases from the experimental and control groups using the procedure described above. At the second step, examination of the pattern of distribution of the least important of the variables

Box 4.4   Matching variables

Domain	Source
Computer matched variables	
1. Cognitive functioning	OBS scale (CARE – Gurland et al., 1977)
2. Physical functioning	Clifton Assessment Procedures for the Elderly (CAPE): Behaviour Rating Scale (BRS) – Physical Disability Subscale (Pattie and Gilleard, 1979)
3. Disturbed behaviour	Clifton Assessment Procedures for the Elderly: BRS-Social Disturbance Subscale (Pattie and Gilleard, 1979)
4. Living environment	Whether living alone or with an involved carer
5. Carer stress	Malaise Score (Rutter et al., 1970). If no family carer, rated as zero
6. Current psychiatric episode	Length of time case open to team when referred for special case management service
Additional matched variables	
1. Gender of client	
2. Gender of carer	
3. Age of client	
4. Relationship of carer to client	

(current psychiatric episode) permitted its relaxation without any adverse effect upon the composition of the two groups and provided eleven more pairs. Third, there was stepwise adjustment of the cut-off points for the main scales which generated a further eleven pairs of cases. The fourth step involved attempting to reduce the discrepancy which had pre-existed between the two groups in the number of older people with dementia whose main carer was their partner. This involved substituting previously matched cases with unmatched cases, first using the computer generated variables and then the four additional variables relating to characteristics of the carer and client. This created one further matched pair, resulting in a total of 43 matched pairs. Thus, the creation of matched groups led to two cases being excluded from the experimental group and seven being excluded from the control group. No statistically significant differences were evident between the two groups on a range of descriptive indicators as illustrated in Table 4.4.

In the subsequent statistical analysis of data, differences between the experimental and control groups were examined using one-way and also two-

Table 4.3   Matching process

Step	Process	Number of matched pairs generated
1	Matched on six variables and cut-off points	20
2	Matched on five variables (relaxing current psychiatric episode variable)	11
3	Stepwise adjustment of key scales cut-offs by up to 2 points	11
4	Reducing matched groups discrepancy with regard to type of main carer by substituting previously matched cases	1
	Total	43

Table 4.4   Case characteristics by matched group

Characteristic	Mean value/ frequency distribution		Significance level p
	E **n=43**	**C** **n=43**	
Age (I) – mean	80.4	79.8	NS[1]
Sex: male (R) – %	30.2	30.2	NS[2]
Socio-economic group (I):			
professional/intermediate – %	34.9	25.6	
skilled non-manual – %	20.9	32.6	NS[2]
skilled manual – %	20.9	9.3	
semi-skilled/unskilled – %	23.3	32.6	
Presence of carer (I) – %	88.4	83.7	NS[2]
CAPE (I):			
Overall BRS – mean	15.7	15.7	NS[1]
Communication disorder – mean	0.72	0.65	NS[1]
Apathy – mean	5.73	5.93	NS[1]

Source: Challis et al. (2002c)

Notes: 1. One way analysis of variance   3. Source of information:
              2. Chi-square test   I= Informant
                                                                               R= Researcher

way analysis of variance for changes over time, using the initial information as a covariate. All results at the five per cent level and below are reported as statistically significant. Although it has been suggested that giving the exact value of p is preferable for medical statistics (Altman et al., 2000), the conventionally given values of p (<0.05, <0.01, and <0.001), were thought to be appropriate in reporting the findings for analysis of variance tests in this study. Statistical control through covariance analysis was employed to adjust and test for differences between the two groups. To minimise loss of information in a relatively small data set, where standard scales were used and where individual items comprising less than 20 per cent of the possible total score were missing, data from the most appropriate other time assessment were substituted. This was likely to attenuate the scale of any changes and differences. For the regression analyses, mean values were employed for missing data on as sensitive a basis as possible, by using appropriate sub-group means. The small number of cases and likely medium to small effect sizes meant that the power of tests was low and there was therefore a reduced chance of finding statistical differences. The case selection and research design process is summarised in Figure 4.1.

Service and Cost Information

A number of approaches and sources of data were employed to describe the process of intensive care management within the scheme and relate it to the service system in which it was placed. First, systematic case records were developed to capture the activities of case managers. Second, analysis was undertaken of the contents of case notes and patterns of services provided to meet particular needs. Third, interviews were undertaken with staff involved in providing and managing the service or immediately affected by it. Finally, the service receipt measures also contributed to the analysis of the practice of case managers and the care packages they established, supplementing other data.

A Case Planning and Review form record system (CAPRE), completed by case managers was used to describe client and carer needs assessed by case managers, the patterns of care planning and the response to needs, resources used and outcomes. It was derived from documentation used in the Kent, Gateshead and Darlington case management projects, (Challis and Chesterman, 1985; Challis and Davies, 1986; Challis, et al., 1995; 2002a) which themselves built on that devised by Goldberg and Warburton (1979). The CAPRE encouraged goal planning and was adapted to make it appropriate for older people with mental health problems. It was divided into two sections, case planning and case review which were completed at two different points in time. The case planning section was in four parts. First, a tick box format was used to identify the main problems, concerns and unmet needs experienced by the older person and carers within the service system. The second part allowed for the identification of the main problem as assessed by the case manager, older person and carers indicating the overall severity of

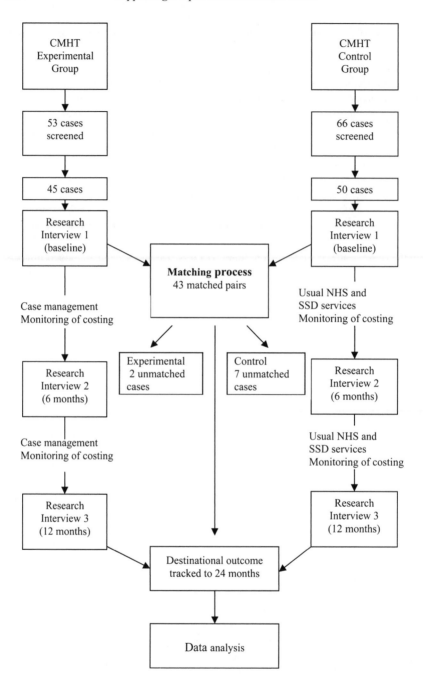

Figure 4.1   Case selection process and research design

the problems highlighted in the domains. The third part was open-ended, for case managers to describe the strengths and resources of the older person and carer as well as an overall formulation of care. The fourth part allowed for care planning, to draw up plans to address identified need domains, strategies and resources to be used and to specify intended goals. The case review section of the form was completed for the vast majority of cases between four and six months after the first section. It included a quantitative measure of the plan's success including comments and conclusions from the case manager with reasons for its positive or negative outcomes. There was a tick box section to summarise the main strategies and resources actually used by the case manager and a review of their input to the case. If the case was to remain open, another review form was commenced at this point to continue with the planning and review cycle as above. Improvements or deterioration of any recorded unmet needs from the previous plan were noted on this form.

As indicated earlier in the chapter, cost information was an important part of the evaluation, integral to the assessment of the costs and effectiveness of the new intensive case management scheme. The approach to cost data collection was that it met the criteria of comprehensiveness, and focused upon opportunity cost as a more general cost concept (Challis and Davies, 1986; Netten, 1994; Challis et al., 1995; Challis et al., 2002a; Byford et al., 2003). Opportunity cost has been described as, 'the value of the alternative use of the assets tied up in the production of the service' (Netten, 1994, 46). Cost analysis requires two elements, careful monitoring of the use of services or resources over a given time period, and adequate estimates of the unit cost of each service or resource.

As indicated in Figure 4.1, comprehensive costing was undertaken during the first year of all service inputs provided for the experimental group in receipt of intensive case management, and the control group receiving standard services. The price of services was obtained locally when possible and cross-validated with national price estimates. All services were costed and where variation occurred due to local circumstances, such as different prices for day care, contributions from a variety of sources were amalgamated into a single figure. The gross costs for services are detailed in Appendix 2. Most of the service receipt data were collected in 'package' form retrospectively. This was derived from service settings and interviews with family carers and paid carers at the second and third interviews. All information was mapped out on a cost form for each client over their first year, recording which services were received in what amounts each week. To further minimise distortion or error in the service receipt data collected, a simple 'diminishing value' principle of accuracy was adopted. The greatest effort to establish validity was given to the highest cost services, where the consequences of even a small error could be substantial. The costing covered all the services provided and all the costs connected with their delivery. Hence cost information collected covered a range of interest groups potentially affected by the intervention and encompassed costs to agencies, costs to carers and costs to society as a whole.

Agency costs were those incurred by each of the purchasers of services, social care and the NHS, and were derived from two sources: the amount of services received by the client and the prices of services. Costs to carers were assessed by taking account of both the direct financial burden of caring and the hours spent caring, and the opportunity cost of this was calculated. Total costs to carers constituted the aggregation of these. Costs to carers other than the main carer were also included. The total costs to society were estimated by combining costs to services, costs to carers, clients' personal expenditures and housing costs. Factors associated with cost variations for older people in both the experimental and control groups were examined using cost function analysis, in order to identify client and carer characteristics or care processes that influenced costs to agencies, costs to society and community package costs. The latter were those costs of services associated with maintaining older people with dementia at home and supporting their carers.

Information was collected on the paid helpers, through the analysis of their recruitment questionnaires and interviews with case managers; by interviews with a sample of ten helpers; and finally using paid helper payment records to construct a picture of the use of paid helpers throughout the scheme. In addition, the case notes of members of the community mental health team for older people, case managers and records within the local social services department were scrutinised in order to gain more information on their contacts with individual cases in both experimental and control groups. These data were used to define service receipt and cost to services, and also to gather further information which could qualitatively describe the practice of members of the community mental health teams for older people and case managers in particular. Furthermore, budget statements by case managers and reviews of care packages set up through the scheme were used to look at the balance between paid helpers and the local authority home care service during the life of the study.

Summary

This chapter has provided a brief overview of the case management study and the context within which it was set, and a description of the research design, methodology and the interview schedules and the measures used therein. It has also described case selection and the detailed methods used to create the two matched groups. Of particular interest is the fact that based upon information relating to characteristics of clients and carers in the experimental and control groups, it was established that there were no significant differences between the two groups following the matching process. The process of gathering costs and service information has also been outlined.

A considerable number of informants were consulted in the process of data collection in order to get the most accurate information and to obtain the best possible picture of the older person's situation. However, in a number of cases, quality of data was not ideal, due to difficulties in collecting information. These methodological dilemmas highlight the particular difficulties associated with the evaluation of research into long-term care arrangements for people with dementia. For example, there are methodological implications for the evaluation of intervention programmes for older people with dementia where high rates of attrition occur due to death or placement in long-term care (Zarit and Leitsch, 2001). Observers have also noted various methodological problems (Gilhooly, 1990; Knight et al., 1993; Levin and Moriarty, 1996) where intervention programmes are likely to impact differentially on older people with dementia on the one hand and on their carers on the other.

The following chapter seeks to examine the case management practice of the Lewisham Case Management Scheme, and how it evolved during the course of the research study. Subsequent chapters describe: the development of the paid helper service and its characteristics; the outcomes of the scheme for the older people with dementia in both experimental and control groups and for their carers; and details of the costs and effectiveness of the case management scheme, illustrating some of the methodological dilemmas referred to above.

Chapter 5
Care and Support at Home for Older People and Their Carers

Introduction

Models of community care in respect of adults with mental health problems have been well developed as compared with those for older people. For example, a meta-review of research literature from 75 studies on case management for people with severe mental illness identified six different models of case management (Mueser et al., 1998). These were: brokerage; clinical case management; assertive community treatment (ACT), intensive case management (ICM), the strengths model; and the rehabilitation model. The focus of brokered case management is on: assessment; referral; co-ordination; monitoring and advocacy. Kanter (1989) described clinical case managers as providing services in four areas: initial phase including assessment and planning; environmental interventions; patient interventions; and patient-environment interventions. ACT is given by a multidisciplinary team for people with severe mental illness and offers low patient/staff ratios, 24 hour community care, shared caseloads, and direct services (Stein and Test, 1980, 1985; Test, 1992). ICM provides practical assistance in daily living, and is similar to ACT except that ICM employs individual rather than shared caseloads. The strengths model focuses on the personal strengths of the individual. The rehabilitation model emphasises the personal goals of the individual and encourages skills to promote community tenure (Anthony et al., 1988).

Arguably the Lewisham Case Management Scheme contains a number of these models. However, if any are to be selected, they are a combination of both the clinical and ICM approaches, replicating the style of case management of the PSSRU pilot projects (Challis and Davies 1986; Challis et al., 1990; 1995), cited in *Caring for People* (Cm 849, 1989) as exemplars of good practice. The responsibilities for assessment, care planning, linking with both carers and the mental health team and for managing crises are consistent with the clinical approach. Furthermore, in terms of target group, the centrality of practical assistance and small caseloads, it resembles intensive case management as described by Mueser and colleagues. There is almost certainly a necessary relationship between intensive case management and the clinical model, whereby the small caseloads of the intensive model are necessary to make feasible the clinical approach. Indeed, this approach to the care of older people has been replicated elsewhere (Eggert et al., 1990), and there is evidence to suggest that smaller caseloads are necessary if case managers are to support older people at home as an alternative to admission to long-term care (Degenholtz et al., 1999). An informed approach to commissioning services for older people is also an important component of case management and, more generally effective, community-based care (Moxley, 1989; Applebaum and Austin, 1990; SSI/SWSG, 1991a,b; Cm 4169, 1998; Cm 6499, 2005; Cm 6737, 2006; Department of Health, 2006), epitomised in this study by the paid helper service, which will be outlined in Chapter 6.

Social workers who possessed a range of skills and experience in working with older people were recruited as case managers to the LCMS. Although no specific training programme was provided at the clinical level, case managers had access to the normal range of training resources available both generally in social work issues and also in some specialist areas which had particular relevance to their client group, including, for example, reminiscence and elder abuse. They also visited one of the earlier care management schemes to learn from staff who had implemented that service (Challis et al., 1990; 2002a). In the development phase of the scheme, attempts were made to achieve a balance between providing a clear model for the case management scheme based on previous studies, together with the opportunity for good practice development. Overall, the aim was to allow sufficient flexibility for the scheme to develop and evolve in its unique setting.

Successful outcomes for the LCMS were defined as: enhancing the effectiveness of care; improving quality of life; reducing stress and ill-being in older people and carers; and allowing people to live where they wished in a manner which was as cost-effective as possible. This chapter examines case management practice which underpinned these goals, as it evolved during the course of the research study, highlighting the principles of case management as compared with more traditional social work practice with older people and their carers (Marshall, 1990; Hughes et al., 2005). The findings discussed in this chapter are based upon those clients who were recruited to the experimental group of the LCMS and receiving case management input. Information was derived from two sources: interviews with practitioners and data derived from the CAPRE documents, completed by case managers when assessing clients and reviewing care plans, as noted in Chapter 4. This work undertaken by case managers is examined in terms of the core tasks of case management: case finding and screening; needs assessment; implementing the care plan and monitoring, review and case closure.

The Process of Case Finding and Screening

One notable difference between the role of social workers in the community mental health team for older people and those social workers employed as case managers was the latter's focus on long-term continuity of care. Figure 5.1 describes the process whereby referrals were made for case management within the community mental health team in Lewisham. Both the community mental health team for older people in which the case managers were based and the home care service provided by the social services department were significant sources of referrals.

The managers of the home care service referred two groups: older people whose care required greater co-ordination in order for them to continue to live in their own home; and older people with dementia discharged from hospital who were adjudged to require more care than was available from traditional services to enable them to live at home. Referrals came from hospital staff through case managers developing close links with the in-patient old-age psychiatry service. In part this was fostered by psychiatrists who worked in both the hospital and the community mental health team.

However, this process, inevitably, had implications for the workload of other members of the community mental health team for older people in which it was based. At the outset of the scheme there were concerns regarding the workload of other team members since all its referrals received an initial mental health assessment. The management of the twin functions of case screening and case finding for the scheme sometimes proved difficult to negotiate within the close-knit multidisciplinary team with what, with the benefit of hindsight, constituted a lack of transparency about both the eligibility criteria for the scheme, and the process itself. However, as the case management scheme developed, other members of the multidisciplinary team were able to focus on more short-term interventions and working relationships were facilitated by the co-location of all team members. As described in Chapter 4, the target population of the LCMS was older people with dementia and related mental health problems, at risk of long-term care in hospital, or a specialist facility. This definition formed the basis of case screening. Case managers selected clients for inclusion onto the scheme and on the basis of experience they learnt to identify those who were more likely to

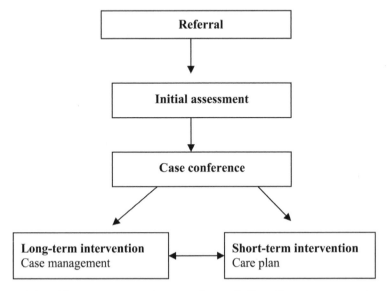

Figure 5.1   Case management: screening and allocation arrangements

benefit from the case management service. Particularly significant in this was the limited resource available of just two case managers leading to a waiting list of older people on occasions. These factors described above which affected both the supply and demand for services are summarised in Box 5.1.

As has been noted elsewhere (Kane, 2000), the main purpose of the assessment within long-term case management is to generate a care plan and this was a key activity for case managers within the LCMS, both when people were initially referred to the service and at review. The importance of the reassessment of need whilst clients were in receipt of assistance co-ordinated by the case managers was clearly evident in the care plan. In part this was a consequence of the deteriorating health of people with dementia and the constant need to monitor and reassess. It also related to significant events, such as planning for discharge from hospital after admission on an emergency basis or a change in the circumstances of a carer, affecting their capacity to contribute to care. Therefore, the case management approach as epitomised in this scheme illustrates how assessment is linked with, and is part of, the intervention process.

Typically, case managers undertook assessments following initial diagnostic assessment by a member of the community mental health team for older people. These focused upon assessment for specific community packages in order to maintain the older person with dementia in their own home. The assessment undertaken by case managers focused around three time periods: past experiences, the present situation and current concerns, and future hopes and aspirations. A history of the older person's previous interests, and likes and dislikes was obtained in order to build up a picture of their previous functioning. Case managers also incorporated carers' attitudes and experiences of caring, and their past and present perceptions of support for the client from statutory services were also incorporated into the assessment. In addition, case managers took account of services already in place in particular those provided by home care workers and paid helpers, whose

Box 5.1   Factors affecting screening, referral and selection

	Supply side: restrictions on availability	Selection criteria Resources available Waiting list Experience from longevity of scheme
Lewisham **Case** **Management** **Scheme**		
	Demand side: source of referrals	Client and carer circumstances Community mental health team Home care service Hospital staff

roles were outlined in Box 3.1. The hallmark of assessments undertaken by case managers was that they: included health and social care issues pertinent to the older person with dementia; focused on their quality of life; and recognised the importance of contributions to the existing care network by both informal and paid carers. The importance of developing supportive and flexible social networks both in traditional social casework practice (Briar and Miller, 1971) and in case management (Trevillion, 1992), has been well documented, and now finds expression in the drive to develop innovative ways of supporting vulnerable users (Cm 6737, 2006; Committee of Public Accounts, 2008).

As described in previous chapters, case managers recorded information in the form of CAPRE documentation for clients receiving case management input. Following the initial assessment, a number of clients required further assessments. Analyses of 42 initial assessments and 72 further assessments, 114 in total, are reported here. In the assessment process, case managers focused on three issues; the problems which had prompted referral to the specialist service; the combination of presenting problems, and identification of the most severe problem. Judgements relating to these issues are detailed in Table 5.1 which examines the content of assessments in terms of nine domains. A distinction is made between the first assessments completed in respect of each client and subsequent ones, for the purpose of analysis. A large and diverse number of problems were identified. Distress and difficulties experienced by carers were the most frequent in both contexts, being noted in over 80 per cent of both first assessments and subsequent assessments. In relation to the older person, the most frequent need noted was in respect of their mental state, present in 79 per cent of first assessments and slightly

Table 5.1   Assessment of needs by domain

	Initial assessments (n=42)		Subsequent assessments (n=72)	
	No.	**%**	**No.**	**%**
Client				
Physical health	22	52	44	61
ADL	30	71	44	61
Mental state	33	79	48	67
Social/leisure	32	76	35	49
Environment	13	31	18	25
Carer				
Distress and difficulties	34	81	60	83
Care Network				
Monitoring	30	71	50	69
Relationships	24	57	40	56
Service provision	11	26	26	36

less, in 67 per cent of subsequent assessments. This is perhaps unsurprising, given the nature of the target population for the scheme. In terms of the care network, the most significant area of need was recorded in relation to monitoring its functioning. Again this was noted in 71 per cent of first assessments and 69 per cent of subsequent assessments, and indicative of the large amount of time which was needed to sustain the care network.

Table 5.2 indicates the case manager's rating of severity of the unmet need within broad domain categories relating to different aspects of client and carer difficulties. Case managers rated the overall severity of problems within the seven domains on a seven point analogue scale ranging from 'none' to 'severe problems'. Clients were assessed as having a 'marked or severe' problem if the problem was rated five or above on this scale. The needs most commonly rated as 'marked or severe' were in the area of their social life, that is, their daily contact with other people where over half of first assessments (52 per cent) were rated as such. Similarly, carer distress and difficulties were rated as 'marked to severe' in half of all first assessments (50 per cent). Interestingly, these two domains also showed the greatest reduction in rated marked/severe need between initial and subsequent assessments. The latter illustrates that the scheme offered support to both clients and their carers. Physical health was, not surprisingly, the only domain which showed an increase in the proportion of cases rated as having a marked or severe problem at subsequent assessments, compared to all the other domains which showed a subsequent reduction. Arguably, this is an area in which case management input is likely to have least impact.

Additional data revealed problems and unmet needs of the older person with dementia and their carers recorded by case managers. Problems with preparing food or a meal were rated as present in half (50 per cent) of all first assessments,

Table 5.2   Severity of need

Assessments of need rated from marked to severe	Initial assessments (n=42)		Subsequent assessments (n=72)	
	No.	%	No.	%
Client				
Physical health	13	31	27	38
ADL and environment	19	45	21	29
Mental state	19	45	25	34
Social/leisure	22	52	13	18
Carer				
Distress and difficulties	21	50	17	24
Impact on life	19	45	20	28
Relationship problems				
Client and carer	11	26	8	11

but in only one fifth (22 per cent) of all subsequent assessments. Similarly, managing laundry and household cleaning were rated as problems in 31 per cent and 26 per cent respectively of all initial assessments. In subsequent assessments, case managers rated these as problems in 13 per cent and 14 per cent respectively of all subsequent assessments. Furthermore, carers were noted to have high levels of mental health problems. Case managers rated the presence of anxiety or depression in 36 per cent of first assessments, but in just 19 per cent of all subsequent assessments.

In summary, initial assessments revealed a high level of need, typically spanning a number of domains, thereby reflecting the nature of dementia, its impact on the older people themselves and those concerned for their care. Needs of the former arising from their mental state were understandably paramount although these decreased in subsequent assessments. Conversely the needs of carers remained uniformly high both at the time of initial assessment and subsequent ones. However, assessments of severity of need suggest a reduction in those relating to both the client's mental health and carer's distress. Indeed the assessments of case managers suggested that overall the severity of need was reduced at second and subsequent assessments.

Implementing the Care Plan

Care planning has been described as, '...a resource allocation process where a service prescription is written for a client' (Applebaum and Austin, 1990, 22) and is recognised as an important function of case management. Case managers were responsible for establishing a care plan, negotiating with a range of providers of services, particularly home care and other services, as well as purchasing support from outside the agency if this was appropriate. This enabled the scheme to offer intensive care packages involving both public and private sector providers and paid helpers. Thus, case managers took account of the current care plan for the older person, and the weekly diary kept in their home, which recorded the assessments completed by colleagues in the community mental health team for older people, and other significant events. These described the person's level of company and stimulation, as well as the structure and organisation of their week. This was relevant since some were unable to comment fully on the help they received. In addition, an understanding of the carer's day and week gave a clear picture of their pattern of activity, and times of difficulty or risk. The data for this section were drawn from information contained in 80 review documents completed in respect of 42 clients with complete data within the experimental group. These contained a total of 254 care plans which detailed goals, interventions employed by case managers and the use of resources. Within the 254 care plans, there were 245 goals, 333 intervention strategies and 414 resources specified. In this context, care plans were defined as strategies which case managers employed to address a particular need or goal.

Often the goals of case management, at either the level of the client and their family or the organisation or system in which it is located, are poorly expressed

(Kane, 2000). However, within the LCMS they were clearly articulated, as detailed in Table 5.3. In the review documentation seven domains were specified, and the most frequently reported goals of intervention were supportive (68 per cent), therapeutic (66 per cent) and practical (56 per cent). Supportive goals were almost exclusively directed for the benefit of carers, the most frequently reported categories were being to relieve carer burden, provide respite and to a lesser extent assist the paid carer. On the other hand, therapeutic interventions were used to benefit both older people with dementia and their carers. For example, this category included strategies to reduce the problem behaviours associated with deteriorating mental state and to provide counselling for carers in supporting the older person with dementia at home. Practical goals were geared towards the individual with assistance with personal care, health care and domestic care being the most frequently reported goals. There were fewer goals formulated of a social nature than might have been expected (40 per cent), bearing in mind the prevalence and severity of the older people's unmet needs in this domain which have been noted earlier. Taken as a whole, Table 5.3 demonstrates that the main objectives of case managers were to support, sustain and enhance the quality of life of the older person with dementia in their own home. The small percentage of reviews (21 per cent), making reference to living situation is evidence of this, and furthermore, in only four cases did the goal of intervention relate to the provision of long-term nursing or residential home care.

The means by which the case managers attempted to achieve their goals are shown in Table 5.4. They directed a great deal of their time to assisting the paid helpers in their task of supporting people in their own homes, a little over 40 per cent of all strategies employed. Another significant group of strategies employed by case managers was directed to maintaining the existing care network, again illustrating the commitment to supporting the older person with dementia in their own home. Closer examination of this table reveals several other points of interest. The significant amount of time employed by case managers in strategies relating to the paid helper demonstrates both the importance and value placed upon a close relationship between what might be termed the micro-level commissioner or purchaser of service (the case manager) and the provider of service (the paid helper). The strategies employed by case managers are also of interest. In maintaining the care network, case managers divided their time equally in terms of direct work with members of the care network and working through others. In some circumstances case managers made use of specific skills, for example, five per cent of the strategies employed came within the broad definition of counselling skills, although it is not unreasonable to assume that case managers used communication skills derived from their professional training in maintaining the care network.

Allied to the intervention strategies used by case managers was their use of resources, detailed in Table 5.5. Four hundred and fourteen resources were categorised from 254 care plans. Over 70 per cent detailed the use of domiciliary care in order to support the older person with dementia at home. The greater part of this assistance came from the paid helpers, specifically recruited to work

Table 5.3   Goals of intervention

Case managers formulations of specific needs and goals of intervention (number in brackets)	No. of goals formulated (n=245)	As a % of reviews (n=80)
Supportive Relieve carer burden/stress (25) Provide respite (20) Support carer (9)	54	68
Therapeutic Reduce problem behaviours (19) Counselling about the situation (14) Relieve distress/anxiety/agitation (11) Improve mental state (9)	53	66
Practical Meet personal care needs (23) Get necessary health care (10) Meet domestic care needs (8) Improve environment (4)	45	56
Preventative Monitoring and reassessment (16) Detect signs of deterioration (11) Prevent crisis (7)	34	43
Social Relieve loneliness/provide social contact (18) Increase social activity/stimulation (14)	32	40
Destinational Maintain in own home as long as possible (7) Enable client to return home (6) Placement in permanent nursing/residential care (4)	17	21
Organisational Create/restructure care package (10)	10	13

Adapted from Challis and Hughes (2000)

with clients of the scheme, 55 per cent in total. This figure compares with 15 per cent for the home care workers supplied by the local social services department. In 37 per cent of care plans the case manager was recorded as a specific resource. In this sense they not only arranged services but were also responsible for the provision of assistance. This was sometimes in the form of specific skills as detailed in Table 5.4 and by facilitating access to more appropriate forms of help, for example a local voluntary organisation specialising in carer support. The care plans detailed inputs from other professional groups, particularly and perhaps unsurprisingly, members of the community mental health team for older people in which the case management service was located. This team accounted for over one quarter of resources specified in care plans within the broad categorisation of professional colleagues.

Table 5.4   Case manager intervention strategies

	Number of strategies used (n= 333)	Percentage
Use of paid helper		
Introduce worker	67	20
Adjust input	43	13
Recruit	15	5
Assist in care	5	2
Train	2	1
Total	132	41
Maintain care network		
Use of self	41	12
Via others	41	12
Total	82	24
Resource uptake		
Refer for services	20	6
Refer for assessment	15	5
Search for services	9	3
Manage medication	6	2
Transfer between services	3	1
Total	53	16
Service co-ordination		
Liaison	32	10
Case conference	7	2
Total	39	12
Specific skills employed by case manager		
Counselling	16	5
Advice	8	2
Reassessment	3	1
Total	27	8

Overall this table reveals that professional colleagues within the health services, particularly members of the community mental health team for older people, community nurses or general practitioners were more likely to be identified as resources in the care plan than professional colleagues in social care (16 per cent compared with 5 per cent). This is perhaps unsurprising in view of the deteriorating mental and physical health of a person with dementia and, with respect to the community mental health team for older people, the close working relationship between team members and case managers. It is also of note that comparatively little use was made of resources outside the home. Only 14 per cent of care plans recorded the use of a day centre in order to provide care for older people and even less (5 per cent) noted the use of respite care in hospital or residential or nursing home care. Moreover, in only one per cent of care plans was long-term care an identified resource. Finally, it is significant to note that in only 11 per cent of care plans were carers identified as a resource (Twigg and Atkin, 1994; Nolan and Keady, 2001), more usually they were likely to play other roles.

Table 5.6 analyses the use of resources by domain of assessed need. It is apparent that the needs of carers and issues relating to the mental state of the older person were the domains of need which received the highest amount of resource input. Closer examination of the use of domiciliary care provides an interesting finding. The table indicates that the paid helpers recruited as part of the scheme were more likely to provide assistance in relation to mental state than in respect of activities of daily living (21 per cent compared to 16 per cent). On the other hand other helpers, most likely to be home care workers employed by the social services department, were more likely to provide assistance in respect of the activities of daily living than in relation to issues arising from the clients mental state (32 per cent compared to 18 per cent). The use made of institutional care is also of interest. Overwhelmingly, this was a response to the identified needs of family carers (58 per cent). However, it was also used to a lesser extent as a response to declining

Table 5.5   Care plan: use of resources

Resource	No. of resources (n=414)	Resources specified as % of care plans (n=254)
Domiciliary care		
Paid helpers (LCMS)	140	55
Home care (SSD)	37	15
Others	7	3
Total	184	72
Case manager	94	37
Professional colleagues		
CMHT for older people	14	6
Community nurse	11	4
GP	10	4
Other health services	4	2
SSD staff	8	3
Other social services	6	2
Total	53	21
Day centre	36	14
Carers	28	11
Care outside the home		
Respite	13	5
Long-term hospital admission	4	2
Long-term residential/nursing home placement	2	1
Total	19	8

physical health (this was noted in respect of 32 per cent of assessed need). Finally, this table provides an insight into how case managers spent their time. In terms of domains of assessed needs, over a third of case managers' interventions were devoted to meeting the needs of carers.

The psychological impact of sharing the care with services and the effect this has on the perceived responsibility of the carer and their relationship to the older person has been recognised (Zarit et al., 1998; Moriarty and Webb, 2000; Duijnstee and Ros, 2004). A feature of the present research was that it demonstrated that how services, dovetailed to a carer's own routine of care, were particularly important for carers living with the older person with dementia. As part of this process, case managers identified tensions in the caring relationship and a number of difficulties around the caring role, particularly for carers living with the older person with dementia but also for paid carers. Examples of these difficulties and their implications for service response, derived from the researchers' observations and discussions with carers are shown in Box 5.2. A number of dilemmas for carers were highlighted: the experience of change and deterioration in the person with dementia, the expertise and skills of carers, their distress and concerns and the psychological aspects and adjustments needed to provide the caring role (Tilki, 1999). An important role for case managers was assisting in the successful management of these situations.

Table 5.6   Percentage use of resource type by domain

Resource type (number of times documented)	Domain of assessed need (percentage)							
	Physical health	*ADL*	*Mental state*	*Social/ leisure*	*Environment*	*Carer*	*Care network relationships*	*Care network service provision*
Domiciliary care: paid helpers (140)	14	16	21	14	2	25	2	5
Domiciliary care: other (44)	14	32	18	5	5	16	2	9
Case manager (94)	12	6	21	4	4	34	13	5
Other professionals (53)	34	17	11	0	9	21	4	4
Day care (36)	8	3	22	47	0	15	3	3
Carer (28)	22	21	21	11	0	0	14	11
Institutional care (19)	32	0	0	0	5	58	5	0
Total (414)	17	14	19	11	4	24	6	5

Box 5.2   Tensions and paradoxes in dementia care and consequences for service delivery

Dilemma	Paradoxes within the caring relationship	Appropriate response
Client behaviour		
Periods of insight and awareness are rewarding for carers who encourage reminiscence, prompting meaningful interaction with client.	This may be a devastating reminder of the loss and deterioration in the client's mental state for the principal carer particularly.	Sensitivity to the balance between the value of reminiscence for the client and the distress it causes the principal carer (Tilki, 1999).
Deteriorating physical and mental health.	Client deteriorates, placement in long-term care may be necessary and ultimately client dies.	Preparation for these transitions in order that the trauma and loss is managed as well as is possible.
Principal carer and care networks		
Carer requires help and support in the caring tasks.	Input is seen as an intrusion on the existing relationship, particularly for couples. Recognition that helping relationships are major interventions and can have significant side-effects.	Help dovetailed to the existing carer-client relationship.
The stress of caring and the quality of life of the client and frustrations expressed by them elicit anxieties in the principal carer.	Anxieties elicited in other carers (paid helpers, other relatives).	Support of all members of the care network recognising that their current contribution is influenced by previous experiences as a carer.

Monitoring, Review and Case Closure

In this section we move from consideration of needs and problems, plans and strategies to reviewing the effectiveness of these plans. It highlights one of the hallmarks of what is known as intensive care management, namely the co-ordination of a variety of related functions over time (Challis et al., 1995; Mueser et al., 1998). The present research incorporated an analysis of practice related to implementing the care plan and monitoring and review, particularly important in the context of a service whose key component is long-term support of people at home. Indeed, Goering and colleagues (1988) noted that two year outcomes of quality of life were more significant than six month outcomes. Moxley (1989) specified the various tasks of case management and described four functions of monitoring: ascertaining the degree to which the care plan has been implemented; whether the objectives of the care plan have been achieved; determining the outcome of support; and identifying any new client needs requiring change to the care plan. Interestingly, as the scheme evolved, case managers in their monitoring of the care plan focused on components of the process as identified by Moxley (1989).

Case managers undertook frequent home visits as well as monitoring through the paid helpers. Reviews were undertaken when appropriate, and, where community-based support was no longer viable, case managers were responsible for organising placement in long-term care for the older person with dementia and facilitating this process. Principal activities for case managers undertaking the monitoring, evaluation and review functions of case management were: visits to clients and carers; contact with paid helpers and home care staff; meetings with members of a care network, for example to facilitate hospital discharge; record keeping; and their own formal supervision which spanned both the clinical and administrative aspects of case management. In essence, these activities focused upon the individual components of the care package, its delivery, its effectiveness and level of needs. They are summarised in Box 5.3, which indicates that the major challenge for case managers was to create and sustain an individual care network over time. The continued involvement of case managers allowed for enhanced knowledge of the older person with dementia and main carer; the smooth running of the care network; and the ability to respond to changing needs. Close monitoring allowed them to react quickly to any changes in circumstances and alter services as required (Applebaum and Austin, 1990). Paid helpers, who were

Box 5.3   Monitoring: components of the care plan

Increased knowledge of client and principal carer	Assess the impact of changes in client's behaviour and health Understand the client's needs, fears, preferences and strengths Help carers discover the assistance they require Place current behaviour in the context of previous life experience
Maintenance of the care network	Balance and review care inputs Encourage the commitment of network members to the client Respect knowledge and commitment of all network members Note emergent ways of relating to client e.g. reminiscence Develop carer's trust in care network Provide respite for principal carer Accumulation of case specific knowledge
Responsiveness to changing needs	Anticipate, identify and quickly respond to crises Monitor and respond appropriately Alert to unanticipated consequences

in close contact with clients, were particularly important in this context as a ready source of information. This long-term close involvement with the care network was an essential component of this case management scheme and it allowed for a complementary relationship to evolve within the care network, with carers as co-workers (Twigg and Atkin, 1994) alongside paid helpers.

Table 5.7 shows the extent to which case managers adjudged themselves to have achieved success in the monitoring stage of the case management process in respect of their goals of the maintenance of the older person at home, in the face of increasing frailty, and the attention paid to the needs of carers. Goals were achieved in relation to assessed needs which related to the older person's physical health and capacity to perform activities of daily living (68 per cent and 62 per cent respectively) and in relation to both the client's mental state and the needs of carers reflecting the assistance received by the latter (74 per cent). In terms of the care network, it was noted that 86 per cent of circumstances where needs were identified with respect to the provision of services, the specified goals were achieved. Overall, case managers felt that in more than two thirds of reviews their goals had been fully, or almost, achieved (68 per cent). Notably, the areas which appeared to have been the most successfully resolved were perhaps the most discrete and achievable, namely those regarding provision of services in the care network, effecting changes within the older person's living environment, responding to their mental state and the needs of carers.

Table 5.8 illustrates changes in the level of problems noted by case managers in between reviews. As such it is a tangible expression of the amount of time invested in the monitoring and review component of case management. In total, 40 per cent of problems in all domains were assessed to have increased. Over one

Table 5.7   Goals achieved by domain of assessed need

Domain	Fully		Partly or not at all	
	No.	**%**	**No.**	**%**
Client				
Physical health	27	68	13	32
ADL	28	62	17	38
Mental state	25	74	9	26
Social/leisure	16	53	14	47
Environment	8	80	2	20
Carer	56	74	20	26
Care network				
Relationships	10	59	7	41
Service provision	12	86	2	14
Total (n=266)	182	68	84	32

(% as a proportion of each domain)

Table 5.8   Change in level of problem by domain

Domain (All completed reviews n=80)	Increased		No change		Reduced	
	No	%	No.	%	No.	%
Client						
Physical health	23	62	11	30	3	8
ADL	18	33	30	55	7	13
Mental state	28	50	20	35	8	14
Social/leisure	9	45	5	25	6	30
Environment	1	13	7	58	4	33
Total	79	44	73	40	28	16
Carer	17	24	28	39	26	37
Care network						
Relationships	9	47	5	26	5	26
Service provision	7	88	0	0	1	12
Total	16	59	5	19	6	22
Total of all domains	112	40	106	38	60	22

third (38 per cent) of all problems were assessed to have remained at the same level, and 22 per cent had significantly reduced. However, since the table refers only to those problems which were current at the time of the review, problems that had been identified and/or resolved between reviews would not be captured in this format. Therefore, the 22 per cent apparent reduction is likely to represent an underestimate.

The level of problems relating to physical health and mental state was notably higher on review, reflecting the progressive nature of the condition. Of particular interest is information relating to the domains of the client's environment and the carer. In both of these the reduction in the level of problems is larger than the reported increase. This demonstrates that case managers perceived themselves as particularly effective in intervening in those domains in which problem resolution is directly attributable to their influence and skill either in the form of service provision or their interpersonal communication skills such as building relationships between people and resource systems. These are long-standing objectives of social work practice (Pincus and Minahan, 1973). In view of the progressive nature of dementia, the maintenance of the status quo in the level of identified problems can also be seen as evidence of effective monitoring of the situation by the case manager, and has been recognised so elsewhere (Applebaum et al., 1980). It is therefore useful to combine the figures of the two right-hand columns of the table, to reflect both no change and reduction. In respect of individual domains, this confirms the findings noted above in respect of living environment (91 per cent) and the assistance given to the carer (76 per cent). Additionally, it suggests that despite difficulties in managing problems associated with deterioration in physical and mental health, case managers through their close monitoring and detailed knowledge of the older person and their circumstances, were able to provide assistance to address problems arising from reduced skills in activities of daily living (68 per cent).

Table 5.9 examines the extent to which problems on assessment were addressed in the subsequent care plans. These findings reveal that case managers were most successful at identifying and addressing the needs of carers. In almost three-quarters of reviews (73 per cent) it was identified that problems relating to carers on assessment had been addressed in the care plan. In relation to the older person with dementia the greatest impact was made on their social life. As noted earlier, this domain describes the extent to which their daytime activities were structured, monitored and facilitated in order to enhance their quality of life. Two-thirds of reviews (67 per cent) identified that where this domain had been specified in the assessment the problem had been addressed in the care plan. In contrast, less than half of reviews (48 per cent) in which problems were identified on assessment in relation to mental state are addressed in the care plan. As noted previously, this is perhaps not surprising since all older people referred to the scheme had been diagnosed as having dementia. In terms of the care network, the problems identified most frequently were those regarding relationships between the main carers, noted in 37 per cent of reviews. Whilst problems within the care network apparently received comparatively little attention, this does not necessarily mean they had a low priority. Issues relating to paid helper input may have been seen by case managers as part of their administrative and management function, which is not so readily captured in a case planning record. This observation is consistent with Table 5.3 which covers the case manager's formulated goals of intervention, where only 13 per cent were defined in organisational terms, namely creating or restructuring care packages.

In the context of their long-term relationship with clients, case managers were on occasion, drawn into the role of advocate. Sometimes, members of the care network – both paid helpers and carers – acted as advocates, although it was often only the case manager who had the requisite specialist knowledge relating to service entitlement. This was apparent at two levels – first, in response to individual circumstances and second, in response to unmet needs of several clients, identified through the case management process. The latter found tangible expression in the development of the paid helper service and is discussed in detail in the next chapter. With regard to the former, case managers exercised their advocacy role on behalf of the older people in the context of a long-term relationship. In this respect the two roles were inexorably linked. The principal components of the advocacy role within the LCMS are summarised in Box 5.4.

Overall, case managers were successful in enabling older people with dementia to continue to live in their own homes, arguably an environment where their needs could be better understood, thereby illustrating the necessity of a biographical

Table 5.9   Outcome by domain of assessed need

Domain (All completed reviews n=80)	Problems identified on assessment	Problems addressed in the care plan	% of reviews where identified problem is addressed
	No.	No.	%
Client			
Physical health	50	29	58
ADL	59	32	54
Mental state	62	30	48
Social life	45	30	67
Environment	19	12	63
Carer	67	49	73
Care network			
Relationships	46	17	37
Service provision	44	11	25

Box 5.4   Advocacy within case management for older people with dementia

Empower as a person
Safeguard from abuse
Assist in decision-making about future care
Access financial and legal entitlements
Ensure provision of high quality services appropriate to identified needs

component for good advocacy, which provides important contextual information about a person's former lifestyle and personal history (Payne, 1995). In this setting they were faced with the challenge of balancing right to self-determination and autonomy with their need for protection. Whilst this dilemma is inherent in case management services for frail older people it is particularly emphasised in respect of older people with dementia, and when undertaking the role of advocate. In these circumstances, the judgement about future care of needs has to be placed in the context of an overall assessment of risk (Department of Health, 2002b; Manthorpe, 2004; Cm 6499, 2005; Cm 6737, 2006; Marshall and Tibbs, 2006).

Case closure has been described as an integral part of the care process, which the case manager can prepare for (Pincus and Minahan, 1977), although in this and similar studies, (Challis and Davies, 1986; Challis et al., 1995; 2002a) termination of care at home was sometimes due to circumstances beyond the control of the scheme, for example due to the older person's deteriorating health or the death of a carer. The most common point of case closure on the LCMS was following placement in long-term care or death, although occasionally people were transferred to mainstream services after receiving support through the scheme. Residential care has often been seen as 'second best' although studies involving former carers have found that they were generally happy with the decision to admit their relatives when re-interviewed at a later date (Pushkar Gold et al., 1995; Moriarty and Webb 1997b; 2000). In this study, on the occasions when admission to long-term care occurred, it was viewed as a positive choice for older people and carers alike, and, following placement and occasionally when a client had died, case managers continued giving support to the carer for a short while.

Summary

A number of issues emerge from this chapter which are worthy of further comment. The location of the case management service within a multidisciplinary team in a secondary health setting critically influenced how case finding and screening and assessment of needs were defined. Members of the community mental health team for older people routinely undertook an initial assessment of mental state and home circumstances within a short period of time. This allowed case managers to undertake a second, more detailed assessment over a longer period of time, focusing on the wider network of care. Arguably this was of crucial importance in facilitating their long-term care in the community.

A second set of issues emerges from the process of implementing the care plan and its subsequent monitoring and review. With regard to the former, it is important to note that goals of intervention were geared to meeting the needs of the older person with dementia and where applicable, their carer. In this sense, the case management service was identifying and assessing the needs of carers in advance of legislative requirement. Moreover, analysis of the case management review documentation suggests that the service was indeed, able to provide effective help to carers. The analysis of the practice of the case managers in this scheme also demonstrates the importance of maintaining regular contact with all those involved in the care of older people with dementia in their own homes. It also shows that case managers required communication skills not only relating to individuals but in managing complicated communication networks. Finally and most importantly, this chapter illustrates that frail older people with dementia can be successfully maintained at home under the auspices of case management.

Chapter 6
Service Development

Introduction

Within the Lewisham Case Management Scheme, the variable and generally progressive nature of dementia led to the requirement for an additional home care service to provide assistance over and above that which was available from the local authority domiciliary care service at that time. In particular, the home care service could not consistently provide the intensity of support required: support at lunchtime, in the afternoon or evening to assist with meals, help with medication or with putting to bed. Thus a new service was developed to fill the gap in service provision and provide greater flexibility and consistency by limiting the number of helpers assisting an individual. Moreover, it had the capacity to offer longer or more frequent visits throughout the day for company and leisure activities for the older person with dementia, which included taking them out of their homes as part of the care plan. As described in Chapter 3, the paid helper service was available solely to those in the experimental group and in receipt of case management, and was designed to complement the home care service, as outlined in Chapter 5. Retrospectively, it can be construed as providing elements to inform a service specification for specialist home care for older people with mental health problems, and an infrastructure to support older people in their own homes under the auspices of care management arrangements (Committee of Public Accounts, 2008). As illustrated in the previous chapter, and as subsequent chapters will demonstrate, the paid helper service played an important role in the positive outcomes for older people and their carers within the experimental group. Furthermore, it may be regarded as a prelude to the development of a specialist home care service for older people with dementia and other mental health problems.

Service development may be judged as the activity of case management most often omitted and frequently referred to only by implication in the literature. It can be conceived of at three levels. The first is at the individual level, the purpose of which is to ensure that services are individually tailored to meet the assessed needs of the individual, arguably a prerequisite for the provision of flexible services as outlined in current policy guidance (Cm 6499, 2005; Cm 6737, 2006). The second is the intermediate/team level, which is to ensure the development of local services to meet the identified needs of client groups. The third is the authority-wide level, which is designed to achieve an infrastructure of services within a community that allows people to live at home as an alternative to long-term care. The importance of service development at both the intermediate and individual level was clearly demonstrated in the early case management pilot projects (Challis and Davies, 1986; Challis et al., 1995; 2002a). For example, in the Darlington project, a domiciliary care service was developed comprising care workers able to undertake health and social care tasks. This service development, available only to those recruited to the experimental group, made a significant contribution to the care of people in their own homes and was therefore one of the crucial factors in the success of the scheme (Challis et al., 1995). Service development has over time been subsumed within the commissioning role of adult social care services (Cm 4169, 1998; Cm 6737, 2006). As such it is no longer undertaken at the intermediate/team level, as evidenced in the LCMS, but at an authority-wide level. Moreover, there is now the capacity for such initiatives to be both jointly commissioned and provided (Cm 4181-I, 2000; Cm 6737, 2006). Irrespective of the commissioning mechanism, there is growing evidence of some specialism within domiciliary care provision (Department of Health, 2005b) with discrete provision for older people with dementia, or more broadly, mental health problems being a target group for such services.

The remainder of this chapter will outline the main characteristics of the paid helper service within the LCMS. The recruitment of paid helpers and the development, management and organisation of the service will be described. Subsequently, the roles of paid helpers in their direct work with older people with dementia and their carers will be examined, illustrating how they meshed with both the support of carers and with the home care service, and influenced the work of members of the community mental health team for older people. In this context it is important to acknowledge that two factors limited its development. First, the financing of the paid helper service was not included in the original costings and hence its development was contingent on the availability of additional monies. Second, much of the development work was undertaken by case managers who did this in addition to the more clinical aspects of the case management service. These were significant constraints on the growth of the service.

Recruitment and Management of Paid Helpers

In their recruitment of paid helpers, case managers identified a number of core skills and attributes. Although predating the requirement for vetting for a criminal record (Department of Health, 2002e), applicants were required to demonstrate: reliability and honesty; tolerance and respect of older people; an ability to cope with difficult problems and issues in response to the different qualities of older people with dementia; and sensitivity to the stresses experienced by carers. Initially a formal advertisement was posted around local shops, churches and in a newspaper, although in the main, recruitment was by word of mouth. Occasionally, neighbours and relatives who were caring for an older person with dementia were used as paid helpers thus formalising an existing arrangement.

As part of the recruitment process, case managers interviewed 58 helpers and the majority were recruited. This ranged from those providing only one or two visits to those supplying hundreds of hours of care. Table 6.1 shows the characteristics of the paid helpers based on their completed recruitment questionnaires. Of the 55 paid helpers recruited to the Lewisham paid helper service, 53 were female as were most of those recruited to the Kent and Gateshead pilot schemes (Challis and Davies, 1986; Challis et al., 2002a). More than half of the recruits to this service were aged between 40 and 60, although one-fifth were aged 30 and under. Most of the helpers had considerable experience of caring in both paid and unpaid roles. Five were trained nurses, 17 had been home helps and many had worked in residential homes and day care as well as having personal experience of caring for relatives. The majority worked in specific localities although a substantial minority were prepared to travel and work anywhere within the geographical boundary of the community mental health team for older people. In terms of personal motivation, recruits to the paid helper service were essentially divided into two groups: those who were keen to work just a few hours but were fairly flexible, and those who were looking for a more rewarding type of work and a regular income. Unsurprisingly, all displayed a high level of commitment to the service.

As in earlier pilot case management projects (Challis and Davies, 1986; Challis et al., 1995; 2002a), paid helpers in Lewisham were contracted to provide a service

Table 6.1   Characteristics of paid helpers on recruitment

	Number	**(%)**
Age		
<20	3	(5)
21-30	8	(15)
31-40	7	(13)
41-50	16	(29)
51-60	15	(27)
61+	6	(11)
Total	55	
Employment status		
None	26	(47)
Full-time paid	14	(25)
Part-time paid	12	(22)
Unpaid work	2	(4)
Student	1	(2)
Total	55	
Caring experience		
Nursing	17	(31)
Paid social care	31	(56)
Relative/family member	26	(47)
Voluntary work or as carer of neighbour	30	(55)

for each older person with tasks specified and a week's notice given for termination of contract, for example, due to admission to long-term care. Their rate of pay was equivalent to home care workers in the area, although they were responsible for payment of their own insurance and tax. At any one point during the evaluation of the scheme the ratio was, on average, 25 helpers supporting 21 clients. A number worked for only a short time because the service had been unable to use them or they had found other work. The paid helper service was introduced prior to the national minimum standards for domiciliary care, when the National Vocational Qualification (NVQ) system was being developed (Department of Health, 2003c). Thus, paid helpers did not receive any formal training on entry, although a number made use of a social service training course and a support group for paid helpers was run for six weeks. These two interventions were valued by paid helpers, and the training opportunities increased their knowledge allowing for the sharing of problems, ideas and mutual support.

There were no clear policies for use of the paid helper service in the LCMS, unlike the case management scheme in Darlington (Challis et al., 1995). In the latter, the support workers were an integral part of the whole organisation, and they worked in teams to support older people. In the LCMS the particular needs of the individual and the availability of helpers governed the contribution of paid helpers. Whenever possible, case managers matched paid helpers with clients and, as noted earlier, limited both the number of paid helpers to one or two key people committed to a particular person, and the number of clients whom helpers visited. This approach enabled them to deal more readily with any sudden crises that occurred. However, although this was deemed the ideal mode of working, it was recognised that it could not always occur due to the small numbers of paid helpers available and the multiple needs of some older people.

There were a number of challenges confronted by case managers in the development and management of the paid helper service. These arose because they were required to both offer a service to clients and discharge obligations to paid helpers for whom they were the representatives of their employers on a daily basis. Case managers, for example, had to liaise with the finance section and secretariat to clarify issues around income tax, insurance and methods of payment to the paid helpers. In addition, they spent time drawing up contracts and codes of practice, and a particular challenge was to mesh the principles and practice of the paid helper service with the home care service provided by the local authority social services department. In the longer term, case managers had to develop skills and awareness in budgeting, and in organising and managing a care workforce. The principal tasks for case managers in the management of the paid helper service were: monitoring the delivery and quality of the service; ensuring payment of the helpers, and recruitment as and when necessary. Thus they were commissioners and regulators of the service at the strategic level, managers of it on a day to day basis, and 'purchasers' of the service in respect of individual needs. As part of the latter role, they made joint visits to clients with paid helpers and used their detailed knowledge of the older person with dementia in each stage of the case management process. In essence, case managers were performing a service development role at both the individual and team level, as discussed earlier in this chapter.

As demonstrated in Chapter 5 (see Table 5.4), the maintenance of the care network was an important activity for case managers, sometimes requiring them to deal with conflicts between various parts of the care network. This was apparent in a number of guises. Occasionally, there were instances when carers who wanted relief from caring nevertheless viewed helper input into the home as an intrusion, or paid helpers assisted case managers in investigating allegations of abuse of older people by carers. In other instances, the older person's vulnerability made it difficult for them to trust new helpers and hence made them resistant to their introduction, or the competing needs of client and carer made it difficult for the paid helper to make an effective contribution to the care plan. Overall, the importance of the case manager's role in maintaining the care network and the pivotal role of the paid helper within it was vital, the latter being an essential cog in the implementation of the care plan.

Role of Paid Helpers

The paid helper service was both a cornerstone of service provision for older people and carers, and also contributed to the process of assessment, especially in the early stages of the scheme as noted in the previous chapter. Chapter 5 (Table 5.5) demonstrated that paid helpers featured in 55 per cent of care plans developed by case managers in a wide variety of roles. Examination of the 80 case reviews completed by the case managers revealed a considerable range of tasks to improve personal and household care and meet social needs, undertaken by paid helpers as shown in Table 6.2. These included a substantial amount of time in providing companionship for clients and carers and assisting in their personal care. Paid helpers were also involved with household activities, undertaking tasks on a daily basis such as cooking, as well as on a weekly basis, for example shopping and housework. Whilst most helper input was carried out in the older person's home, it also involved escorting them, in order to encourage their attendance at a day centre or hospital, or to supervise their safety, for example when shopping or visiting relatives. Paid helpers worked on average with two clients and for fourteen hours a week. Each older person had an average of two helpers, although this concealed quite a large variation, a reflection of their different needs and in the work patterns of individual helpers.

The care provided by paid helpers was characterised by its responsive and proactive nature. Moreover, it was available in the evening as well as during the day, and at short notice. As noted previously, they contributed to the assessment and monitoring of the client's well-being, typically becoming involved within one week of their entry into the service. Sometimes they were involved in the follow-up of clients upon discharge from hospital. On these occasions they were given training by hospital staff in how to help the older person following their discharge home,

Table 6.2   Principal paid helper tasks identified in case reviews

	Percentage of reviews n=80	
	No.	%
Companionship		
Client	36	45
Carer	14	18
Personal care		
Wash/dress	26	33
Rise and retire	25	31
Take to toilet	14	18
Household activities		
Cooking	28	35
Shopping, housework	12	15
Respite		
Day sitting	17	21
Night sitting	9	11
24 hour respite	3	4
Other		
Escort client	26	33
Information gathering for assessment	16	20
Monitor by frequent day-time visits	7	9

in advance of the current hospital discharge schemes now encompassed within the framework of intermediate care (Cm 4818-I, 2000; Department of Health, 2002f). Paid helpers were also involved in monitoring and gaining access to clients who had previously refused to accept help. Of particular importance was the capacity of the service to provide a night-sitting service for a defined period of time. In some cases, paid helpers had a 'key carer' role, acting as a 'cognitive surrogate' (Challis, 1993), through their empathy and capacity to interpret and articulate the person's requirements.

Overall, the paid helper service offered a more flexible and varied level of service and complemented the more traditional approach available from the home care services at that time, as illustrated in Table 5.6. Whereas the former focused primarily on the mental health needs of the older person, the latter was more concerned with the physical needs. For those in the experimental group the paid helper service was available in addition to the community nursing service and the home care services provided by the local authority. In contrast, only the latter two services were available to the control group. Examination of the total number of hours of care calculated from service receipts over the course of one year showed that clients in the experimental group received on average fourteen hours a week, often from a number of carers. This was almost three times the average weekly input of around five hours a week for those in the control group.

The contribution from paid helpers to the care plans of those in the experimental group meant that the experimental and control groups received different levels of service input, which had consequences for the contribution of carers. This is shown in Table 6.3 which compares the ratio of service input to carer input in terms of time and tasks, using information taken from the informant interview. It illustrates that, for example, for each hour of care provided by a carer to a client in the experimental group and living alone, there were 3.5 hours input of paid care. In contrast, for each hour of care provided by a carer to a client in the control group and living alone, there were just 1.6 hours input of paid care. Furthermore, there was a marked difference between the experimental group and the control group in the relative role of formal services (domiciliary care and the paid helper service) and carers in carrying out various tasks of daily living. This was applicable for both older people living with carers and those living alone. For clients in the experimental group and living alone, paid carers assisted with an average of 2.4 tasks of daily living for each one task undertaken by a carer. This compared with an average of 1.5 tasks provided by paid carers to assist with activities of daily living for each one task undertaken by a family carer of a client in the control group and living alone. Carers living in the same household as the older person undertook the majority of the tasks of daily living, regardless of whether they were in the experimental or control group. However, overall the level of support to carers in the experimental group was markedly greater than to those in the control group.

Table 6.3   Ratio of paid helper service and domiciliary care provision to carer input after one year

Assistance provided	Clients living alone		Clients living with carer	
	E n=23	C n=24	E n=10	C n=14
Hours of care [service input hours ÷ family carer hours]	3.5	1.6	1.0	0.4
Daily living tasks [service input tasks ÷ family carer tasks]	2.4	1.5	0.6	0.2

Table 6.4 categorises indicative care packages received by both the experimental and control groups and demonstrates the different patterns of support received by the two groups. It is derived from average service receipt over one year. To permit comparison between the two groups, professional oversight of the care package is defined as a visit from a case manager or member of the community mental health team for older people. The table reveals that half (50 per cent) the experimental group received 21 or more hours of care per week in contrast to around one tenth (11 per cent) of the control group. It is interesting to note that nearly three-quarters (73 per cent) of the control group received lower overall care packages and were

Table 6.4   Types of care package over 12 months

Care package categorisation	E n=34 No. (%)	C n=38 No. (%)
Receiving ≥21 hours care per week and ≥1 case manager/team† visit per month	15 (44)	1 (3)
Receiving ≥21 hours care per week and <1 case manager/team† visit per month	2 (6)	3 (8)
Receiving <21 hours care per week and ≥1 case manager/team† visit per month	8 (24)	6 (16)
Receiving <21 hours care per week and <1 case manager/team† visit per month	9 (26)	28 (73)

† Note: experimental group received case manager visits, control group received visits from members of the community mental health teams for older people, e.g. community psychiatric nurses

visited infrequently (i.e. less than monthly) by a member of the community mental health team for older people. Where the experimental group received fewer visits by a case manager, irrespective of the level of home care received, they may have been supported by a 'key carer', able to report back to the case manager if problems arose, emphasising their contribution as a 'cognitive surrogate', as discussed earlier in this chapter.

Early work suggested that provision of paid care could lead to a reduction in informal care. It was reported that, '... there is impressive evidence to confirm the existence, hitherto, of a negative relationship between care provided *by* the community for its own members and care provided *in* the community by public authorities; that is the latter erodes the former.' (Abrams, 1977, 136). Subsequently, the relationship between service inputs and carers has been the focus of research and reviews to determine whether paid services substitute for or complement carers of frail elders (Kemper et al., 1987; Arber et al., 1988; Lyons and Zarit, 1999; Wanless, 2006), and to what extent formal service provision approaches the level of input provided by carers (Moriarty and Webb, 2000). Box 6.1 illustrates how the LCMS redistributed the burden between carers in the experimental group and the home care service and where applicable, the paid helper service and contrasts it with that for the control group provided by traditional services. For those living alone in the control group, carers could be described as 'sharing' the care input with paid services. In contrast, for those in the experimental group and in receipt of the case management scheme, effectively the paid helper service became the main input, taking responsibility for providing the majority of care. For carers who lived in the same household as the client, it appeared that there was much greater sharing of care for those in the experimental group, whereas in the control group, carers carried out the majority of care tasks. This suggests that carers living with clients and in the experimental group, and as described by Twigg and Atkin

Box 6.1   Styles of care

		Group	
		Experimental	**Control**
Client living arrangements	*Alone*	*paid helper*, carer, and home care services	*carer* and *home care services*
	With carer	*paid helper, carer* and home care services	*carer* and home care services

Note: italics = locus of care responsibility

(1994), could be regarded more as 'co-workers', rather than simply a resource as appears the case for carers of those in the control group.

In respect of paid helpers' perceptions of the service they provided, there were similar views expressed in both the LCMS and the Gateshead care management scheme (Challis et al., 2002a). In each of these schemes they enjoyed the worthwhile nature of the job, its flexibility, and the level of pay and disliked its lack of guaranteed work. Nevertheless, in both the payment of helpers enabled the services to be distinguished from purely voluntary or 'good neighbour' schemes, and also gave helpers some form of paid status among other members of the care network. Many gained satisfaction from working in people's homes and providing social support, in particular those who had not undertaken this type of work before. The value of developing rapport and the importance of companionship for both the older person with dementia and their paid carer has been reported elsewhere (Ryan et al., 2004).

Evolution of the Service

Historically, it has been acknowledged that most support schemes specific to people with dementia, develop in response to local need and the type of people and carers involved (Levin et al., 1994) and this was the case with the LCMS. Almost from its inception, it was a characteristic of the scheme that it was for older people with dementia whom statutory services found difficult to support, and this was undoubtedly one of its most important features. The lack of a sufficiently flexible home care service for dementia care led to the much greater development of the paid helper service than expected at the outset and that which evolved was more extensive than the less formalised input of a previous service (Challis and Davies, 1986). One case manager felt that the home care service was better in carrying out personal care with very frail clients, but that paid helpers were better in assessing situations and establishing relationships where commitment was important. Analysis of the care plans illustrated in Table 5.6 of Chapter 5 supports this. As noted earlier in this chapter, in contrast to the Kent, Gateshead and Darlington projects (Challis and Davies, 1986; Challis et al., 1995; 2002a) where there were regular advertisements, most workers in Lewisham were recruited by word of mouth, from other helpers who worked on the scheme or through other service providers' knowledge of the scheme. Nevertheless, overall in terms of the characteristics, variability, turnover and motivations of the recruits to the Lewisham paid helper service, they showed most similarity to helpers recruited to the Kent scheme. The recruitment of the latter has been described as allowing,

> ... a balance to be struck between drawing into care a large number of persons each offering a few hours ... and having a small corps of easily administered, experienced and versatile quasi-employed helpers with formalised conditions of service. (Qureshi, et al., 1989, 210).

Over time, management arrangements for the paid helper service changed, and it became part of the local authority home care service. Initially, the paid helpers formed the core of a team of home care workers with their own manager who provided care to older people with dementia within the local authority home care service. Case managers therefore began using two different types of home care service provided by the local authority social services department: a standard service and a specialist service for people with dementia which employed workers originally recruited to the paid helper service. In each case a service-level agreement was drawn up based on lessons learnt from the pilot scheme. As before, the matching of the home care workers from the specialist team to an individual was still given special consideration as was their role in both assisting the older person and supporting family carers. For both the specialist home care service and the standard service, longer hours of availability from 7.30 a.m. to 10.00 p.m. became the norm. Initially, it did not appear that the clients of the LCMS experienced any reduction in the duration of home care provision as a result of the changes. In fact it was noted that after integration of the paid helper service with the local authority domiciliary care service, a significant number continued to receive more than 20 hours care from the home care service each week. Paid helpers who subsequently joined the local authority home care service received training and access to the NVQ system. They also benefited from the support of a home care organiser on a day-to-day basis. Moreover, case managers still maintained close liaison with care assistants and their organisers to allow for good quality monitoring and service information in respect of older people with dementia and contributed to the training of the home care workers in the specialist team. The subsequent evolution of the paid helper service is discussed in the final chapter.

Summary

The paid helper service was developed during the course of the research study as an additional service available for the experimental group. A number of points of particular interest are demonstrated in the development and management of the paid helper service. It is an example of service development arising as a consequence of needs identified through the case management process, specific to older people with dementia which the structure and style of the traditional home care service could not meet. The contribution of this service was central to the success of case managers in maintaining people in the experimental group at home, providing an early example of the value of a change to the traditional pattern of service which achieved benefits for those using it (Cm 6499, 2005; Cm 6737, 2006). Indeed, this example of service development at the intermediate or team level facilitated its development at the individual level thereby permitting the creation of individualised packages of care in response to client need. Over time, this became an authority-wide service, part of the infrastructure of support for vulnerable older people with mental health problems.

It also highlighted the challenges and opportunities for case managers in undertaking a service development role in addition to other tasks within the case management process more directly concerned with the provision of care to a specific individual in their own home. Whilst the care managers' responsibilities for management of the paid helper service was undoubtedly time consuming, it offered a unique opportunity to, as far as possible, match needs with the skills and strengths of paid helpers. In effect, case managers were responsible for both commissioning and providing services within the case management process. In terms of the study, it was an important factor, making a significant contribution to the continuity of care for older people with dementia in their own homes. The outcomes of this study for both the older people with dementia and, where appropriate, their carers, are described in the next two chapters.

Chapter 7
The Experience of Older People

Introduction

The research findings of the Lewisham Case Management Scheme from predominantly the perspective of the older person are detailed in this chapter, and in the next, those relating to the carer are highlighted, along with an assessment of the scheme's effect on both client and carer outcomes. Together they illustrate the capacity of intensive case management to maintain and support older people with dementia at home as an alternative to care home admission, an objective of national policies in a number of countries (Carpenter et al., 2004; Wanless, 2006; Committee of Public Accounts, 2008). This chapter first discusses the most salient issues in respect of admission to residential or nursing home care for older people and their carers. It then explores current developments in helping to maintain the independence of older people in their own homes. Subsequently, the outcomes for the clients in both the experimental and control groups in terms of placement in care homes over the two years of the study, and the predictors of placement for each of the two groups are reviewed. It also describes the success of the scheme in meeting needs and finally discusses outcomes for the older person with dementia and the effect of the scheme on their well-being and their quality of life. It will be recalled from Chapter 4, that all those in the research study met the same inclusion criteria, however, those recruited to the experimental group received the specialist case management input, whilst the control group received standard care from statutory services.

Care in Residential Settings

For a number of years concerns have been expressed about the quality of care provided to older people in residential and nursing homes. For example, in the USA throughout the 1990s programmes were implemented which focused on staff training and the use of problem-solving techniques to address challenging behaviours of residents with dementia. A number of homes introduced separate units which were tailored to meet their needs, sometimes involving segregation from the remainder of the establishment by means of locked units (Lacey, 1999). Subsequently there has been growth in the use of residential care/assisted living (RC/AL) facilities for older people who do not require medical care (Zimmerman et al., 2005). Interestingly, research has found that outcomes over 12 months for older people with dementia in terms of health, cognition, behavioural problems, depression and social functioning were the same in both RC/AL facilities and nursing homes (Sloane et al., 2005). It has been suggested that people with dementia with stable medical conditions can fare just as well in residential or assisted living facilities (Sloane et al., 2005; Zarit and Zarit, 2006).

Similar developments in quality of care for older people in care homes have been noted in the UK. An initial drive to improve standards and quality of care within the residential sector (Centre for Policy on Ageing, 1984; Department of Health/SSI, 1989) was extended with the publication of the Consultation Document *Fit for the Future* (Department of Health, 1999b) on National Standards for Residential and Nursing Homes. Further standards were developed following the policy commitment to greater consistency and regulation in care across England (Cm 4169, 1998) with National Minimum Care Standards as enshrined in the Care Standards Act of 2000. This was designed to shift towards standards that 'focus on the key areas that most affect the quality of life experienced by service users, as well as physical standards' (Cm 4169, 1998, para 4.48). These not only address structural measures such as environment and staffing, but also process measures such as health and personal care, as well as daily life and social activities (Department of Health, 2002g; 2003c). In a study of service provision in care homes in England, specialist homes for people with dementia were found to perform only slightly better than non-specialist homes (Reilly et al., 2006). Both types met high standards in relation to person-centred care and privacy, but neither did so in relation to rehabilitation such as activities and interaction, or support for carers. In the future, the development of small-scale and homely accommodation for older people with dementia is regarded as an important area for service development in the UK (see Woods, 2008).

Following admission to a care home it has been suggested that residents remain socially isolated from their wider community (Willcocks et al., 1987) and the term 'islands of the old' has been coined as a metaphor for care homes (Reed, 1998). Davies (2001) described this in terms of residents' lack of contact with their local community, and their view that they no longer have anything useful to contribute to society. Ball and colleagues (2000) found that a major consideration in residents' quality of life was the 'goodness of fit' between a resident and a care facility's social and physical environment. This increased when residents and their families had sufficient knowledge about what the facility offered in relation to residents' own needs, thus emphasising the necessity for prospective residents to plan ahead, and for facilities to provide clear information about their services, amenities and philosophy of care. With regard to older people with dementia, the importance of designing 'homely' surroundings which also help such residents to function at the highest level possible has also been stressed (Marshall, 1999).

Most importantly, the views of older people, and older people with dementia, reflect a desire to remain in their own homes (Moriarty and Webb, 2000), which is particularly pertinent given the increased mortality and morbidity associated with admission to care homes in people with dementia (Cohen-Mansfield et al., 1999; Aneshensel et al., 2000; Mozley et al., 2004). More generally, loss of independence has been cited as an important reason by community-dwelling older people for rejecting residential care (Qureshi and Walker, 1989). Indeed, quality of life interviews conducted with residents of care facilities have indicated that residents often experience loss of their valued independence and autonomy (Ball et al., 2000). However, some community-dwelling older people can experience social isolation and loneliness (Tunstall, 1966; Phillipson et al., 2001; Victor et al., 2005) which may be alleviated following admission to a care home (Allen et al., 1992; Mozley et al., 2004). On the other hand, carers may experience a reduction in levels of burden (Meiland et al., 2001) and improvement in their psychological health (Wells and Jorm, 1987) following their relative's admission to long-term residential care although an increase in carer burden following admission has also been reported (Tornatore and Grant, 2002). Taking account of both the burden experienced by carers and the wishes of older people with dementia who require care in order to live safely, it has been suggested that residential care and community care should be regarded as part of a continuum of care rather than two polar opposites (McKee, 1999).

Supporting Older People at Home

The value of supporting older people with dementia or cognitive impairment at home in preference to their admission to a care home has been demonstrated over a substantial period of time (Gilleard, 1984; 1992; Levin et al., 1989; Allen and Perkins, 1995; Andrew et al., 2000). Within a continuum of care (McKee, 1999) the provision of community care in the form of 'substitution services' such as home care, meals-on-wheels, respite care or other services, it has been argued, can reduce decline in the older person and/or reduce carer burden. This can then delay or prevent care home admission, which in turn reduces government expenditure (Gilhooly, 1990). However, there has been little or inconclusive evidence in both the UK and North America that provision of services at home or respite care necessarily prevents admission (Lieberman and Kramer, 1991; Gilhooly et al., 1994; Zarit et al., 1999; Gaugler et al., 2003a; Arksey et al., 2004). The importance of providing interventions that are both appropriate and sufficient in intensity in order to assist the carer in maintaining the person with dementia at home has also been noted (Zarit et al., 1999; Zarit and Leitsch 2001; Zarit and Femia, 2008).

In England, government policy promoting the values of independence and choice (Cm 849, 1989; Cm 4169, 1998) was followed by guidance which proposed that older people with complex mental health needs should be supported in the community using outreach facilities including telecare and environmental technologies (Department of Health, 2001b, 104–5). More recent policy (Cm 6737, 2006) has acknowledged that assistive technology (AT) offers possibilities in supporting people in their own homes. It has been defined as 'any item, piece of equipment, product or system that is used to increase, maintain or improve the functional capabilities and independence of people with cognitive, physical or communication difficulties'

(Marshall, 2000). For older people with dementia, it has a variety of applications including smart housing, telecare, and low-level technology (Cash, 2006). Telecare, which is a combination of equipment, monitoring and response, can be used to help individuals remain independent at home (Cm 6737, 2006). It includes assistance that is supportive – such as keyless entry systems or medication reminder systems; preventative – such as falls predictors or room occupancy monitors; and responsive – such as smoke detectors or gas monitors. Although it is important to distinguish between interventions that are purely rehabilitative and those whose goal is to improve independent living (Andresen et al., 2000), it has been suggested that AT is inexpensive compared with care staff costs, but needs to be introduced as soon as possible after diagnosis to encourage familiarity before cognitive skills decline too greatly (Audit Commission, 2004).

So what is the relationship between AT and case management? They are not mutually exclusive, but rather, complementary (Marshall and Tibbs, 2006). However, it does not have the capacity to replace the components of a care plan provided by carers; rather it has the potential to assist in the management of risk, often associated with older people with dementia living in the community (Woolham, 2006). Seen in this light, AT could conceivably enhance the potential of case management to enable older people with dementia remain in their own homes, which more importantly, is often their stated preference (Commission for Social Care Inspection, 2006). It is also relevant in terms of the cost of care since for some, the cost is higher in a care home, which is of particular concern in view of the projected increase in the number of older people with dementia (Knapp et al., 2007). Moreover, AT aimed at alleviating care tasks or reducing carer burden in order for carers to spend more time with the person with dementia may be regarded as beneficial (Baldwin, 2006). Nevertheless, concerns have been expressed about the use of AT in the care of older people with dementia in their own homes. Marshall and Tibbs (2006) suggested that a combination of the increasing numbers of older people with dementia living at home, a diminishing workforce and government policies will mean AT may become a more routine part of many care plans and with the possibility that technology will replace individual contact. They add a cautionary note that it should not replace existing services, but rather supplement or support them as part of a comprehensive care plan. It has also been argued that more generally, less attention may be given to person-centred approaches, and to the ethical or legal issues particularly regarding consent (Woolham, 2006).

The remainder of this chapter examines the study's outcomes, in which an intensive case management scheme for older people with dementia was compared to a similar group of people receiving statutory services alone. Whilst the study predated the advent of the increasing use of AT described above, nevertheless older people in both the experimental and control groups benefited from devices which increased their safety and lessened the risk to themselves and others by the use of items such as smoke detectors, and medication reminder systems. Implicitly, this is an evaluation of the capacity of the LCMS to provide a viable alternative to care home admission for older people with dementia.

Admission to Care Homes

Dementia Severity and Placement

Dementia may be regarded as a clinical syndrome whose core features can include impairment in areas of cognitive function, social or occupational functioning, and in the ability to perform activities of daily living (ADLs) (Eastley and Wilcock, 2000), and which follows a typical clinical course. It has been described in terms of different discrete stages such as; pre-dementia or minimal; mild or early stage; moderate or middle stage; and severe or late stage (Roth et al., 1988; Audit Commission, 2000; Förstl, 2000; National Audit Office, 2007). However, it has also been argued that such a clinical model of dementia described in distinct stages may detract from a person-centred approach to caring (Marshall and Tibbs, 2006). Nevertheless, late stage or severe dementia, characterised by impairment of all cognitive and expressive functions, disrupted daytime patterns and inability to wash, dress, or care for oneself, often necessitates long-term nursing or residential care or high levels of community support.

All clients in this research study were assessed using the Organic Brain Score (OBS, Gurland et al., 1977) which measures cognitive impairment, with a higher score indicating greater impairment. Seventy-two per cent of older people in the experimental group and 76 per cent of those in the control group scored 6 or more on this measure, corresponding to 'severe dementia'. The differences between OBS scores of people in the experimental and control groups and their subsequent placement in care homes are illustrated in Table 7.1. Although the numbers of cases observed in each group were small, it appeared that clients scoring less than six on the OBS scale were admitted to care homes in roughly the same proportion in both groups, approximately half. However, those in the control group scoring 6 or more on the OBS were almost twice as likely to be admitted as those in the experimental group. Twenty-seven per cent of the experimental group and 53 per cent of the control group for those scoring 6 or 7 on the OBS were placed in care homes, and 30 per cent in the experimental group compared with 56 per cent of the control group scoring 8 or more, were placed. For those scoring 6 or more on the OBS, there was a statistically significant difference between the experimental and control group with regard to destinational outcome, (χ^2=4.27, p<0.05). This suggests that the case management scheme was successful in providing care at home to older people with more severe cognitive impairment. Indeed, the capacity of intensive case management to provide care at home for older people with severe cognitive impairment has also been noted elsewhere (Challis et al., 2002a). Similarly, Lindesay and Murphy (1989) demonstrated that older people with fairly severe dementia, living alone and with no carer, stayed at home for longer when supported by a specialist domiciliary scheme, than did those receiving the normal range of services.

Table 7.1   Care home placement and OBS score

OBS score	Experimental group n=43 Placed in care home/OBS score (%)		Control group n=43 Placed in care home/OBS score (%)	
<6	7/ 12	(58)	5/ 10	(50)
6–7	3/ 11	(27)	9/ 17	(53)
8+	6/ 20	(30)	9/ 16	(56)

Placement Rate

As noted previously, the LCMS was designed with the aim of supporting older people with dementia in the community. Nevertheless, case managers occasionally facilitated admission to a care home as a more appropriate form of long-term care than continued residence in the community. One example involved a couple both suffering from dementia, where the paid helper's reports of abuse resulted in the placement of the husband in a long-term care establishment, to allow his wife to continue living in safety at home. However, such an intervention was not customary, as demonstrated below.

The study recruited 45 cases to the experimental group and 50 to the control group, as previously described in Chapter 4. From these groups, 43 pairs were identified and matched. It is upon these matched pairs that the comparisons of destinational outcome are made. Table 7.2 indicates this at 6 monthly intervals over the two-year period for the 43 matched pairs. This is in effect a measure of 'prevalence' of placement, i.e. a record of where the clients were living at particular points in time during the period of research. At the end of a year around three-quarters of each group of older people remained in their own homes, 19 per cent had been placed in care homes and seven per cent had died. Comparable rates of placement in residential and nursing care homes in both the experimental and the control groups appear to have occurred during the first year of the research study. In the second year appreciable differences between the two groups in the rate of placement became evident. This is an effect which is somewhat masked in Table 7.2 but is clearly demonstrated in Figure 7.1, which is a graphic representation of the first two columns of this table. Table 7.2 illustrated that by eighteen months 56 per cent of those in the experimental group and 51 per cent of those in the control group remained in their own homes. At the end of two years 51 per cent of the experimental group remained at home compared with just 33 per cent of the control group.

In respect of Table 7.2 it is also notable that the mortality rates of seven per cent in the first year and 28 per cent over the two years in the experimental group are low compared with some other studies of dementia, be they epidemiological studies or service populations. A community study offering additional support

Table 7.2 **Destinational outcome at six month intervals over two years for matched groups**

No. of months	In nursing or residential home		At home		Dead	
	E	C	E	C	E	C
	No.(%)	No.(%)	No.(%)	No.(%)	No. (%)	No.(%)
0	0 (0)	0 (0)	43 (100)	43 (100)	0 (0)	0 (0)
6	5 (12)	3 (7)	37 (86)	39 (91)	1 (2)	1(2)
12	8 (19)	8 (19)	32 (74)	32 (74)	3 (7)	3(7)
18	12 (28)	12 (28)	24 (56)	22 (51)	7 (16)	9(21)
24	9 (21)	14 (33)	22 (51)	14 (33)	12 (28)	15(35)

Source: Challis et al. (1997a)
n=43 matched pairs

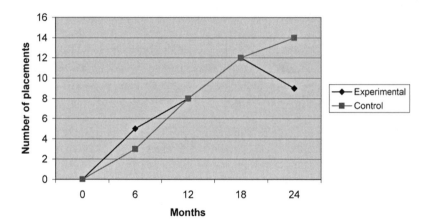

Figure 7.1 **Number placed in long-term care**

to older people with dementia reported mortality rates of 29 per cent after the first year, and 43 per cent by the second year (O'Connor et al., 1991), and in the US, a demonstration study of older people with dementia eligible for case management had a mortality rate of 35 per cent after three years (Miller et al., 1999). However, in England, a more recent study which followed up a group of older people suffering dementia, found that 15 per cent had died eighteen months later (Moriarty and Webb, 2000), a finding similar to that of the experimental group in the present study.

Table 7.3 provides an indication of 'incidence' of placement in residential and nursing home care when treating the two years as separate. In these circumstances, incidence is defined as the number of new instances of an occurrence in a study sample over a defined period of time. In year one there were nine placements in the experimental group and ten in the control group, whereas in year two there were seven placements in the former group (22 per cent of those at home) and 13 in the latter group (41 per cent of those at home). Over a two-year period there were 16 placed in the experimental group compared with 23 in the control group. This provides further evidence to suggest that the effects of the scheme upon placement in care homes occurred in the second year with a reduced rate of placement for the experimental group in this period of time.

It is important to understand the reasons for the slightly faster rate of placement among the experimental group cases in the first six months of the scheme, followed by a relatively slower rate in the next eighteen months, in comparison with the control group as shown in Figure 7.1. A number of factors concerning the selection of cases are likely to be pertinent. These have been described in Chapter 4 and summarised here to assist in the interpretation of the findings relating to destinational outcome. Despite the matching process, there appeared to be different subgroups of cases in the two matched groups. The evidence of this and of a previous study (Challis and Davies, 1986) suggests that the presence of an alternative form of care, such as case management, can attract a special subgroup of cases, some of whom it is able to support with success, but some of whom it cannot support since the most appropriate course of action has been postponed in favour of referral to the scheme. Typically such cases have reached the point where placement is almost inevitable. The inclusion of these cases in the experimental group will have a negative effect on the overall impact of intervention (Challis and Darton, 1990). It appeared therefore, that whilst the two groups were well matched on objective measures which are regarded as determinants of continued community residence, some within the experimental group were to a greater extent at the point

Table 7.3   Outcomes in the first and second years after referral

Number of people alive and at home at beginning of year (base for %)		Number surviving at home at end of year (%)		Number placed during year (%)		Number dying at home in year (%)	
E	C	E	C	E	C	E	C
Year 1	43	43	32 (74)	32 (74)	9 (21)	10 (23)	2 (5)	2 (5)
Year 2	32	32	22 (69)	14 (44)	7 (22)	13 (41)	3 (9)	5 (16)

Source: Challis et al. (1997a)

Note: In the control group 1 case placed and subsequently discharged in year 1

of transition, despite comparable levels of disability and disturbance. There were also those within the experimental group who were discharged home from hospital with the help of the case managers, an intervention that could not be recreated in the control group. Inevitably, this early placement effect has implications for the cost analysis. The placement pattern illustrated here suggests that some important cost outcomes will occur over two years and longer in determining the relative efficiency of case management compared with standard services.

Risk of Care Home Admission

Factors which might have prompted admission to a care home for older people living in the community were explored utilising information derived from client and carer circumstances. Four of these related to the client, and one to the carer's circumstances. These were: risks associated with the level of carer distress; the client's activities of daily living, including their risk of falling using evidence over the past 6 months; behavioural difficulties such as wandering; their health; and environmental factors.

As shown in Table 7.4, older people in the experimental group were rated to be at greater risk than those in the control group at referral in all but one of the domains. After six months it was estimated that there had been a decrease in the incidence of risks overall among the experimental group while there was little overall change among the control group. The reduction in risks over 12 months for the experimental group was greatest in relation to the clients' activities of daily living and behavioural problems. It is also of note that the proportion of cases where the carer's level of distress constituted a serious risk was halved in the experimental group over 12 months. In contrast, there was very little change in the control group in this domain over the same period. This is despite the fact that carer distress was rated as present in almost the same proportion of cases in both

Table 7.4   Overall risk: care home placement

Domains of risk	At referral		At 6 months		At 12 months	
	E n=37 %	C n=42 %	E n=29 %	C n=36 %	E n=25 %	C n=29 %
Carer circumstances Level of distress	41	40	28	42	20	38
Client circumstances Activities of daily living	59	31	21	25	27	31
Behavioural difficulties	46	38	41	39	15	28
Health	30	31	28	31	23	28
Environmental factors	11	5	7	6	0	10

Researcher rating

the experimental and control group at referral. This suggests that greater support to carers was provided by the case management scheme.

An overall risk score was derived from the aggregate of the five factors rated as present by the researcher, plus a sixth, 'other' risk area. Table 7.5 shows that the mean change in score between initial assessment and six months follow-up was a reduction of 0.72 for the experimental group but a small increase of 0.22 for the control group and the average scores altered little between the six and 12 month follow-ups. This difference in change scores between the experimental and control groups was statistically significant at both six and 12 months. On the whole, factors which might have prompted admission to a care home were rated by the researcher as present in similar proportions for both the experimental and control group at referral. However, by six months there had been a much greater reduction in these risk factors among those in the experimental group and receiving case management and this was maintained over 12 months. Thus, the case management scheme demonstrated some success in reducing the risk of placement in a care home, as assessed by researchers.

Table 7.5   Overall risk score: care home placement

	Change by 6 months			Change by 12 months		
	E **n=29**	**C** **n=36**	**p**	**E** **n=25**	**C** **n=29**	**p**
Mean score	-0.72	0.22	<.01	-1.11	0.10	<.01

Researcher rating

Predictors of Care Home Admission

The effects of the LCMS on admissions to long-term residential and nursing care were investigated by identifying which factors were most influential in enabling older people with dementia to remain in their own homes. Logistic regression was undertaken with the dependent variable being location after two years, that is, whether residence was in their own home or in a care home. For those who had died, their permanent location was taken to be that at the time of death. This type of analysis allows the prediction of a discrete outcome from a set of appropriate variables. The selection of these variables was based upon their relevance to the home-based care of older people with dementia and their carers. For example, a number of individual measures of functioning were used in preference to a global measure of cognitive impairment which, it was felt, did not usefully discriminate between cases. The variables chosen were taken from a list describing the characteristics of clients and carers as detailed in Box 7.1.

Box 7.1   Variables used in logistic regression analyses

Client variables	Carer variables
Descriptive factors Gender Presence of carer Socio-economic group Two clients in household	*Descriptive factors* Age Gender
Quality of life ADL need shortfall Client activity score Overall risk Perceived change in activities and company Risk behaviour	*Quality of life* Carer desires placement Health affected by caring Malaise score Overall strain Presence of severe malaise
Dependency Ability to transfer ADL functioning Behaviour rating scale (CAPE) Incontinence severity Physical health problems Risk of falling	*Caring role* Carer reluctance to accept help Main carer hours input Other carer hours input Tension in relationship between carer/ client
Mental health Aggressive exchanges Communication impairment Depression (CARE) Duration of memory problems Night disturbance Recent deterioration in behaviour Signs of distress and disturbing actions Single diagnosis – Alzheimer type	
Care process Client uncooperative with services Number of months at home	

Experimental Group

Four characteristics were predictors of placement in a care home for those in the experimental group. The three client characteristics were: the duration of memory problems, defined as the number of months before the initial interview that the informant first noticed memory problems; incontinence severity based on the CAPE summary measure for incontinence, and socio-economic group (semi-skilled or manual). The carer characteristic, desire for placement, was based on their response to the informant interview question, 'If you could arrange permanent care for (the client) in a home or hospital or if it was offered would you accept it?'

As Table 7.6 shows, the most significant predictor of placement was the carer's view on the need for care home admission for their relative. This supports the findings of other studies (Levin et al., 1989, 1994; Moriarty and Webb, 1997b; Cohen and Pushkar, 1999; Davey et al., 2005). The three client characteristics combined with the carer characteristic could successfully predict location at two years of 84 per cent of the experimental group. Whilst the client characteristics noted to be influential in the placement process were only at borderline levels of significance in statistical terms, factors in their lifestyle and behaviour in combination with the carer's view were important in terms of risk of admission to a care home.

Control Group

Initial analysis of predictors of permanent placement in a care home for clients in the control group indicated that the most important component was the presence of a carer. This effect had such a big association with reduced probability of placement that it swamped other effects. Therefore, this variable was later omitted as a predictor in order to investigate the influence of a wider range of factors. Table 7.7 illustrates

Table 7.6   Experimental group: predictors of permanent placement

Variable	Co-efficient β	Odds Ratio	(95% Confidence Interval for odds ratio)		Wald statistic p
N=43			Lower	Upper	
Client characteristics Duration of memory					
problems	0.020	1.02	1.00	1.04	0.056
Incontinence severity	0.713	2.04	0.97	4.31	0.062
Socio-economic group	1.774	5.89	0.90	38.67	0.065
Carer characteristics Desire for placement	2.180	8.85	1.99	39.23	0.004
Constant	-3.411	0.00			0.002
Model chi-square 16.72 p<0.01 Correct – not placed 89% – placed 75% – overall 84%					

Odds ratio – the factor by which the probability of placement should be multiplied when a particular characteristic is present
Wald – tests the statistical significance of coefficients in the model

Table 7.7   Control group: predictors of permanent placement

Variable	Co-efficient β	Odds Ratio	95% Confidence Interval for odds ratio		Wald statistic P
N=43			Lower	Upper	
Client characteristics					
Physical health problems	0.857	2.36	1.13	4.90	0.022
ADL need shortfall	0.490	1.63	1.01	2.64	0.045
Client activity score	0.171	1.19	1.00	1.41	0.054
Signs of distress and disturbing actions	0.259	1.30	0.97	1.73	0.079
Carer characteristics					
Age	0.233	1.26	1.06	1.51	0.010
Other carer hours input	-0.507	0.60	0.41	0.89	0.011
Constant	-20.760	0.00			0.008
Model chi-square 34.05 p<0.001 Correct – not placed 86% – placed 82% – overall 84%					

Odds ratio – the factor by which the probability of placement should be multiplied when a particular characteristic is present.
Wald – tests the statistical significance of coefficients in the model

that two aspects of client functioning were strongly associated with increased probability of placement. These were, physical health problems and shortfall in the meeting of needs associated with ADLs as rated by the researcher, and both were statistically significant ($p<0.05$). Two other predictors less strongly associated with placement in a care home were: a higher client activity score; and a higher score on the signs of distress and disturbing actions measure, based on Platt et al.'s (1980) Behaviour–Mood Disturbance Scale. These effects reflect the difficulty of managing the care of restless people at home. Two carer characteristics, namely, age of the carer and input of carers other than the main carer, were also significantly associated with increased probability of placement.

Overall, these four client characteristics combined with two carer characteristics could successfully predict location at two years of 84 per cent of the control group. The influence of carers is particularly interesting in this model in two respects. First, with regard to the age of the main carer, it appeared that the older the carer, the greater the probability of placement in a care home for the client. This may reflect the greater frailty of older carers who were generally their partner. This finding is consistent with other research (Bergmann et al., 1978) which found that people with dementia being cared for by an elderly spouse were less likely to remain in the community. However, another study (Lieberman and Kramer, 1991) found an association between younger caregivers and subsequent placement, particularly if the caregiver was a son or daughter caring alone or with relatives. Second, the contribution of carers other than the main carer was associated with maintaining older people with dementia at home for longer. This perhaps indicates that they provided support for the main carers. Nevertheless, it should be borne in mind that the most crucial component in reducing the likelihood of admission to a care home was simply the presence of any carer, which concurs with the findings of a study of older people with dementia and their carers where the presence of a co-resident carer had a highly protective effect (Banerjee et al., 2003).

In comparing the regression equations of the experimental and control groups, it is apparent that both had high predictive validity, although none of the characteristics were common to the two groups as might have been expected. They were dominated by carer-related factors: the extent to which the carer wanted the client to be placed in a care home in the experimental group; and presence of a carer in the control group, a factor with such a large association that it was removed from the analysis because it swamped all others. Only one factor in the experimental group regression equation was significant at the one per cent level, namely desire for placement, suggesting that the case management scheme appeared to substitute successfully for problems arising from the absence of carers, and to provide care for clients with a high degree of health and behavioural problems. Indeed, one of the hallmarks of the LCMS was its success in maintaining older people at home who did not have carers, which is discussed further in Chapter 8, where the contribution of carers is considered more fully. More generally, the research highlights the critical contribution carers make to decisions about the admission of older people with dementia to care homes. As reported elsewhere the attitude of the carer was one of the key variables in predicting placement (Levin et al., 1989; Pot, 2004).

Outcomes of Care

Outcomes for older people described in this section have used material derived from interviews with clients, carers and the assessments of researchers. The analyses have sought to explain differences in the extent to which the LCMS met the needs of the experimental group, compared with the control group. As such it represents an attempt to measure many of the unique features of the case management scheme using items specially selected for this purpose. Inevitably, due to attrition, through factors such as death, decline in health and placement in long-term care out of the area, it was not possible to re-assess all clients or carers during the follow-up period of two years. Therefore all remaining cases were used for the comparison of change measures. Measures of change over time are illustrated in a number of tables, from baseline to 6 months and baseline to 12 months and were tested using analysis of variance. Descriptions of the measures or variables used are referenced in Appendix 1.

The results reported in Table 7.8 not surprisingly demonstrate that there was an overall deterioration in functioning over 12 months in both the experimental and control groups with regard to independence in undertaking ADLs as indicated by an increase in score. At 12 months, ability to communicate had declined, physical disability had increased and level of apathy generally had increased in both groups as measured by the Behaviour Rating Scale sub-scales (Pattie and Gilleard, 1979). These differences between groups were not significant. However, signs of distress and disturbing actions (Platt et al., 1980), including misery, restlessness, over-dependence, anxiety and aggression were reduced more in the control group than in the experimental group, which reached a statistically significant difference over the first six months (p<0.05). The reasons for these findings are unclear but the improvements seen for those in the control group may have been due to factors exogenous to the scheme.

Table 7.8   Overall functioning

Client functioning	Change by 6 months			Change by 12 months		
	E	C	p	E	C	p
ADL functioning	0.78	0.81	ns	2.70	2.38	ns
Behaviour rating scale (BRS) Subscales:	0.89	-0.74	ns	0.81	-0.38	ns
Communication difficulties	0.18	0.13	ns	0.21	0.13	ns
Physical disability	0.08	-0.11	ns	0.36	0.50	ns
Social disturbance	0.10	-0.97	ns	-0.25	-0.93	ns
Apathy	0.45	0.19	ns	0.93	0.10	ns
Signs of distress and disturbing actions	0.14	-1.91	<.05	-0.94	-1.97	ns

Informant rating

E: min=29 max=39. C: min=31 max=46

Carers' views of clients' unmet needs that were present initially and at twelve months are detailed in Table 7.9. Sample sizes were small due to missing information at 12 months. Twenty 'need' areas were identified, covering personal care, household chores, daytime supervision, respite and health needs. Carers were asked which of these activities or chores they were happy to do and which they would like to be relieved of, or receive more help with, or think that the older person with dementia needed more help with. The strength of carer anxiety about clients being left alone is reflected in the fact that on referral, the two most frequently identified needs in both the experimental and control groups were for someone to visit to provide companionship in their own home, and for day care. A need for daytime company was identified in 81 per cent of those in the experimental group, and 72 per cent of those in the control group on referral. Similarly, the requirement for day care away from home was expressed in 59 per cent of those in the experimental group and 73 per cent of those in the control group.

This table reveals that in the experimental group, there was a reduction in all but one of the areas of unmet need at 12 months compared with the proportion at referral. Conversely, in the control group there were seven areas showing a slight increase in perceived need at twelve months. The proportion of clients with an identified need in three areas of personal care, namely help with washing, dressing and help going to bed, was higher in the experimental group and declined more over

Table 7.9   Carer rating of client unmet needs

Areas of need	E n=22		C n=26	
	On referral %	After 12 months %	On referral %	After 12 months %
Personal care to client				
Washing	55	9	12	19
Bathing	55	14	31	31
Dressing	50	0	8	15
Help getting up	36	0	12	12
Help going to bed	36	5	8	15
Prepare meals (food and hot drink)	32	5	38	23
Help with toilet	23	0	4	4
Medical attention	15	26	37	41
Maintenance of the home				
Housework	55	27	35	27
Laundry	32	9	15	23
Medication	18	5	12	12
Shopping	14	0	4	4
Finances	14	0	4	8
Move around indoors	5	0	0	4
Additional care				
Day time company	81	32	72	65
Day care	59	23	73	42
Respite overnight (away)	50	10	46	31
Respite overnight (at home)	50	6	26	20
Escort outside the home	41	30	44	32
Night sitting	14	5	13	10

12 months as compared to clients in the control group. This increase in personal care needs reflects both the progress of the disease and the difficulties for existing services in responding to these changed circumstances. The need for daytime company was a successful feature of the scheme, since at 12 months only 32 per cent of those in the experimental group but 65 per cent of those in the control group were identified as having unmet needs in this area. The increased need for medical attention may be a reflection of the general physical deterioration in both groups by 12 months.

The researchers' ratings on client needs associated with their ADLs (Challis et al., 1995) are summarised in Table 7.10. The ADL needs were rated in four domains; rise and retire; personal care needs; daily domestic chores, and weekly domestic chores such as heavy cleaning and shopping. The overall ADL need shortfall was derived from the combination of the four domains. The table shows statistically significant differences between the two groups in the reduction of overall ADL need at both six months ($p<0.01$) and 12 months ($p<0.05$). It is notable that the improvement was achieved swiftly, within the first six months and maintained over 12 months. The gains for the experimental group over the control group as measured by changes at six and 12 months were higher in the areas relating to rising and retiring and weekly domestic chores. Although gains over the control group were also apparent in the areas of personal care and daily domestic chores, these differences did not reach a statistically significant level at either six or 12 months. These findings are important particularly in respect of the domain rising and retiring, in that they reflect the unique contribution of the paid helper service to clients in the experimental group and its capacity to provide care outside of normal working hours.

In real terms the average number of hours in a day (6 a.m. to 6 p.m. including weekends) that those in the experimental group spent on their own was nearly two hours per week less on average after 12 months than the control group. For

Table 7.10   Activities of daily living: shortfall

	Change by 6 months			Change by 12 months		
	E n=39	**C** n=47	**p**	**E** n=34	**C** n=39	**p**
ADL need shortfall	-2.85	-0.55	<.01	-2.74	-0.79	<.05
Subscales:						
Rise and retire	-1.00	-0.19	<.01	-0.88	-0.33	ns
Personal care needs	-0.77	-0.28	ns	-0.79	-0.15	ns
Daily domestic chores	-0.49	-0.13	ns	-0.41	-0.33	ns
Weekly domestic chores	-0.59	0.04	<.05	-0.65	0.03	<.05

Researcher rating

those living alone, the experimental group on average spent three hours a day less on their own at 12 months compared with those in the control group. Although clients in the experimental group spent less time alone compared to those in the control group when measured over time, these differences did not reach statistical significance. As described in Chapter 5, case managers rated social life and leisure as being a marked or severe problem in 52 per cent of first assessments, but just 18 per cent of subsequent assessments. This may indicate an inverse relationship between the number of daytime hours spent alone, and the perceived quality of social and leisure activities for clients in the experimental group.

Particular importance was attached to gaining the views of the older person with dementia themselves in regard to their own quality of life and a variety of measures were used. However, there were difficulties with this due in part to the small numbers with complete data, as fewer older people could be successfully interviewed for comparative purposes as time progressed. Therefore, to complement this, the views of both paid and family carers involved in supporting clients at home were also recorded in the informant interview schedules. These are reported in Table 7.11 and show changes in the client's quality of life over six and 12 months on a range of indicators. At six months, those in the experimental group were significantly more satisfied with their home environment. However, there were no statistically significant differences found between the two groups with regard to either level of depression using the CARE measure (Gurland et al., 1984) or in the frequency of client activities at home, as perceived by the informants. On the other hand, the informant-rated perceived change in activities and company, recorded improvements for the experimental group at both six and 12 months ($p<0.05$).

Table 7.11   Changes in quality of life

	Change by 6 months			Change by 12 months		
	E	C	p	E	C	p
Satisfaction with lifestyle within the home (CL)	0.67	-0.39	<.05	0.11	-0.06	ns
Depression (CARE) (CL)	-1.5	-0.54	ns	0.33	-0.95	ns
Client activity score (I)	0.81	1.00	ns	-0.03	0.46	ns
Perceived change in activities and company (I)	0.91	0.30	<.05	1.54	0.47	<.05

CL=client   Experimental min n=9 max n=29

I=Informant   Control min n=16 max n=38

Summary

In this chapter, outcomes for older people have been explored in the context of the two options available to them: care in residential settings and care in their own homes. For those clients within the LCMS, it achieved: success in maintaining care at home for older people with more severe dementia; a low placement rate in care homes; a reduction in the perceived level of risk of placement; a reduction in unmet needs as perceived by carers; higher levels of company and social activities; and better quality of life in terms of greater satisfaction of lifestyle within the home. It appears that the issue of the location of older people with dementia, as described earlier in this chapter, whether receiving care in their own homes or in care homes is of great importance. The scheme was characterised by high survival rates in terms of community tenure, and low placement rates in respect of care home admissions for the older people with dementia in both the experimental group and the control group over the first year. In the second year of the scheme its effects began to show in lower rates of admission to residential or nursing home care for the experimental group, than under standard arrangements for the control group. There was also an observed reduction in the level of risk of placement in a care home for the older people receiving the case management input. Objective measures of client circumstances at the outset revealed a high level of unmet need across a broad spectrum that was reduced much more for the experimental group in receipt of case management than for the control group. The scheme was particularly effective in meeting the personal care needs of clients and providing daytime company, although the lack of impact on their behaviour is not surprising given the progressive nature of the illness.

These findings should, however, be placed in context. Problems associated with measuring quality of life generally, and in particular with older people with more severe dementia have been recognised (Downs and Zarit, 1999; Bauld et al., 2000a). It was not possible to re-interview all clients who had been interviewed initially due to the deteriorating nature of their disease and increased physical frailty, and assessing changes in quality of life over time was also difficult with this particular client group. Only one measure showed significant change in the client's subjective perception of their quality of life for those in the experimental group, namely greater satisfaction with their lifestyle at home by six months. However, objective measures revealed a reduction across a broad spectrum of need, which was greater for the experimental group than the control group, since the carers' perception was of an improvement in the amount of activities and company that the clients enjoyed. It is noteworthy that within the research study, attention was given to addressing the social needs of both clients and carers, and in particular, it was apparent that older people living alone appeared to receive more company and social activity as a result of case management input. Thus, this chapter provides only a partial account of the outcomes of this research study since a key element of intervention in dementia care is to support the carers as much as the older person. The impact on carers is the subject of the next chapter.

Chapter 8

The Experience of Carers

Introduction

The demands placed on the carers of older people with dementia and the burden of coping with the effects of the condition is indeed high and often affects all areas of the carer's life. In addition, the effects of the emotional stress of coping with the changes in the person as the disease progresses have been well documented (Gilleard, 1984; Moriarty and Webb, 2000; Zarit and Zarit, 2006; Zarit and Edwards, 2008). The differential effects of gender on caring have also been widely reported with research suggesting that female carers generally experience higher levels of stress than their male counterparts (Parker, 1990). Husbands caring for their wives reported lower emotional distress (Zarit and Whitlach, 1992), and lower subjective caregiver burden than wives caring for their husbands, even when controlling for coping resources and level of social support (Thompson et al., 2004). Citing evidence to indicate that female caregivers suffer greater psychiatric morbidity as a result of caring has led some researchers to advocate targeting them early in the care-giving process as an 'at risk' group (Yee and Schultz, 2000). In England, it would appear that caring is still more likely to be undertaken by females (Wanless, 2006) and as discussed in Chapter 4, the majority of family carers in this study were females caring for partners or parents. Thus, reducing the emotional distress associated with caring for an older person with dementia was of fundamental concern in the study reported here.

This chapter briefly reviews the efficacy of carer intervention programmes, the use of service interventions for older people with dementia and their carers and the utilisation of respite services for carers. Subsequently, the outcomes of the Lewisham Case Management Scheme are described with regard to: how the overall needs of clients and carers changed; the extent to which carers were relieved of the tasks of caring and in the time spent in this role; and how this related to the burden of care. It also examines the influence of the scheme on the carer's quality of life, and their own perception of their level of strain experienced due to their caring role. In contrast to Chapter 7 which focused on the experiences of older people, this chapter examines the effect of the scheme on different members of the care network, for example main carers, other carers, and paid carer services. Furthermore, outcomes for carers who lived with the older person, and carers who did not, are also examined. Thus, as a consequence, the findings presented in this chapter are more complex and, particularly in terms of carers' quality of life, illustrate more subtle changes.

Carer Interventions

A number of studies have been undertaken that examine the provision of support to carers of older people with dementia, and which report varying levels of success. Most of these were designed to improve the psychological well-being of carers by reducing anxiety (Akkerman and Ostwald, 2004); depression (Mittelman et al., 2004; Teri et al., 2005); or carer burden (Marriott et al., 2000; Ulstein et al., 2007). However one criticism noted is that interventions defined by particular health indicators such as depression or burden which are not present in all carers recruited to the study, means the research may fail to produce significant results (Zarit and Femia, 2008). Such studies have also varied considerably in their content and in the duration of intervention. In the majority, carers received information about dementia, but additional interventions ranged from education and training programmes (Brodaty and Gresham, 1989; Onor et al., 2007); therapy or self-help groups (Mohide et al., 1990; Mittelman et al., 2004; 2006; 2007); problem-solving (Teri et al., 2005; Ulstein et al., 2007); and counselling (Marriott et al., 2000; Akkerman and Ostwald, 2004; Mittelman et al., 2004; 2006; 2007). Although most were conducted on-site, for example in clinics or psychiatric units, a number were carried out in the carers' own homes (Mohide et al., 1990; Teri et al., 2005; Moniz-Cook et al., 2008). Such variations arguably make comparisons between studies in terms of their efficacy a complex issue. However, it has been suggested that interventions which combine three treatment techniques: information; problem-solving; and support can be useful resources for carers (Zarit and Zarit, 2006).

Clearly the needs of older people and carers are intertwined and the well-being of the latter depends to a large extent on the practical needs of the former being met (Levin et al., 1989; 1994; Venables et al., 2006). Nevertheless, although many carer intervention studies have not had any direct impact upon the older person with dementia, some have reported significant reduction in the frequency and severity of behavioural problems (Marriott et al., 2000; Teri et al., 2005; Moniz-Cook et al., 2008) and improvements in mood and socialisation of the person with dementia (Onor et al., 2007). The effect of carer interventions in some studies has been to delay placement in a care home (Brodaty and Gresham, 1989; Mittelman et al., 2006). A selection of carer intervention studies that were of a longer duration and recruited larger samples of carers are summarised in Box 8.1. Variations in the interventions provided and the populations sampled makes comparison of these research studies difficult. Most importantly, carers and caregiving are typified by a good deal of heterogeneity in all parts of the caring process (Zarit and Femia, 2008; Zarit and Edwards, 2008). However, it would appear that there are four pertinent observations which appertain to many carer intervention studies. First, is the importance of using reliable and accurate measures of carer well-being and the types of intervention that will usefully help carers. Second, the differential effect of an intervention upon carers and the older person with dementia should be considered. Third, programmes designed to reduce psychological distress in carers or which delay placement in long-term care may only have a limited effect (Zarit et al., 1999; Zarit and Leitsch,

Box 8.1 Carer intervention studies: older people with dementia

Authors	Intervention	Outcomes
Brodaty and Gresham, 1989	Carer programme: training in coping skills. Memory retraining programme: for older person with concurrent 10 days carer respite.	Lower level of psychological stress in carer programme after 12 months. 65 per cent of older people still living at home in carer programme compared to 26 per cent in memory retraining programme.
Mohide et al., 1990	Carer support group: education, problem-solving, in-home respite, self-help support group. Control group: conventional community care.	Carer support group more satisfied with caring role and spent longer caring prior to placement than controls. No change in levels of anxiety or depression in either group and similar placement rate in long-term care for both groups at 6 months.
Marriott et al., 2000	Family intervention group: carer education, stress management and coping skills training. Two control groups: neither received specific intervention although one group received the Camberwell Family Interview allowing an opportunity to talk and express feelings.	Significant reduction in psychological distress and depression in intervention group compared to control groups at 9 and 12 months. Modest positive effect on behavioural disturbance of older person with dementia at 9 months but not at 12 months and improvement in activities of daily living at 12 months in intervention group. Information alone had no effect on carer burden.
Mittelman et al., 2004

Mittelman et al., 2006

Mittelman et al., 2007 | Enhanced group: Carers provided with individual and family counselling and support groups. Control group: Normal service provision; support and counselling only on request. | Significantly fewer depressive symptoms in carers in the enhanced group. Effects were sustained for over 3 years and continued after placement or death of older person. Carer's level of depression was higher when dementia severity of older person was greater. There were significant delays of around 1.5 years in nursing home placement for the older person with dementia whose carer was in the enhanced group. This was achieved by improved carer well-being and tolerance of behaviour problems exhibited by the older person. Self-rated health of carers in the enhanced group significantly better compared to controls 4 months after baseline and maintained for two years. Both groups showed a decline in health but this was less in the enhanced group. |
| Ulstein et al., 2007 | Intervention group: dementia education and structured problem solving programme. Control group: usual treatment from memory clinic. | Over 12 months no effects of intervention were found in relation to carer burden or psychological symptoms. Carer burden increased in both groups. More relatives of carers in the control group were admitted to care homes however the difference was not statistically significant. |
| Moniz-Cook et al., 2008 | Experimental group: systematic psychosocial interventions (PSI) from trained Community Mental Health Nurses (CMHNs). Control group: usual practice from CMHNs. | Problem behaviours in the older people with dementia were reduced in the experimental group families although this was associated with certain individual CMHNs. By 18 months control group families reported reduced coping abilities and higher depression levels. Patient cognition declined in both groups. |

2001). Fourth, intervention programmes carried out with older people with dementia need to set realistic and achievable goals in order to have a positive effect upon carer outcomes (Woods and Clare, 2008).

Support for Carers

In Europe, support for older people with dementia and their carers has been described as patchy and inadequately resourced and cultural differences have been identified in respect of their care (Marks and Sykes, 2000; Manthorpe and Moriarty, 2007). In Sweden, for example, the expectation is that the health and social care system will assume the principal role in care provision. In contrast, other countries such as Italy and Portugal where the role of the family is paramount, the additional absence of resources in some areas means that carers provide the bulk of support (Marks and Sykes, 2000). A European Union-funded study (AdHOC) of community care recipients has found variations across 11 European countries (Carpenter et al., 2004; Carpenter, 2005). In Italy low levels of formal care for older people supported at home contrasted with high dependency levels and significant levels of carer burden. Although Germany had lower dependency levels, carer burden was the highest across the countries. A possible explanation was the inflexible regulations in place for formal care provision. Despite these differences, it has been suggested that across Europe, in respect of case management, delay in diagnosing dementia often results in referrals to services when informal carers are already under stress. This has been argued to need Europe-wide interventions to help support carers (Manthorpe and Moriarty, 2007). Furthermore, the influence of gender may be also apparent in respect of service provision since research in England conducted with the carers of older people appeared to confirm that caring was disproportionately expected of women, with male carers being allocated higher priority for services (Bywaters and Harris, 1998).

With regard to giving support to carers, research has underlined the importance of care programmes or service provision that not only target all carers but also educate them and their relatives about accessing services as early as possible (Zarit and Zarit, 2006). Taking account of the care-giving trajectory, individuals who have provided more years of caring could be exhausted and thus, receipt of services at a late stage may have little impact in reducing carer stress. Conversely, acceptance of services at this stage may in fact speed up the process of placement in a care home for their relative (Lyons and Zarit, 1999). Interestingly, recent research has countered the 'wear and tear' hypothesis (Townsend et al., 1989) which suggested that longer duration of care increases likelihood of psychological and emotional distress in the carer. Gaugler and colleagues (2003b) found that carers of older people with dementia who gradually progressed into their caregiving roles were less likely to place their relatives in long-term care, possibly because their coping and managing styles had been defined long before the most difficult aspects of dementia symptoms in their relatives, had emerged. Nevertheless, carers in the earlier stages of caring may benefit more from formal services and delay institutionalisation of their relative (see Gaugler et al., 2005a). The targeting of specific subgroups of older people and carers has also been advocated (Knight et al., 1993), in order to tailor services to the specific needs and problems faced by the carers of older people with dementia.

Respite services are a type of support aimed directly at the carers of very dependent people allowing them to take a break from caring (Levin and Moriarty, 1996; Moriarty and Levin, 1998); the assumption being that a short-term break will alleviate the associated stress of caring and thus enable carers to continue in their role for longer (Montgomery and Rowe, 2007). The terms 'short stay care' or 'short term break' are used in some literature in preference to respite care. Respite care or short term breaks include a range of services which typically include day care, day or night sitting services in people's own homes, and relief care in a care home, or exceptionally, hospital. In England, residential respite care may be used as a transitional service, acting as a link between community services and residential care (Levin et al., 1994; Moriarty and Levin, 1998). Research has found that respite services can be used in three distinct ways; to provide direct support to carers in their caring role; to help those who use respite services to care for their relative at home for longer; and to prepare carers planning a permanent place in long-stay care for the older person (Levin and Moriarty, 1996).

Studies investigating the use of respite services have reported diverse outcomes. Research with the carers of older people with Alzheimer's disease who used respite services at an earlier stage, found they experienced a reduction in stress and the older person was likely to remain at home for longer (Chu et al., 2000). Similarly, in a review of the effectiveness and cost-effectiveness of services to the carers of older people in England and Wales, both day care and respite care in a care home have been found to be effective in reducing negative psychological symptoms in carers, and in some cases delaying admission to care homes (Pickard, 2004). By comparison, another study found that the use of in-home respite and day care were associated with increased placement although those who had cared for longer were no more likely to place their relative in long-term care. The authors recommended the targeting of services at those at risk of placement, using interventions which reduce carer depression and teach effective management of problem behaviours (Whitlach et al., 1999). It has been acknowledged that respite services are most beneficial when the type of service and amount provided are carefully matched to the perceived needs of the carer and when services are utilised at the appropriate time (Montgomery and Rowe, 2007). An Australian review of the effectiveness of respite care for older people with dementia concluded that carers found it useful, although its effectiveness varied according to how much respite was given, where it took place, and on the individual circumstances of the user (Brodaty and Gresham, 1992). In the USA, research found that respite services can speed up placement in long-term care by helping carers transfer responsibilities to formal services (Zarit et al., 1999; Gaugler et al., 2003c), although subsequent research suggested 'out of home' respite care delayed placement (Gaugler et al., 2005b).

Carer Perception of Client Needs and Assistance with Care

The impact of the LCMS on the carer network should be viewed in the context of the intrinsic difficulties of evaluation of this aspect of service provision. In this study, support provided to carers was examined in a number of ways, and the remainder of this chapter reports the outcomes for carers in terms of their perception of older people's needs and assistance with caring tasks. It also examines the effect of the scheme on carer quality of life and on risk to the older person with dementia by remaining in the community. First, the needs of carers for assistance with the older person's physical health problems and deteriorating mental state, and for help in undertaking the activities of daily living which the older person with dementia could no longer carry out independently are reported. It was these activities, together with the need to supervise a very confused person, which consumed most of the hours of attention required from carers and, as illustrated in Chapter 5 Table 5.6, these were the domains of need which received the greatest resource input. Furthermore, Table 7.9 in Chapter 7 illustrates that the case management scheme was particularly successful in meeting the needs of clients in terms of daytime company, day care, and overnight respite both at home and away from home. The range of respite services available to carers in the LCMS were the same in terms of statutory services, since those in both the experimental and control groups resided in adjacent geographical areas and both groups received care from the same providers of health and social care.

As mentioned in the previous chapter, it was not possible to re-interview all older people and their carers during the two year follow-up period for reasons such as illness, death or placement in long-term care out of the area. Therefore, in order to maintain as large a sample size as possible for statistical analyses, unmatched groups were again used for the comparison of change measures. Similarly to Chapter 7, the tables in this chapter measure change over time from baseline to 6 months and baseline to 12 months using analysis of variance tests. Descriptions of the measures or variables used are referenced in Appendix 1.

The change in the overall needs of clients with carers is shown in Table 8.1. This was calculated using domains identified in Table 7.9 and shown in Box 8.2. There was a statistically significant reduction in the number of overall needs rated for those in the experimental group as compared with those in the control group. This was evident in the first six months of the scheme and was maintained over the first twelve months. Thus the effect of case management input on clients in the experimental group was to reduce the actual physical burden on carers on a daily basis, by relieving them of some aspects of the client's daily care needs.

Changes that occurred in the level of assistance from the main carer and other carers in relation to the contribution of paid carers and professional staff were explored. The burden of caring was assessed by examining the contribution of the main carer, any other carers and paid carers, to activities in each of fourteen domains relating to domestic routine, as detailed in Box 8.3. In each case the main carer was asked whether they provided regular help in relation to these domains,

Box 8.2   Client need domains

Personal care	Maintenance of the home	Additional care
Washing	Housework	Day care
Bathing	Laundry	Daytime company
Dressing	Medication	Respite overnight (home)
Help getting up	Shopping	Respite overnight (away)
Help going to bed	Finances	Escort outside the home
Prepare meals (food and hot drink)	Move around indoors	Night sitting
Help with toilet		
Medical attention		

Table 8.1   Overall need of clients with carers

	Change by 6 months			Change by 12 months		
	E n=23	C n=32	p	E n=22	C n=26	p
Overall need	-4.22	-0.25	<.001	-5.14	-0.62	<.001

Informant rating

whether other carers provided regular help, and whether formal services did so. For those in the control group and receiving the standard service, the majority of formal care services were in the form of paid carers who were part of the local authority home care service. Those in the experimental group were able to access this service in addition to the specialist paid helper service. Table 8.2 shows changes in the number of caring tasks undertaken by the main carer, other carers and paid services for the client. Negative values indicate a decrease in the number of tasks undertaken to help them and positive values indicate an increase. The input of main carers in both the experimental group and the control group decreased over time, and although the difference between the two groups was not statistically significant, the impact appeared greater for those in the experimental group. For carers other than the main carer the impact of the scheme was significantly greater. Both the main and other carers in the experimental group experienced a reduction in their caring input over 12 months. However, for those in the control group it appeared that main carers experienced a slight reduction in caring input but this may have been at the expense of other carers who it seemed, increased their input of care, in addition to increased support from statutory services.

Table 8.2 also demonstrates that over time, more activities were carried out by paid services for clients in both the experimental group and control group. Whilst the difference between the two groups was statistically significant at 6 months, it

Box 8.3   Client domestic routine domains

Personal care	Maintenance of the home
Washing Bathing Dressing Help getting up Help going to bed Prepare meals (food and hot drink) Help with toilet Transfer in and out of chair Eating and drinking	Housework Laundry Shopping Finances Move around indoors

Table 8.2   Support activities by carer and other members of the care network

Contribution to client care	Change by 6 months			Change by 12 months		
	E	C	p	E	C	p
Main carer	-0.85 (n=33)	-0.30 (n=37)	ns	-1.00 (n=27)	-0.07 (n=27)	ns
Other carer	-0.58 (n=33)	0.16 (n=37)	ns	-1.07 (n=27)	0.41 (n=27)	<.01
Paid services	2.59 (n=32)	1.06 (n=36)	<.05	3.96 (n=27)	2.39 (n=28)	ns

Note: Carer rating

was not the case at 12 months. Nevertheless, looking at the 'change by 12 months' figure, on average almost four more activities were being carried out by paid services with those in the experimental group, compared to the baseline input. For the control group, on average, two more activities were being carried out by paid services. However, overall, there was a shift in balance from carer to community services whether the client was receiving the standard service in the control group, or the case management scheme in the experimental group.

The number of hours per week main carers spent in contact with, or doing things on behalf of clients was calculated, and is shown in Table 8.3. Their input at 12 months and the change in their contribution over a 12 month period can be seen as a proxy indicator for the physical burden experienced by carers. The calculation included the time spent on such tasks as travelling, laundry and telephoning as well as personal care, indeed all activities additional to spending time with the older person. The table shows that over 12 months, there was a reduction in the number of hours spent caring by carers in the experimental group. By comparison, carers in the control group experienced a lower reduction in the number of hours spent caring. Indeed, by 12 months, carers in the control group were providing nearly eight hours per week care more than those in the experimental group.

It is also of interest to note that, within the main carer group, there was an average reduction of six care hours (20 per cent) of input by co-resident carers in the experimental group, compared to an average increase of almost five hours (11 per cent) per week from co-resident carers in the control group. There was also an average reduction of three hours a week spent by carers in the experimental group supporting those living alone. Conversely, carers in the control group living apart from the client increased their input by just over three-quarters of an hour a week on average over the year, a difference which was statistically significant ($p<0.05$). Thus overall, the support provided by the case management scheme in the form of regular visits by paid helpers markedly reduced the hours of input provided by carers in the experimental group.

The nature of dementia can create tensions not only between those most directly involved in the care of an older person with dementia, but also among family and neighbours. This can be an important additional factor in the burden of carers. A rating of the tension in the relationship between the client and carer derived from Brown and Rutter (1966) was made by the researcher. At referral, 31 per cent of carers in the control group (n=42 overall) and 22 per cent of carers in the experimental group (n=37 overall) reported regular episodes of relationship difficulties with the older person. A smaller cohort was re-interviewed and at one year, the proportion of those experiencing relationship difficulties had increased by one quarter in the control group (n=29) but decreased by half in the experimental group (n=24), although the difference was not statistically significant.

Table 8.3   Number of hours contact per week by carers

	Change in carer hours over 6 months			Change in carer hours over 12 months		
	E **n=36**	**C** **n=38**	**p**	**E** **n=36**	**C** **n=38**	**p**
Main carer input	-5.92	-1.34	ns	-9.60	-1.65	<.05
Total carer input	-6.55	-1.84	ns	-11.19	-3.15	<.05

Note: n values = cases with carers

Quality of Life Measures

This section evaluates the effect of the LCMS in terms of its impact on the quality of life of carers. Carers completed a scale which measured levels of malaise, or lack of well-being, as part of the research study. Their quality of life was also measured subjectively in terms of their own description of the level of strain experienced, and by looking at how carer burden, that is the demands of caring, affected their lives. Changes over time were measured and comparisons were made between those in the experimental group receiving the case management service and those in the control group receiving the standard service from the community mental health team for older people. Carers were asked to complete the Malaise Inventory (Rutter et al., 1970), which is a 24-item questionnaire covering areas of psychological and somatic health. The physical and psychological symptoms subscales of the Malaise Inventory were also examined. The former relates to the stress experienced by carers caused by the physical demands of caring whereas the latter relates to the nature of the carers' responses to their role, for example feeling out of control or unable to relax (Nolan et al., 1990).

In Table 8.4a, data are presented for all carers; Table 8.4b shows the data for the group of carers who lived apart from the client, and Table 8.4c presents data for the group of co-resident carers. In each case, the tables show the outcomes for the carers of those who were still living at home at 12 months, that is, excluding carers of those who had died or been placed in nursing or residential homes by 12 months. From Table 8.4a, it would appear that after 6 months, there were no statistically significant differences in change scores between carers in the experimental group and carers in the control group with regard to their level of distress experienced, as expressed in their Malaise Inventory scores and sub-scores. However, there were statistically significant differences found between Malaise Inventory total scores of all carers in the experimental and the control group, for changes measured over 12 months with the carers of those in the experimental group having lower scores. However, there were no statistically significant differences between the groups in respect of subscale scores at either six or 12 months.

For the group of carers who lived apart from the clients, there were no statistically significant differences in change scores between carers in the experimental group and carers in the control group as expressed in their Malaise Inventory total scores or sub-scores at either six months or 12 months. These are illustrated in Table 8.4b. Clearly, small numbers influence these observations.

Table 8.4c shows that for the group of co-resident carers who lived with clients, there were no apparent differences between the experimental and control group in their change scores at 6 months. However, there were statistically significant differences in change scores by 12 months, for the Malaise Inventory and also for the physical and psychological sub-scores. Again, carers in the experimental group had a significantly greater reduction in their Malaise scores, an effect which was gradual, only appearing after 12 months. Again, these data are influenced by small numbers.

Table 8.4a   Carer malaise: all carers (client still at home at 12 months)

All carers	Change by 6 months			Change by 12 months		
	E n=27	C n=36	p	E n=22	C n=29	p
Malaise Inventory score	-0.48	-0.36	ns	-1.77	-0.10	<.05
Malaise physical sub-score	0.03	0.26	ns	-0.38	0.03	ns
Malaise psychological sub-score	-0.45	-0.58	ns	-1.24	-0.26	ns

Note: Carer rating

Table 8.4b   Carer malaise: carer lives apart (client still at home at 12 months)

Carer lives apart	Change by 6 months			Change by 12 months		
	E n=17	C n=19	p	E n=14	C n=16	p
Malaise Inventory score	-0.88	-0.47	ns	-1.29	-0.12	ns
Malaise physical sub-score	-0.13	-0.22	ns	0.15	-0.07	ns
Malaise psychological sub-score	-0.71	-0.16	ns	-1.00	0.00	ns

Table 8.4c   Carer malaise: carer living with the client (client still at home at 12 months)

Carer lives with client	Change by 6 months			Change by 12 months		
	E n=10	C n=17	p	E n=8	C n=13	p
Malaise Inventory score	0.20	-0.24	ns	-2.63	-0.08	<.05
Malaise physical sub-scale	0.40	0.65	ns	-1.25	0.23	<.05
Malaise psychological sub-scale	0.00	-0.76	ns	-1.75	-0.23	<.05

More generally, carers were asked to rate their level of overall strain on a seven point scale (Morris et al., 1988) ranging from 'no strain' to 'severe strain' in answer to the question 'How much strain do you feel because of the way (the client) is nowadays?' They were asked to rate presence of life burden in five domains. These were: sleep; finances; work; relationship with the client; and social life/leisure. Carers were also asked a single question regarding any improvement to their feeling of burden over time. The findings are reported in Table 8.5. In this, negative values indicate a decrease in the carer's perception of strain and in their life burden, and positive values in carer felt burden indicate their view of improvement. There were few apparent differences between carers in the experimental group and in the control group with respect to their levels of overall strain, both groups showing a reduction in their perceived level of strain. There was a reduction in carer life burden for those in the experimental group which was roughly twice that of those in the control group at both six and 12 months, although these effects did not reach statistical significance. In terms of felt burden, there was no difference observed at six months between the two groups. However, between six and 12 months there was less felt burden for carers in the experimental group compared to slightly more felt burden for those in the control group, a difference which reached significance ($p<0.05$). Overall, therefore, changes to carers' strain and life burden over time were slight with only felt burden showing a significant difference between the two groups at the end of the year. This lack of change may reflect the carer's emotional reaction to the unalterable fact of their relative's decline. This finding is similar to that of an American study in which carers of older people with dementia eligible for case management showed a statistically significant but very small reduction in burden compared to the control group (Newcomer et al., 1999).

Table 8.5   Carer overall strain and life burden

	Change by 6 months			Change by 12 months			Sample size	
	E	C	p	E	C	p	E	C
Carer overall strain (7 point scale)	-0.68	-1.05	ns	-1.00	-1.19	ns	26	32
Carer life burden (objective) (5 domains)	-0.77	-0.38	ns	-1.08	-0.64	ns	24	32
				6–12 months[1]				
Carer felt burden (improved)	0.35	0.58	ns	1.46	-0.39	<.05	25	32

Note: Carer rating

[1] First and second 6 months treated separately

The greatest reduction in carers' burden and psychological stress as shown by other studies (Levin et al., 1989, 1994; Levin and Moriarty, 1996) occurs when the older person is placed in long-term care. However, this study provides little evidence to support this since, as demonstrated in Chapter 7, comparatively few clients moved into long-term care during the course of the study. Moreover, the researchers were limited in their capacity to follow up these older people. Therefore, comparisons between the outcomes for these older people, and in particular their carers, and those remaining in the community can only be indicative since there are insufficient data to support these observations. Nevertheless, it appeared that admission to long-term care reduced the burden and strain of carers who were relieved of the responsibility and concern about the meeting of basic care needs of clients. Carers receiving assistance from a case manager appeared less dissatisfied with the process of placement and case managers were seen as offering useful support to carers, as the person they cared for made the transition to long-term care. The evidence also suggested that carers of clients in the experimental group were better able to resume a more 'normal' social life when the latter were admitted to long-term care. Nevertheless, carer distress as measured by the Malaise Inventory, showed no significant difference between the carers of those in the experimental group admitted to residential or nursing home or remaining at home, each improving somewhat compared to carers in the control group.

Summary

This chapter began by examining the vital role played by carers of older people with dementia and has reviewed the efficacy of some of the wide-ranging interventions undertaken to support carers, and in some cases the older people with dementia, and has discussed the outcomes of respite services for carers. In this study, the LCMS achieved a reduction in the physical burden of care experienced and an improvement in quality of life by reducing levels of distress. The scheme both supported older people with dementia in their own homes, and lessened the physical burden of care experienced by carers and relieved them of some of the tasks of caring. More specifically, there was a significant reduction in the rating of older people's unmet needs as perceived by the carers, for those supported by the case management scheme. In terms of the support offered by carers and other members of the care network, one positive effect of the scheme was that after 12 months main carers and other carers in the experimental group were able to reduce their care contribution. These findings complement those of the previous chapter which demonstrated that the LCMS was able to support older people with dementia who had correspondingly high levels of need with some degree of success.

The difficulties inherent in using quality of life measures with carers have been widely reported. The importance of using reliable measures which have been standardised with non-carers has been described (George and Gwyther, 1986) and it has been recognised that improving carer well-being or reducing levels of carer stress may not always be a realistic outcome of intervention (Zarit et al., 1998; Zarit and Leitsch, 2001). It has also been acknowledged that the concepts of carer 'stress' or 'strain' are sometimes interchangeable or confusing (Gilleard, 1984). Indeed, in this study, carers often did not perceive any significant change in their levels of strain or burden over time. The reduction in carer stress is a relative rather than an absolute gain. The aim was to make a larger impact than did existing services. Nevertheless, the impact of case management on carers' well-being was apparent, since it appeared that over 12 months, the case management scheme had most impact on co-resident carers. This can be seen both in benefiting carers in their difficult task and in reducing carers' potential negative reactions when inappropriate responses to behaviour can contribute to further deterioration in the person with dementia (Kitwood, 1997).

Chapter 9
The Cost of Care – Multiple Perspectives

Introduction

It has become widely acknowledged in government policy and other literature that the long-term care of older people with dementia has attained a higher priority as it represents a major challenge to health and social care with an ageing population and rising costs (National Audit Office, 2007; Knapp et al., 2007; Committee of Public Accounts, 2008; Department of Health, 2008b). An expected increase in the numbers of older people with dementia, and in particular those aged 75 and over, means that service costs associated with dementia are far higher than those associated with other mental health problems in England, currently accounting for 66 per cent of all mental health service costs (McCrone et al., 2008). With regard to the cost of dementia care the biggest component of cost relates to care home accommodation (Knapp et al., 2007; Committee of Public Accounts, 2008).

In this and the following chapter, the costs associated with the implementation of the Lewisham Case Management Scheme are explored. This chapter analyses the costs of care of older people with dementia receiving an intensive care management service compared to those incurred by a similar group receiving the usual modes of care. The next chapter examines the personal and care characteristics of individuals receiving the case management scheme and those receiving the standard services in order to identify which ones were most associated with variations in costs. Despite the obvious importance of costing any new programme of care, there are a number of difficulties associated with such an analysis. Calculating the actual costs of services can be problematic and thus deriving the full costs of care can be complex (Comas-Herrera et al., 2006; Bowes, 2007) and the costing of services may be inexact and such data should be used with caution (Curtis, 2007). In addition, calculating the costs incurred by informal carers can be difficult (Lowin et al., 2001) and these are not always fully accounted for in cost analyses, apart from estimates of loss of wages which are not appropriate for retired carers (Zarit and Leitsch, 2001). However, the importance of studying the various components of cost separately has also been noted, for example, in an innovative service, both professional time use and relevant service costs should be determined in order that different flows of resources can be identified and effectiveness broadly judged (Challis et al., 2008).

Notwithstanding these difficulties, it was, nevertheless, possible in this study to carry out a comprehensive costing of all service inputs received by those in the experimental group and receiving case management input and by those in the control group receiving the standard service, during the first year of contact with services. Similarly, a full costing of the contribution of carers was also undertaken taking information from a range of sources. The comparison in this research study is between the relative costs of the experimental and control groups (Challis et al., 2002a) and hence the price base itself is less important. This chapter describes the derivation of these costs, in terms of costs to agencies, costs to carers and aggregated costs to society. It then presents the different types of care provided in terms of the proportion of people in each of the two groups who received them and the costs per year of these services. A breakdown of costs to each of the agencies, to family carers and to society is illustrated.

Derivation of Costs

Agencies

This material was derived from two components: services received, and the unit cost of services. Both types of data were usually obtained from two sources, allowing cross-validation, with greatest validation effort being given to the highest cost services such as residential and nursing home care, so as to minimise the effect of any error. Full details of the services and their source of record of receipt and derivation of price are shown in Appendix 2. Most service receipt data were collected in 'package' form from interviews with either or both carers and paid carers supplemented by special collection from service settings. Costs were allocated to all items of service. In respect of both residential and day care provision, estimates included revenue costs (salary, supplies, and central overheads) and capital costs (building, land, equipment and durables). Additionally, costings for day care included a travel component and those for residential care, a component for personal expenditure. For unit costing, local figures were used wherever possible, supplemented by data from other sources and for all items, London regional multipliers were used if local costs were not used directly.

Figures in relation to both day care and residential care encompassed the concept of opportunity cost, which is based on the judgement that this is the cost forgone by using a resource in one way rather than in an alternative way. Not surprisingly, in practice such an approach may have to build upon available cost information, but in making judgements about which capital elements to include, consideration of opportunity costs can be helpful to ensure that different accounts are treated similarly (Knapp, 1984; 1993). For example, in respect of local authority residential care, estimates of capital expenditure incorporated projected rebuilding costs. In line with the principle of opportunity costs, assumptions were made that the building had a life span of sixty years and replacement costs would increase at a rate of six per cent per annum. This formed the basis for the notional building costs included in the calculation of capital expenditure in the estimation of the cost of residential care. The local service context was also incorporated into the calculation of the cost of residential and nursing care by the inclusion of the occupancy levels of homes during the course of the study. Furthermore, it should be noted that in respect of care homes, costings were developed for specialist provision for older people with dementia in recognition of their special needs which are additional to those who were predominantly physically frail.

For professionals undertaking home visits, costings were based on a unit cost per visit using relevant team activity records generated within the project (von Abendorff et al., 1994), and including salaries, overheads (managerial and clerical), capital costs where appropriate, and travel costs. It was assumed that case managers' time was exclusively dedicated to their caseload whether related to direct contact or indirect activities. In contrast, it was recognised that a small proportion of the work of other members of the community mental health team for older people was attributed to work outside of the team's remit. As a consequence, for the purpose of this costing exercise, a nominal figure of eight per cent of team members' time was attributed to outside work and the appropriate adjustment was made in the calculation of costs. Costs for residential and nursing home care included central overheads which incorporated an appropriate element for social work provision. Finally, it is relevant to note that paid helpers' costs included central overheads and administration on top of their basic pay, to which was added their travel costs.

Carers

Two separate dimensions of costs to carers were calculated. First, the direct financial burden borne and reported by carers, and second, the hours they spent caring and the associated opportunity cost of this were assessed. These were aggregated to draw out the total cost. Direct financial burden was based on the accounts given by the main carer. The main component to this was lost earnings, and opportunity costing of this took no account of what would have been paid in tax. It did, however, include a number of other components, for example, laundry, transport, telephone use and purchase of services where they related specifically to the needs of the older person. Where carers could not estimate costs, standard rates were derived, where appropriate, from state benefit rates.

In addition, the costs to all carers in the care network were examined, including costs to the main carers, and where appropriate, other carers including partners of the carer, relatives and neighbours. Since the study was looking at opportunity costing rather than gross costing, an attempt was made to evaluate how time could alternatively have been used, instead of simply focusing on time spent caring. Therefore the costing of the contribution of carers excluded the 'normal' time together that for example partners would have spent together as part of a relationship. In this context notional costings were developed on the basis of estimates of the care given to a person with dementia by their partner as a consequence of the former's illness. Three levels were categorised – 'low' up to 28 hours per week, 'medium' between 29 and 56 hours, and 'high' between 57 and 84 hours – for the purpose of this costing exercise. To define financial cost to carers an average figure was used, based on the local market rate for basic care or help with practical tasks bought privately at that time. Time components included for example, face to face contact, night-time disturbance, time spent on laundry and travel specifically associated with the caring role. This contact time was estimated by the researcher and placed into one of the three levels. It was based on the level of disturbing behaviour of the client, their caring needs and tasks specific to them, and any respite provided. Therefore, at one extreme if a person's behaviour was disturbed, for example preventing the carer from even watching television, with little respite afforded, this was rated at the high level of contact time. At the other extreme, where the person was less impaired, capable of doing things together with their carer, with a good quality of life and relationships, the time spent caring would be rated at four hours a day (28 hours per week). Likewise night-time contact between the carer and the client was quantified and apportioned to one of two categories; either under 10 hours a week, or more.

Society

In essence, costs to society were an aggregation of four components: costs to agencies; costs to carers; personal expenditure of the older person; and housing costs. However, three small but significant amendments were made. First, to avoid double-counting the costs of older people's and carers' contributions towards services, both were combined and attributed to the former since they were calculated as part of the service costs. This may slightly underestimate carer costs as it excludes costs to carers of services being used specifically for their benefit. Second, personal expenditure generated from the Family Expenditure Survey (Central Statistical Office, 1994) was included for older people living at home and during the first six weeks after placement in long-term care. Thereafter, personal expenditure cost was estimated for those placed permanently in care homes, as the personal allowance from the appropriate schedule of benefits. Third, housing costs were taken into account for the first six weeks of a placement in long-term care. Again, applying the concept of opportunity cost, if the older person lived alone all the costs were taken into account or alternatively if they lived with a carer, only 50 per cent of costs were taken into account. If the older person was placed permanently in long-term care, after six weeks they were adjudged to have no housing costs since it was assumed that either their home and assets were sold or disposed of or all housing costs were attributed to the carer who remained in the house.

Service Receipt and Associated Costs

Tables 9.1a and 9.1b summarise the receipt and costs of a range of care services received by the experimental and control groups. The proportion of older people who received a particular service, the amount received and the cost of that service are shown, the latter two being the mean units of service received by matched groups, as appropriate to the nature of the service. Presenting costs as a proportion of the period of time alive standardises the effect of any variance in survival rates between the experimental and control groups, so as to allow for direct comparison between the groups with regard to expenditure.

Less than a quarter in either group used long-term care facilities over the year, predominantly from the independent sector. Differences between the groups in terms of destinational outcome were explored previously in Chapter 7 and the figures demonstrate there were no significant differences between the groups in the first year. For those who did receive a long-term care service, Table 9.1a illustrates this in terms of days per year alive. Those in the control group received on average 25 days of long-term care compared to 31½ days in the experimental group. This finding may be accounted for by factors relating to the selection of cases, described in Chapter 4, and which suggests that those who were more difficult to support were specially referred to the case management study (Challis and Darton, 1990).

There were no significant overall differences between the groups in the use of acute hospital care, covering acute psychiatric and medical care. However, there was greater use of in-patient medical care by the experimental group (49 per cent compared with 37 per cent). It is possible that older people in the experimental group were more likely to be discharged home following an in-patient psychiatric stay and subsequently readmitted to an acute medical bed with cost implications for the NHS, whereas those in the control group admitted to the same type of facility were more likely to be discharged to a care home. The latter effect may be conceived of as part of the historic shift in the burden of costs of long-term care from health services to social services (Wistow, 1995) and was identified in a study of dementia care costs as older people with dementia move from home into long-term care (Schneider et al., 2003).

One third in each group used overnight respite care, mainly in local authority homes, in the year. There was no statistically significant difference between the two groups in the proportion of time spent in respite care away from home, although this was higher in the control group than in the experimental group, 10 days compared to six days per year. As noted in the previous chapter, research has reported that respite services predominantly away from home, are used just prior to placement (Levin et al., 1989; 1994; Moriarty and Levin, 1998). This suggests that the service offered by case managers to those in the experimental group may have prevented this process happening to an extent, particularly since they were able to offer respite relief overnight for carers in their own homes, an option that was unavailable to the control group. There were no differences in the receipt of day care, with around two fifths in each group receiving this service.

As shown in Table 9.1b, all older people received at least one visit from a professional worker. However, the overall number of visits received per year showed a statistically significant difference between the groups. Those in the experimental group received on average 63 visits compared to just under 34 visits on average for the control group. This is accounted for by the visits of case managers and a

Table 9.1a   Mean service receipt and costs: long-term care, acute hospital care, respite care and day care

Type of care provided	% who receive service		Days per year alive		Cost per year alive	
	E	C	E	C	E (£)	C (£)
Long-term care						
NHS psychiatry	4.7	2.3	0.9	0.6	107.09	73.27
NHS medical	0	2.3	0.0	5.5	0	572.93
Local authority specialist[1]	2.3	7.0	0.8	7.1	49.47	445.08
Local authority generic	0	2.3	0	0.5	0	26.47
Independent sector residential	4.7	2.3	4.4	0.3	163.34	12.03
Independent sector nursing	14.0	11.6	25.4	10.8	1279.30	544.20
Total	20.9	23.3	31.4	24.9	1599.20	1674.98
Acute hospital care						
Psychiatric	14.0	14.0	12.4	7.0	1655.63	947.68
Medical	48.8	37.2	18.3	13.7	2917.56	2108.03
Total	58.1	41.9	30.7	20.7	4573.19	3055.71
Respite overnight away from home						
Hospital	2.3	0	1.0	0	119.17	0
Local authority specialist[1]	7.0	11.6	1.1	2.7	71.30	170.25
Local authority generic	11.6	25.6	2.7	5.8	147.47	313.41
Independent sector	4.7	4.7	0.7	1.4	25.38	65.07
Adult family placement	7.0	2.3	0.5	0.2	28.26	12.11
Total	32.6	34.9	6.0	10.1	391.58	560.84
Respite overnight in own home	7.0	0	1.4	0	57.03	0

	% who receive service		Days per week alive		Cost per year alive	
	E	C	E	C	E (£)	C (£)
Day care						
Local authority specialist[1]	32.6	35.6	0.69	0.23	1433.79	496.01
Other local authority	9.3	23.3	0.09	0.38	139.84	616.27
Other[2]	11.6	11.7	0.07	0.02	163.40	45.72
Total	41.9	42.2	0.84	0.63	1737.03	1158.00

Adapted from Challis et al. (2002c)

Note: all matched cases n=43

[1] An institution catering specifically for older people with mental health problems particularly dementia

[2] Includes day hospital care

Costs based on 1993/94 prices

Table 9.1b   Mean service receipt and costs: professional visits, domiciliary care and other services

Type of care provided	% who receive service		Visits per year alive		Cost per year alive	
	E	C	E	C	E (£)	C (£)
Professional visits						
GP	79.1	69.8	3.3	2.9	95.44	85.53
Other health professional	81.4	72.1	3.7	2.4	56.43	38.77
Auxiliary nurse[1]	27.9	18.6	16.0	4.6	445.01 *	265.85
District nurse[1]	55.8	58.1	15.3	10.9		0
CMHT[2] for older people	65.1	81.4	2.7 **	6.9	212.13 **	548.42
Case manager[3]	95.35	0	16.7	0	1558.86	0
SW assessor	34.9	44.2	1.1	1.5	45.21	61.33
Home care officer	37.2	30.2	3.7	2.1	0	0
Other	16.3	30.2	0.3	0.6	9.74	18.89
Outpatients	27.9	30.2	0.6	1.6	32.25	92.31
Total	100	100	63.3 **	33.5	2455.07 **	1111.10
	% cases who receive service		Hours per week alive		Cost per year alive	
Domiciliary care						
LCMS: paid helper[3]	90.7	0	7.4	0	2069.92	0
: purchased private sector[3]	16.3	0	0.4	0	157.29	0
Local authority home care	81.4	72.1	4.0	3.6	2139.67	1925.81
Private sector home care purchase by family	8.6	9.3	1.3	1.0	331.14	275.61
Crossroads	11.6	7.0	0.2	0.1	81.78	49.39
Volunteer	2.3	4.7	<0.1	<0.1	0.99	8.61
Total	97.7	81.4	13.3 ***	4.7	4780.79 ***	2259.42
Other						
Support groups (client and carer)	7.0	9.3	N/A	N/A	32.68	6.05
Meals on wheels	62.8	44.2	N/A	N/A	467.31	361.35

Adapted from Challis et al. (2002c)   Costs based on 1993/94 prices

Note: all matched cases n=43

[1] Combined and including travel costs

[2] CMHT: Community Mental Health Team

[3] Experimental group only

*One-way analysis of variance significance level $p < 0.05$

** One-way analysis of variance significance level $p < 0.01$

*** One-way analysis of variance significance level $p < 0.001$

greater input from the community nursing service to the experimental group. The control group received significantly more visits from the community mental health team for older people, suggesting that case managers' contributions reduced some of that required from NHS personnel within the multidisciplinary team.

Another statistically significant finding was the greater number of hours of care at home overall supplied to the experimental group, reflected in the high use of paid helpers. In both the experimental and control group there was evidence of families purchasing additional private help from the independent sector, around 9 per cent in each group. A significantly greater number of home care hours per week were supplied to the experimental group, just over 13 hours on average, compared to those in the control group, with just under five hours. Unsurprisingly, the costs of care at home were significantly higher for the experimental compared to the control group, both for professional visits and domiciliary care with both achieving statistical significance. There was no difference noted in the use of support group activities between the two groups. However, whereas over 60 per cent in the experimental group made use of meals on wheels throughout the year period, only 44 per cent of those in the control group did so, although this difference was not statistically significant.

Table 9.2 details the costs apportioned to the various service providers contributing to the care of people with dementia at home. It is a subset of that included in Tables 9.1a and 9.1b with additional information relating to the location of the older person at 12 months. In this way, the impact of the case management scheme is clearly discernible. As would be expected from the services received, the two service sectors which accounted for statistically significant differences between the experimental and control groups were professional visits and domiciliary care.

Table 9.2   Mean costs of services

Services provided	All		Placed at 12 months		At home at 12 months	
	E (£) n=43	C (£) n=43	E (£) n=9	C (£) n=10	E (£) n=34	C (£) n=33
Long-term care	1599	1674	7640	7202	0	0
Acute hospital care	4573	3056	7232	8796	3869	1316
Respite care (overnight)	449	561	488	767	438	498
Day care	1737	1158	1461	1271	1810	1124
Professional visits	2455 **	1111	1542	1211	2690 ***	1040
Domiciliary care	4781 ***	2259	2245	1265	5452 ***	2561
Goods (inc. meals-on-wheels)	561	424	221	252	651	476
Other services[1]	189	241	114	190	208	257
Total	16344 ***	10484	20943	20954	15118 ***	7272

Costs based on 1993/94 prices

Note: [1] Includes additional items not costed in Tables 9.1a/b.
** One way analysis of variance significance level p <0.01
***One way analysis of variance significance level p<0.001

In both cases the experimental group received significantly more, both in respect of all older people and those at home at 12 months. When examining only those still at home after one year, the increased use of acute hospital care in the experimental group, accounted for almost one-third of the cost differential between the groups, contributing to the statistically significant increased level of service use overall.

Costs

Agencies

The costs to different agencies are shown in Table 9.3 which reveals the costs incurred by providers of health and social care, clients and the voluntary sector. For all, the cost to health and social services was greater for the experimental group although the only statistically significant difference between the groups was the cost to social services. When costs to the NHS and the social services authority are aggregated for the experimental and control groups (derived from the first two rows of columns 1 and 2), the higher level of expenditure in the former is apparent. From the differential of £5670 between the two groups, the respective cost excess to each agency can be calculated. For social care this proportion is 73 per cent compared with 27 per cent for health care. The cost excess to the NHS is accounted for by the higher acute medical inpatient cost of those in the experimental group compared to the control group, as demonstrated in Table 9.1a. The cost excess to social services in the experimental group may be accounted for by case manager visits and by domiciliary care in the form of the paid helper service. Neither of these services was available to the control group. In respect of those still at home at 12 months, differences in costs were statistically significant

Table 9.3   Mean annual costs by agency

Agency	All		Placed by 12 months		At home at 12 months	
	E (£) n=43	C (£) n=43	E (£) n=9	C (£) n=10	E (£) n=34	C (£) n=33
NHS	6038	4507	8395	11436	5414 *	2407
Social services authority	8815 ***	4676	8997	7151	8767 ***	3926
Other local authority services	6	8	0	0	7	11
Department of Social Security	318	225	1522	969	0	0
Other statutory services	15	11	35	31	9	5
Voluntary sector services	90	80	15	70	109	83
Client	1060	947	1980	1296	817	841
Total	16342 ***	10454	20944	20953	15123 ***	7273

Costs based on 1993/94 prices

Note: * One way analysis of variance significance level p<0.05.
         *** One way analysis of variance significance level p<0.001

for both the NHS and the social services authority. Overall, for those remaining at home over the year the costs to health and social care in the experimental group was twice that of the control group.

Carers

There has been an increasing recognition of the implications of the policy of community care for carers (Cm 4169, 1998; Department of Health, 2001b; HM Government, 2008). In this study, a broad definition of carers was adopted. As described in Chapter 4, it encompassed all those actively involved in the care of the older person with dementia and receiving no payment, even if this involved visiting only on a once a month basis. Carer input has been costed and described in the same way as other inputs using opportunity cost principles in order to provide a description of the relative magnitude of the support provided.

As an important component of the costs to society, the contribution of carers is identified in Table 9.4, which shows mean weekly cost to carers per client for both the experimental and control group. This composite figure has two elements: direct financial costs borne by carers and indirect costs primarily due to the time involved in caring tasks. However, it is likely that figures for both the experimental and control group may be underestimates since evidence was based on retrospective analysis of questionnaires and global views expressed by carers rather than, for example, a prospective diary-based study, as recognized in other cost data (McCrone et al., 2008). Although the difference between the two groups in respect of costs to carers was not statistically significant, it is apparent that carers in the control group incurred higher costs per week. This finding supports an observation noted in the previous chapter relating to outcomes for carers. In this, it was noted that there was a reduction over twelve months in the number of hours spent caring, for carers supported by the LCMS, suggesting that there were cost savings for these carers compared with the control group.

Further analysis revealed that the main component for financial cost borne by carers was the time involved in caring. The main carer usually provided this and most of this was in a face to face role. The majority of older people with carers had another carer providing some input. One sixth of the financial costs borne by carers in both the experimental and control group was due to direct financial costs. Although a small percentage of total costs, it was significant since this measured real costs borne by carers. There were a number of components of this: earnings loss; services purchased; transport; food; laundry; clothing; fuel; and telephone calls. However, by far the highest gross component of cost was earnings loss, recorded by nearly a quarter of carers. This outcome concurs with that of a subsequent study which showed that the biggest component of the cost of caring for an older person with dementia was care-giving time and carers' earnings (Moore et al., 2001). Other research has found that informal care accounts for one-third of the annual cost of dementia care (McCrone et al., 2008), suggesting, as hypothesised above, that the estimates of the costs incurred by carers within the LCMS are conservative.

Society

Table 9.4 illustrates the component parts of costs to society: the costs to agencies in terms of services provided; costs to carers; personal expenditure of the older person; and the costs of housing. The difference in mean total costs per week per client between the two groups was £73, a figure which almost reached statistical significance (p=0.059), with the weekly cost for those in the experimental group being higher. The cost of providing services to the older people with dementia was higher in the experimental group compared to the control group, a difference which reached statistical significance. This was to some extent offset by the lower costs incurred by carers in the experimental group. The balance of costs between carers and services is important as an indicator of the extent to which the scheme appeared to offer some redress in terms of provision, cost reduction and outcome to carers, since one of the aims of the community care reforms was to provide sufficient care to carers (Cm 849, 1989) and has been emphasised in subsequent guidance (Cm 4169, 1998; Department of Health, 2003a; HM Government, 2008).

Table 9.4   Mean costs to society

Component	Cost per week		Cost per year alive	
	E (£)	C (£)	E (£)	C (£)
NHS & Social Services	311**	201	14853**	9183
Carers	82	111	3916	5072
Personal expenditure	65	68	3104	3107
Housing	32	37	1528	1691
Total	490	417		
Society as a whole			23401	19053

Matched pairs n=43   Cost based on 1993/94 prices
** One way analysis of variance significance level $p < 0.01$

Summary

Overall, the LCMS provided care that was more expensive than standard services. Nevertheless, some components of costs were higher for those in the control group receiving standard services, as shown in Box 9.1. There were higher costs to the NHS in respect of acute hospital care for those in the experimental group, possibly attributable to the needs of older people who may otherwise have been admitted to a long-term care setting where their acute medical needs may have been met without recourse to hospital admission had they not received intensive case management. Overall, costs to the control group were higher in respect of long-term care admissions, primarily to residential and nursing home care, reflecting the paucity of domiciliary care compared to that available in the experimental group primarily in the form of the paid helper service. Since professional visits and domiciliary care were costs accrued by social services, this explains why costs to this agency were significantly higher for those in the experimental group. Greater use of respite care and higher associated costs in the control group may reflect a lack of available care to people in their own homes, whereas day care which accrued higher costs in the experimental group perhaps indicates a focus on support to carers. There were more home visits in the control group by members of the community mental health team thereby accounting for higher costs, whereas case managers visited older people in the experimental group undertaking their monitoring role either directly, or through close contact with paid helpers. With national policy focusing upon the early identification of, and intervention with older people with dementia there is a recognition that in order to successfully provide support at home, there needs to be not only an increase in the number and extent of home care packages including traditional 'home help' services, but also opportunities for older people and their carers to access personal budgets and direct payments (Knapp et al., 2007; Department of Health, 2008a,b; 2009a).

Box 9.1   Service costs per year alive

Higher in experimental group	Higher in control group
• Acute hospital care • Day care • Professional visits • Domiciliary care	• Long-term care • Respite away from home • Visits by community mental health team for older people

It could be argued that the scheme has demonstrated its cost-effectiveness since, when all costs to society are accounted for including informal care, the weekly cost of supporting older people with dementia and their carers is not significantly higher for those receiving intensive case management, although the main component for services is much greater, reflecting findings illustrated previously. It must be noted that the cost data were collected only over a one-year period. In Chapter 7 it was clear that the reduction in admissions to care homes were only evident in the second year, and some cost estimates for that period suggest that differences between the groups diminish as a consequence (Challis et al., 2002c). With regard to family carers, it would seem that the documented weekly costs incurred by carers in the experimental group were lower than for the carers in the control group, although this difference also did not reach a significant level. In the next chapter factors which are associated with variations in costs such as client and carer characteristics and the care process itself, are examined in more detail.

Chapter 10
Predictors of Costs – Individual Characteristics

Introduction

One of the key purposes of analysis of costs data is to determine for whom, in terms of individual characteristics, and in which circumstances is one type of intervention more cost effective than another (Challis et al., 1988). It has the potential to be of use in a number of ways as the development of the concept of personal budgets evolves (Department of Health, 2008a; 2009a). First, such an evaluation is relevant in the context of an increased emphasis within policy guidance of the value of local data to inform service commissioning across the public, private and voluntary sectors. Indeed, recent guidance suggests local information can be used to establish population needs and develop the social care market (Cm 6737, 2006). In conjunction with demographic details for a defined population, the data can be used to identify and estimate the costs of the components of care and support in respect of particular characteristics of older people and their carers. Agency costs provide information relating to factors which influence the cost of care, and allow comparisons to be made between the two types of service. Costs to society, including accommodation, personal and specific carer costs, would fulfil a similar purpose. In addition, the inclusion within costs to society of data relating to carers, provide evidence of help offered to this group of people and permit their incorporation into the evaluative and strategic planning process. Second, cost data is pertinent to the development of an infrastructure to support personal budgets, an approach which seeks to combine individual characteristics and costed services, to inform the associated resource allocation process and thereby promote the equitable and transparent use of resources (Cm 6499, 2005; Cm 6737, 2006). Third, the data described in this chapter could, for example, be of use in financial planning, particularly if used in conjunction with the concept of indicative care packages (Challis et al., 1997b), providing a benchmark for monitoring expenditure on care management. Finally, the data might be used to expand the development of local performance measures (Challis et al., 2006b) by, for example, identifying indicators specifically for carers in addition to those already routinely required (HM Government, 2008).

To examine the factors associated with variations in costs, this chapter again distinguishes between those individuals receiving the case management scheme and those receiving standard services. Information is presented relating to costs in two different ways. First, estimates are derived from regression equations predicting variations in cost. In these tables, the material is organised into four broad domains of factors influencing costs: outcomes or change indicators; client characteristics; carer characteristics, and the care process. Second, using the equations, illustrative examples of care package costs are provided for different combinations of client and carer characteristics. Factors associated with variations in costs for the experimental and control groups are described separately and these predictors of costs used to illustrate the costs of care for a variety of individual characteristics. The value of analysing costs in this way is that the separate equations can provide some evidence of which factors in the care process are of significance in determining the cost and use of services in respect of those receiving a case management service in the experimental group and those receiving the standard services in the control group. Thus, the intention is to identify the determinants of variation in costs associated with the characteristics of the older people, their carers and the effects of services upon well-being, or outcomes. The underlying premise of this approach is that the ways in which costs vary are determined by the need characteristics and the outcomes of services such as changes in well-being over time.

Approach

Cost function analysis was used to identify factors which caused the costs of care to vary, an approach used in previous evaluations of case/care management (Challis and Davies, 1986; Challis et al., 1995; 2002a). This approach incorporated regression analysis, a multivariate technique 'designed to simultaneously tease out the many influences on cost' (Netten and Beecham, 1993, 64). Analyses were carried out using forward step-wise multiple regression. A range of independent variables were taken from the list of client and carer variables shown in Box 7.1, Chapter 7. They were selected from the following domains: dependency and mental health; descriptive factors; the caring role; and the care process. Six variables were chosen as outcome measures from the list, and were selected on the basis that they were not only relevant to the cost of care, but more importantly, were also outcomes of value both to older people and carers. Each outcome measure was expressed as a change score, being the value of the change over time between the baseline interview and follow-up interview conducted at 12 months. These are shown in Box 10.1. For the analysis, where information was missing, the mean value for cases in that group was used. This approach supports the central tenet of the study which has been to explore the multiple issues involved in the care of an older person with dementia and where appropriate for their carer.

The independent or predictor variables were explored in conjunction with three sets of cost variables applied to the experimental group and control group separately. First, at the micro level, care package costs were estimated based on the total agency costs but excluding the cost of acute hospital and long-term placement, thus estimating the average cost of care packages for those remaining at home. The community care package describes the costs of services primarily orientated to maintaining the

Box 10.1   Outcome measures used in cost equations

Client variables	Carer variables
Change in ADL need shortfall (R) Perceived change in activities and company (I) Overall risk (R) Reduction in depression (CL)	Perceived reduction in overall strain (C) Reduction in Malaise (C)

C = carer rated
CL = client measure
I = Informant rated
R = researcher rated

person with dementia at home and supporting their carers. It includes respite care but excludes acute hospital care and long-term care. For this calculation, it was not possible to match the two groups due to differential survival in the community and therefore unmatched groups were used in order to maximise the numbers available for analysis and increase statistical power. Separate models were produced for the experimental and control groups, containing 34 and 37 cases respectively, and these are shown in Tables 10.1 and 10.2. These measured the relationship of community care packages to outcomes.

Second, at the macro level similar calculations were made in respect of agency costs and costs to society based on average cost per week, in this case using matched groups. The dependent variable of agency cost for both health and social care was based on the total service cost per week. This included private sector care purchased by statutory services, for example case managers' use of the independent home care sector. In contrast, the dependent variable of cost to society based on average cost per week included: costs to health and social care agencies; costs to housing; and the additional costs incurred by clients and carers. As noted earlier in the chapter, the value of the data lies in the fact that these incorporate carer costs and in this respect are the most inclusive data. Analyses undertaken in respect of agency costs and costs to society are illustrated in Tables 10.3a to 10.6a. These were used to predict the costs of care for various combinations of client and carer characteristics and circumstances for those in the experimental and control group respectively. Based upon the variables which proved to be significant, six different client typologies were developed from each equation and these are shown in Tables 10.3b to 10.6b. For economy and relevance of presentation, fewer client and carer attributes have been selected for the client typologies than appear in the accompanying regression analyses, although all have an effect on costs. In most cases, the effects of these attributes on any client type can be assessed by adding or subtracting the relevant co-efficient detailed in the companion table.

Overall, these findings, and particularly those relating to care packages detailed in Tables 10.1 and 10.2 and agency costs illustrated in Tables 10.3b and 10.4b could be set against the comparable local cost of residential and nursing home care. In particular, average costs for different case characteristics indicates how achieving outcomes for people with different combinations of circumstances and characteristics leads to different costs. For example, using local prices from data collected for the study, nursing home care in the independent sector cost £281 per week and residential care in a specialist local authority home cost £390 per week (1993/94 figures). The enduring relevance of these data is illustrated by the fact that Schneider and colleagues (2003) found residential or nursing care to be more cost-effective for older people with moderate or severe dementia than community care. Similarly, research conducted in Taiwan (Chiu et al., 2000) noted that community care was less cost effective for people with higher levels of disability when compared to nursing care. The approach described in this chapter, irrespective of when the data were collected, would permit similar judgements to be made about the relative cost effectiveness of care at home compared with that of residential care for older people in different circumstances.

This is of particular importance since in the UK there has been a move away, partly for financial reasons, from the predominance of institutional types of care with a reduction in the availability of care home places following rapid growth in the 1980s and early 1990s (Warburton and McCracken, 1999; Bauld et al., 2000a; Netten et al., 2003; 2005; Darton, 2004). Consequent changes focused on a policy of community care enabling people to remain in their own homes and, by implication, this was to be achieved in a more cost-effective framework than had been the case previously (Cm 849, 1989). Like the UK, many countries have financial incentives in place to delay for as long as possible the admission of an older person to a care home. Thus, with respect to older people with dementia, studies carried out in a number of European countries, Canada and the USA found many country-specific processes by which this group of older people entered care homes (Coleman, 1995; Payne et al., 1999).

Care Packages

In the initial analyses of the costs of care packages, female carers in the experimental group were associated with reduced costs for community care. However, this appeared to be artifactual since after further examination, it was found that male carers in the experimental group cared for much frailer people compared to carers in the control group. This finding may either be chance or the result of targeting. Nevertheless, as a consequence, this variable was then excluded to allow possible entry of other variables.

Tables 10.1 and 10.2 show the factors associated with variations in average weekly community care package costs for respectively the experimental group receiving case management, and for the control group receiving standard services. In the experimental group both client and carer outcomes were associated with increased costs, namely reduced risk overall for the older person, and perceived reduction in life strain for the carer. However, in the control group, only one client outcome, positive change in activities and company for the older person as perceived by the carer, was associated with increased costs. It is noteworthy that neither carer outcomes nor carer characteristics entered the regression equation in the control group. In both groups the presence of a carer living in the same household was, unsurprisingly, associated with a reduction in the cost of the care package. Conversely, in both groups recent deterioration of behaviour was associated with increased costs. A fairly strong prediction of the cost of care packages was obtained for the experimental group receiving intensive case management (adjusted $R^2 = 0.60$) although this was less so for the control group receiving standard services (adjusted $R^2 = 0.41$).

Table 10.1   Experimental group: community care package costs per week

Variable	Cost effect £	SE	p
Outcomes			
Client: reduction in overall risk	43.42	10.86	0.0005
Carer: perceived reduction in overall strain	23.20	6.03	0.0007
Client characteristics			
Two clients in household	-97.42	37.95	0.016
Presence of carer – other than spouse	-144.32	41.57	0.002
Recent deterioration in behaviour	80.61	34.15	0.026
Carer characteristics			
Main carer hours input	2.49	0.98	0.018
Reluctance to accept help	-97.31	36.81	0.014
Constant	151.45	28.22	<0.00005
F=7.99, R^2=0.68, Adjusted R^2=0.60, p <0.001			

Table 10.2   Control group: community care package costs per week

Variable	Cost effect £	SE	p
Outcomes			
Client: perceived change in activities and company	15.68	7.78	0.053
Client characteristics			
Presence of carer	-44.21	21.77	0.051
Communication impairment	14.44	7.90	0.077
Recent deterioration in behaviour	62.93	24.49	0.015
Risk of falling	25.87	13.30	0.061
Depression	-15.34	6.10	0.018
Constant	95.56	29.86	0.003
F=5.17, R^2=0.51, Adjusted R^2=0.41, p <0.001			

Costs to Agencies and Society

Agency Costs

Table 10.3a reveals that a single diagnosis of Alzheimer-type dementia, with no other psychiatric diagnoses, was associated with lower costs for the experimental group, indicating that less complex mental health needs were less costly. Depression too was associated with lower costs. However, as illustrated in Table 10.4a, there were no such characteristics which greatly reduced costs for the control group. Support to females, and carers' desire for placement were variables common to both equations, and they were associated with higher agency costs in both groups. Unsurprisingly, a carer's reluctance to accept help resulted in lower costs, although this characteristic appeared in the control group alone (Table 10.4a). With regard to costs to agencies, the equation for the experimental group explained 40 per cent of the variation; 57 per cent of variation in costs to agencies was explained by the control group equation.

The accompanying Tables 10.3b and 10.4b present details of the costs of care for various combinations of characteristics using outcome variables identified in the regression equations for agency costs. The three categories within the outcome variables of 'None', 'Some' and 'Considerable' represent the degree of change in value for these variables. 'None' represents no change in values or change within the lower quartile; 'Some' represents change within the median range of values; and 'Considerable' represents change in values within the upper quartile. Table 10.3b demonstrates the influence of a diagnosis of Alzheimer-type dementia, compared with the more complex picture of a multiple diagnosis, that is, diagnosis of dementia

Table 10.3a   Experimental group: average agency costs per week

Variable	Cost effect £	SE	p
Outcomes			
Client: reduced ADL need shortfall	25.19	9.17	0.009
Carer: perceived reduction in overall strain	18.50	9.11	0.05
Client characteristics			
Female	141.49	48.32	0.006
Depression (CARE)	-38.25	19.48	0.057
Single diagnosis – Alzheimer type	-100.71	44.76	0.031
Carer characteristics			
Desire for placement	79.62	38.36	0.045
Constant	50.32	90.48	0.582
F=5.71 R^2=0.49			
p <0.001 Adjusted R^2=0.40			

Adapted from Challis et al. (1997a)

Table 10.3b Experimental group: average agency costs per week for different case characteristics

Characteristics		Reduction in ADL need shortfall					
		None		Some		Considerable	
		Carer's perceived reduction in overall strain					
		None	Consider-able	None	Consider-able	None	Consider-able
Client	Carer	£	£	£	£	£	£
Single diagnosis of dementia-Alzheimer type							
male, moderate depression,	no desire for placement	15	89	65	139	115	189
female, moderate depression,	no desire for placement	156	230	206	280	257	331
female, no depression,	no desire for placement	233	307	283	357	333	407
Dementia and other psychiatric morbidity							
female, moderate depression,	no desire for placement	257	331	307	381	358	432
male, no depression,	carer desires placement	271	345	322	396	372	445
female, no depression,	carer desires placement	413	487	463	537	514	588

(£ at 1993/94 prices)

and another psychiatric disorder, on the cost of care for the experimental group. It also reveals that the presence of depression reduces the agency cost for clients in this group. Support given to females increases agency costs for those in the control group, as can be seen in Table 10.4a. It is also apparent from these tables that duration of memory problems has little influence on cost, although it appears that night disturbance, poor ADL functioning and carer's desire for placement increase agency costs for those receiving the standard services.

Table 10.4a   Control group: average agency costs per week

Variable	Cost effect £	SE	p
Outcomes			
Client: reduction in overall risk	29.36	13.33	0.035
Client: reduction in depression (CARE)	39.10	13.61	0.007
Client characteristics			
Female	126.29	44.07	0.007
ADL functioning	8.26	4.12	0.053
Night disturbance	24.92	14.63	0.098
Duration of memory problems	-1.23	0.44	0.009
Carer characteristics			
Reluctance to accept help	-117.19	57.26	0.049
Desire for placement	33.59	22.46	0.144
Constant	-153.61	105.80	0.156
F=7.95 R²=0.65			
P <0.0001 Adjusted R²=0.57			

Adapted from Challis et al. (1997a)

Table 10.4b Control group: average agency costs per week for different case characteristics

Characteristics	Reduction in overall risk					
	None		Some		Considerable	
			Reduction in depression (CARE)			
	None £	Considerable £	None £	Considerable £	None £	Considerable £
male, 5 yrs memory problems, moderate ADL score, no night disturbance, carer desires placement	15	94	45	123	74	152
female, 5 yrs memory problems, moderate ADL score, no night disturbance, carer desires placement	142	220	171	249	200	279
male, 2 yrs memory problems, considerable ADL score, moderate night disturbance, no desire for placement	159	236	118	266	217	295
female, 2 yrs memory problems, considerable ADL score, moderate night disturbance, no desire for placement	285	363	314	392	343	421
male, 2 yrs memory problems, considerable ADL score, moderate night disturbance, carer desires placement	192	270	221	299	251	329
female, 2 yrs memory problems, considerable ADL score, moderate night disturbance, carer desires placement	318	396	348	426	377	455

Note: moderate ADL score = adequate ADL functioning. considerable ADL score = poor ADL functioning

(£ at 1993/94 prices)

Costs to Society

Tables 10.5a and 10.6a illustrate the factors associated with variations in costs to society per week over one year for the experimental group and control group respectively. There were two outcome indicators entering the equation for the experimental group and just one for the control group associated with costs to society. In the experimental group these were, perceived change in activities and company for the client and reduced malaise for the carer, and in the control group, reduction in depression for the client. Client characteristics associated

Table 10.5a   Experimental group: costs to society

Variable	Cost effect £	SE	P
Outcomes			
Client: perceived change in activities and company	62.39	27.51	0.03
Carer: reduced malaise	15.15	7.48	0.052
Client characteristics			
Female	258.92	42.17	<0.00005
Social class 1 or 2	71.44	37.52	0.066
Single diagnosis – Alzheimer type	-80.84	41.77	0.062
Duration of memory problems	-1.06	0.43	0.02
Behaviour Rating Scale (CAPE)	12.49	3.68	0.002
Depression (CARE)	-56.79	14.63	0.0005
Aggressive exchanges	64.58	32.22	0.054
Care process			
Number of months at home	-16.78	5.94	0.008
Client uncooperative with services	-66.41	27.88	0.024
Constant	96.81	111.44	0.392
F=8.89 R^2=0.76			
p <0.0001 Adjusted R^2=0.67			

Table 10.5b Experimental group: average costs to society per week for different case characteristics

Characteristics	Client: Perceived improvement in activities and company					
	None		Some		Considerable	
	\<Carer: Reduction in malaise score\>					
	None £	Considerable £	None £	Considerable £	None £	Considerable £
Single diagnosis - Alzheimer type						
male, high BRS score, cooperative with services	224	239	255	271	287	302
female, low BRS score, uncooperative with services	329	345	361	376	392	407
female, high BRS score, uncooperative with services	417	432	448	463	479	494
Complex diagnosis of dementia						
male, low BRS score, cooperative with services	218	233	249	264	280	295
male, high BRS score, uncooperative with services	239	254	270	285	301	316
female, low BRS score, cooperative with services	477	492	508	523	539	554

(£ at 1993/94 prices)

Note: BRS score = Behaviour Rating Scale (CAPE) score Low score = low dependency

Table 10.6a   Control group: costs to society

Variable	Cost effect £	SE	p
Outcomes			
Client: Reduction in depression (CARE)	37.27	11.89	0.004
Client characteristics			
Female	115.91	40.29	0.007
Social class 1 or 2	72.33	37.68	0.063
ADL functioning	10.57	3.56	0.005
Night disturbance	15.00	6.35	0.024
ADL need shortfall	54.11	12.53	0.0001
Carer characteristics			
Reluctance to accept help	-112.29	52.75	0.041
Age	5.13	1.38	0.0007
Constant	-398.14	137.23	0.007
F=11.48 R^2=0.73			
p <0.0001 Adjusted R^2=0.67			

Table 10.6b   Control group: average costs to society per week for different case characteristics

Characteristics					Client- Reduction in depression (CARE)		
Sex	*ADL score*	*Night disturbance*	*ADL needs shortfall*	*Social class*	*None £*	*Some £*	*Considerable £*
male	moderate	low	none	Not social class 1 or 2	110	147	185
female	moderate	low	none	Not social class 1 or 2	226	263	301
female	moderate	low	none	Social class 1 or 2	298	336	373
male	considerable	high	moderate	Not social class 1 or 2	342	379	416
female	considerable	high	moderate	Not social class 1 or 2	535	572	609
female	considerable	high	moderate	Social class 1 or 2	607	644	681

Note: moderate ADL score = adequate ADL functioning   (£ at 1993/94 prices)
            considerable ADL score = poor ADL functioning

with a reduction in costs to society were unsurprisingly the same as those which emerged in the agency costs, namely single diagnosis of Alzheimer's disease and client depression. By way of comparison, the only characteristic in the control group associated with a reduction in costs to society was the carer characteristic of reluctance to accept help (Table 10.6a). It is, however, also of note that carer outcome indicators were only related to costs to society in the experimental group equation, as was the case in respect of costs to agencies (Table 10.4a). Interestingly, variables related to the care process such as length of time remaining at home, also emerged as predictors of costs to society, though this was only in relation to the experimental group. It was possible to obtain fairly accurate predictions of costs to society for both the experimental group and the control group, with 67 per cent ·of the variation explained by each equation.

Table 10.5b shows that in the experimental group, the effect of gender is apparent, with females being more expensive to support. Arguably, this effect masks the influence of other variables selected from Table 10.5a, particularly the effect of a single diagnosis of dementia. In Table 10.6b, it appears that the characteristics of ADL functioning, night disturbance, ADL need shortfall, as well as social class, have an upward effect on costs to society for those in the control group.

Cost Predictors – Comparison and Utility

As described earlier in this chapter, cost predictors have the potential to be used by social care agencies to promote the equitable and transparent use of resources to target them in response to identified need. In this study, a number of factors influenced the costs of care packages, costs for agencies and costs to society for both the experimental group receiving the case management scheme and the control group receiving statutory services. Overall, three important points appear to emerge from the predictors of variation in cost illustrated in Tables 10.3a to 10.6a, for both groups in relation to: client dependency and mental health; support of female clients; and carer characteristics, both their contribution and well-being. First, in respect of client dependency and mental health, the costs of community care packages were higher in both groups where there was deterioration in behaviour. A single diagnosis of an Alzheimer's-type dementia was associated with lower agency costs and costs to society for the experimental group. This may suggest that these cases demanded a lower level of intervention than where there was greater complexity of the psychiatric needs arising from multiple diagnosis of, say, dementia and depression. The influence of depression on these analyses of costs is multi-faceted and should be viewed in the context of the findings regarding depression in Chapter 7. In respect of client outcome, a reduction in depression seemed to raise agency costs and costs to society in the control group. Conversely, presence of depression appeared to reduce care package costs in the control group, and reduce agency and social costs in the experimental group. Thus, the presence of depression had a cost lowering effect, but to achieve an improvement increased costs, a finding complementary to other research relating to the treatment of depression in vulnerable older people (Banerjee and Macdonald, 1996).

Second, there were higher costs to agencies and to society involved in the support of female clients for both groups. This may be more easily understood in terms of there being reduced costs for male clients due to the greater proportion of them who lived with a carer. Males were more likely to have female carers, who may have refused services or had fewer services provided. Other research which investigated gender differences in the amount of support offered to carers found a difference in some care managers' responses to female and male carers, with greater expectations being made of female carers, despite male carers having lower dependency needs themselves (Bywaters and Harris, 1998).

Third, in respect of the caring role, the presence of a carer, unsurprisingly, had the effect of lowering community care package costs in both the experimental and control groups, whilst a carers' desire for placement increased agency costs in both groups. It is also of note that the effect of being a female carer on care package costs was so strong that this variable was subsequently removed from the experimental group equation. Another detail of interest was the association between a carer's reluctance to accept help and reduced costs. In the control group, this was related to lower costs to agencies and to society, whereas in the experimental group this was related to lower care package costs. Furthermore, carer outcomes relating to perceived reduction in overall strain and reduced malaise were only apparent in the experimental group. However, they were found in each of the three analyses – care package, agency, and costs to society – and were associated with a small increase in expenditure. This may indicate that the extent of carer outcome in the experimental group was associated with the degree of resource provided and therefore the level of help given, an observation supported by the findings described in Chapter 5, which highlight the tangible aspects of the help carers received from the LCMS.

Overall, this approach incorporating predictors of cost also has the capacity to assist in the targeting of assistance to permit optimal outcomes, thereby promoting the cost-effective use of resources. This has been demonstrated in another way in respect of the North American 'Channeling Demonstration' projects, referred to in Chapter 2. These projects concluded that community-based services were not particularly successful at reducing the costs of long-term care for older people (Kemper et al., 1987; Hedrick et al., 1993; Weissert and Hedrick, 1994). However, Greene and colleagues (1998) analysed the programmes to ascertain whether the targeting strategies employed affected their cost effectiveness. Using optimal allocation of home care services, they produced a hypothetical 10 per cent reduction in long-term care costs for the population of older people served by the Channeling Demonstration, in contrast to the 12 per cent net cost increase produced by the intervention itself. The savings were achieved by a model which used tighter targeting of services on those at higher risk and by altering the mix of available services. Others in the US have argued that there is a lack of clarity in terms of how much care is sufficient, and at what point the marginal costs of additional care begin to exceed marginal benefits (Weissert et al., 2003). The authors not only believe that targeting is a 'flawed process' and should be substituted by wider eligibility in conjunction with care that is clearly calibrated to risks, but that more of the variation in care should be explained by individual characteristics. The approach to financial modelling adopted by the LCMS has the capacity to do this and to take account of client and carer views as distinct to those described above. However, as Greene and colleagues acknowledged, although a net reduction in long-term care costs and in nursing home care is an important outcome in the evaluation of an intervention programme, its ability to improve or at least maintain quality of life for older people living at home, should also be valued. Arguably the inclusion of client and carer outcomes in the analyses of costs described in this chapter is a proxy for this.

These conclusions from the LCMS and the programmes described by Greene and colleagues have the capacity to promote informed commissioning and service development. As such they may be linked with other approaches which seek to identify groups of older people who could receive care in more appropriate settings and the resource implications of providing such care. Such studies, which explore how best to meet the needs of frail older people at the margins of care, reflect the concept of the balance of care and have been characterised as having three defining features. These are: the inclusion of data on the dependency characteristics of those groups of people at the margins of care; details of service use; and data on the costs of care in different settings at the level of the individual. It is intrinsic to the practical application of the concept of the balance of care in a strategic planning framework that all three of these components are included (Mooney, 1978). The value of this approach is that it provides data to facilitate consideration of whether the existing use of resources between locations of care is 'optimal' and in which of these locations any increase or reduction of resources should be made (Hughes and Challis, 2004). Whilst data from the LCMS lacks the full range to permit judgements to be made about optimality it does have a clear utility. It provides a rational basis for the allocation of scarce resources in an area in which high costs are incurred both in terms of public and personal finance and where there is a comparative dearth of data to inform decision-making at both the individual level and in the strategic commissioning of services. As such, it is an example of an intervention study which can influence the balance of care by improving the appropriateness of placement decisions (Hughes and Challis, 2004). Finally, and most powerfully in an English context, the setting in which the research was undertaken, and reflecting recent policy concerns, this information demonstrates the association between components of care packages and outcomes (Department of Health, 2000a; Cm 6499, 2005; Cm 6737, 2006).

Summary

The analyses described in this chapter provide some indications of the types of individuals for whom case management might be the most appropriate form of intervention. The use of multiple outcomes in the regression analyses, as discussed earlier, allowed for the inclusion of carer outcome variables. However, this approach also restricted the feasibility of some direct comparisons between the experimental and control group. Despite this, the cost predictions which were produced from these equations using different typologies provide useful information about which individual characteristics are important in determining cost. As mentioned previously, such data can be used to inform strategic planning in terms of the costs incurred in supporting different types of individuals. Whilst data from the study are not conclusive, they provide information that could assist in targeting case management for a small group of vulnerable older people assessed as requiring a substantial package of care at home following a comprehensive assessment (Department of Health, 2002b). However, they are based on probabilities and do not include variations in individual preferences, regarded as important in recent policy initiatives (Cm 6499, 2005; Cm 6737, 2006). Nevertheless, the data suggest that such an intensive case management scheme could make a cost-effective intervention both in the lives of older people with dementia and their carers, particularly in situations where the carer has a desire to support the older person remaining in the community. This is in accord with the rationale of earlier studies of case management (Challis and Davies, 1986; Levin et al., 1994; Challis et al., 1995), and suggests that the most effective case management interventions are those which are targeted on a highly specific group in terms of their needs and specialised nature of their problems.

Chapter 11
Evaluation and Evolution

Introduction

This chapter draws together the main findings of the evaluation of the Lewisham Case Management Scheme and considers some of the implications for the development of care management for older people with dementia and their carers in the context of policy initiatives to promote integrated health and social care provision and the personalisation of care. As described previously, the scheme was designed as one of a family of case management projects, targeted upon vulnerable older people. In this research study, a quasi-experimental design also termed a 'non-equivalent control group' was used (Campbell and Stanley, 1966). The same approach was adopted in the Kent, Darlington and Gateshead projects, with the experimental and control group subjects recruited from adjacent but similar demographic areas within the same catchment area for the provision of health and social care, therefore reducing the risk of service-related differences (Challis and Davies, 1986; Challis et al., 1995; 2002a). All four studies were designed to provide an effective and realistic alternative to long-term placement in care homes for vulnerable older people, increasing the range of choices available.

The Production of Welfare (POW) approach (Davies and Knapp, 1981) provides the conceptual framework for the research methodology for all the studies. It offers a means of examining the causal processes and outcomes consequent on the development of case management. Within it there are five interrelated components: resource inputs, non-resource inputs, intermediate outputs, final outputs and costs as is illustrated in Figure 11.1. On the one side of the production relationships are supply side factors, comprising resource inputs and non-resource inputs. In this study, the former, in the main, comprises the contributions of staff and carers. Non-resource inputs, on the other hand, are the determinants of intermediate and final outputs which are not physical or tangible and in this study comprise the process of case management and the background attitudes and experiences of the key actors in the provision of care on a daily basis. In this example, costs embrace services provided by both staff and carers and less tangible costs such as carer burden.

On the other side of the production relationship are the final and intermediate outputs of care. Both are significant in the context of measuring the effectiveness of policy initiatives. Intermediate outputs attempt to capture what social care services are striving to achieve for carers and older people, such as provision of assistance and development of services. On the other hand, final outputs measure the effects of the supply side factors, both resource inputs and non-resource inputs,

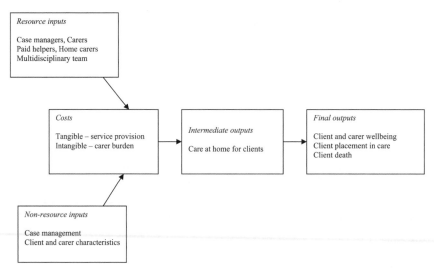

Adapted from Davies and Knapp (1981)

**Figure 11.1   The Lewisham Case Management Scheme and the Production
of Welfare approach**

on those who are identified as the principal beneficiaries of service in this study. Unsurprisingly, in this research and others within this family of case management projects, much of the focus of the evaluation of the intervention related to the costs, both of service provision and the more intangible carer burden, and intermediate outputs such as the provision of care at home for older people thereby promoting their continued community tenure. Measures of final output included in this study related to the rate of placement in residential or nursing home care, the death rate and well-being of the older person and carer.

The value of applying this framework is that it facilitated the exploration of the extent to which case management was a viable alternative to placement in long-term care for older people with a diagnosis of dementia. It provided a means of examining the relationship between the components of service provision, their cost, and the impact on both individuals and services. This chapter first reviews key outcomes in respect of the four research questions previously described in Chapter 4. Subsequently the evolution of the case management scheme into a mainstream service is described. Finally, the relevance and value of the scheme is drawn together in the light of current plans for the development of dementia services and for the implementation of the policy of personalisation for people with dementia.

Principal Research Findings

In Chapter 4, four research questions were formulated concerning the potential impact of the LCMS on the older people with dementia and their carers, the wider care network, and of the purchasers and providers of health and social care. The first two related to outcome and costs, and the last two related to the care process.

- what are the outcomes for older people and their carers of a new intensive care management service?
- what are the costs of care in an intensive care management service compared with the usual modes of care?
- what kinds of practice interventions and strategies do care managers develop for older people with dementia?
- and what forms of service development do care managers initiate to meet need?

These are reviewed in the light of the experience of the scheme, thereby summarising the principal findings of the study.

Outcomes for Older People and their Carers

Box 11.1 describes the main findings of the LCMS with regard to outcomes and costs of the intervention from the perspective of the older people with dementia, their carers, the researchers, and others involved in the care network. In respect of the outcomes of the scheme, it was apparent that by the second year its effects began to show in a lower rate of admission to care homes for older people with dementia in the experimental group, than for those in the control group. This reflects the finding of another study evaluating the impact of integrated care and case management with a group of older people in receipt of community services which also found reduced admission rates in addition to lower rates of functional decline. In this, the intervention group received no additional community services, indicating that the role of the case manager working within an integrated care system was paramount (Bernabei et al., 1998). As discussed more fully in Chapter 8, it appeared that the older people with dementia in receipt of case management had benefited in terms of a reduction in their levels of unmet needs and had gained more daytime company. It is also noteworthy that the quality of life measures used showed little overall change over time except for reported greater satisfaction with lifestyle within the home for the older person. However, the measurement of change in quality of life over time is difficult with this group (Bauld et al., 2000b; Watt, 2001), especially when the desired outcomes of older people with dementia may differ from those typically identified in quality of life measures (Bamford and Bruce, 2000).

Box 11.1   Outcomes and costs of the Lewisham Case Management Scheme

	Outcomes	**Costs**
Older people with dementia in receipt of case management	• Lower admission rate to care homes by second year of scheme • Reduction in the level of unmet needs particularly personal care needs and provision of daytime company • Older people without carers received more company and social activity • Few changes recorded in quality of life measures save for greater satisfaction with lifestyle at home • No reported change in behavioural problems	• Lower costs for long-term residential care and respite away from home • Lower costs in terms of reduced need for visits from community mental health team members • Higher costs of domiciliary care with provision of specialised home care • Higher costs of professional visits (specifically cost of nursing and care manager visits), day care and acute hospital care • Costs of community care packages higher for both case management and control groups where older person with dementia exhibited behaviour problems
Carers of older people with dementia receiving case management	• Relieved carers of some of the physical tasks of caring • Both main carers and other carers enabled to reduce their contribution to the caring network in terms of number of hours caring • Reduction in level of carer Malaise (measuring the physical and psychological symptoms of stress). This effect particularly apparent with carers who lived in the same household as the older people with dementia • No changes in perceived level of carer life burden or strain	• Lower direct financial costs and lower indirect costs due to reduction in time spent caring, incurred by carers • A carer's desire for the placement of the older person with dementia in long-term care increased agency costs (experimental and control groups)

The importance of the role of carers in maintaining an older person with dementia in their own home has been widely demonstrated (Levin et al., 1989; O'Shea and O'Reilly, 2000; Spruytte et al., 2001; Brodaty et al., 2003; Gaugler et al., 2005a; Zarit and Femia, 2008). However, caring may have a negative physiological and psychological effect on the carers' health (O'Rourke and Tuokko, 2000; Patterson and Grant, 2003; Zarit and Edwards, 2008). This study indicates that there were tangible gains for the carers of those in receipt of case management, apparent in terms of relief from some of the physical tasks of caring and in the number of hours spent caring. There was also a reported reduction in carer malaise, or 'ill-being' although there was little change observed in the quality of life measures for carers over time, particularly in carers' perceived levels of burden and strain. Elsewhere, it has been suggested that not only are some of these concepts, particularly carer 'stress' or 'strain', sometimes indistinguishable or unclear (Gilleard, 1984) but there is also a great deal of variety in the types of indicators of carer well-being used in evaluative studies of carers (Gottlieb and Wolfe, 2002). Indeed, it has sometimes been acknowledged that improving carer well-being or reducing levels of carer stress may not always be possible (Zarit et al., 1998; Zarit and Leitsch, 2001).

The Costs of Care

As detailed in Chapters 4 and 9, the LCMS used an opportunity costing approach. This describes the cost of using a resource in a particular way, not necessarily the monetary cost, but, 'the benefit forgone (the opportunity lost) by losing its best alternative use' (Knapp, 1993, 11). In terms of comparing types of care and resources that may be scarce, this method provides information that allows a choice to be made between alternative services (Knapp, 1993). In this study, when all costs to society were accounted for including informal care, the weekly cost of supporting older people with dementia and their carers was not significantly higher for those receiving intensive case management, although the cost to statutory agencies was much greater. The findings thus appear to indicate that a case management scheme could be cost-effective for older people with dementia and their carers, particularly in situations where the carer has a desire to support the older person remaining in the community. As summarised in Box 11.1, the lower rate of admission to residential and nursing home care for older people with dementia receiving the case management input resulted in lower associated costs for residential care compared with the older people receiving standard services. In Ireland, it has been estimated that family carers bore around 50 per cent of the economic and social cost of caring for older people with dementia, whilst community care provision accounted for just 10 per cent of the overall cost of dementia (O'Shea and O'Reilly, 2000). The Dementia UK report (Knapp et al., 2007) estimated informal carer cost overall at 36 per cent of the cost of care for people with dementia, but markedly higher for those living in the community. It is therefore interesting to note that in this study there was a positive effect on the carers of those in receipt of case management with regard to costs, since financial and other costs were lower for this group compared to carers of those receiving standard services. However, it was not possible to differentiate between the costs of informal care of those who lived with the older person with dementia and those who did not due to the relatively low numbers involved. Nevertheless, it has been established elsewhere that costs borne by co-resident carers of older people with dementia are higher than costs for non-resident carers and these also consistently exceed the costs of formal services (Schneider et al., 2003).

A number of factors may account for the relatively high costs identified in both the experimental and control groups. The scheme operated in an area where services may be judged to be more expensive than in other parts of England (Derbyshire, 1987; Allen and Beecham, 1993) including higher weekly community care package costs for older people with dementia (Moriarty and Webb, 2000). It has also been suggested that the costs of setting up and developing a new service will be proportionally high for the number of people recruited to a scheme in its early stages when development work is high and numbers are relatively low (Kane et al., 1991; Challis et al., 1993). For example, the 'Channeling Demonstration' projects (see Chapters 2, 9 and 10) were a series of case management programmes set up in the US to determine whether provision of specific home care services would lower nursing home admissions and thus long-term care costs for frail older people. Evaluation of these costs found insufficient evidence of nursing home savings to offset the cost of the services (Carcagno and Kemper, 1988). However, it has been subsequently argued that such findings merely suggest that *on average* the cost of home care provision is higher than nursing home expenditure, but this *average* loss may disguise a variety of *individual* gains. Many people receiving demonstration services offset the costs of home care services by a reduction in actual or expected nursing home use (their italics) (Greene et al., 1998). In this research study, a variety of individual characteristics were shown to be significantly related to cost, thereby identifying those who were more financially costly to care for at home compared to residential or nursing home care. Thus the costs of care were, to some extent, related to particular characteristics of the older person and in certain circumstances those of their carers, reflected in individually tailored care packages, as illustrated in the present study in Chapter 10.

Practice Interventions and Strategies

The case management process has been described as a series of core tasks: case-finding and screening, assessment, care planning, monitoring and review. The LCMS has been reviewed using this model, shown in Box 11.2. Three aspects of this warrant further discussion in the light of national policy guidance: assessment; provision of a needs-led response; and the monitoring and review of care plans.

It is of interest to review the approach to assessment adopted within the LCMS in relation to the Single Assessment Process (SAP), which was introduced to ensure that older people received 'appropriate, effective and timely responses to their health and social care needs' (Department of Health, 2001b; 2002b). It specified four types of assessment described in Chapter 2. One of these, the comprehensive assessment, was recommended as the most appropriate for older people with dementia since it was identified as a prerequisite for residential and nursing home placements and intensive community support, or where substantial packages of care at home are required. Completion of the CAPRE, a structured

Box 11.2   Practice interventions and strategies for clients and the care network

Practice interventions and strategies	Client	Care network	
		Carer	Paid helper
Case finding and screening: targeting of appropriate cases	Diagnosis of dementia: referral by members of the multidisciplinary team to case managers		
Assessment: structured approach severity of need assessed	Long-term care needs central to the assessment process, complementing initial clinical assessment by multidisciplinary team. Incorporated assessment of physical and mental health, ADLs, social/leisure activities and home environment	Integral to the process both in terms of their needs and their contribution to the process. Carers' experiences of distress and/or difficulties assessed	Informants to the process. Within the carer network, the assessment addressed relationships and service provision
Implementing the care plan: goal defined; strategies of intervention and resources identified	Strategies to manage problem behaviour and assistance with personal care and activities of daily living paramount	Reduced contribution to client care, active support from case manager	Substitute for carers and closely involved in monitoring mental state
Monitoring, review and case closure: achievement of goals re-assessed problems reviewed outcome by domain of assessed need evaluated	Care plan adjusted in relation to changed circumstances by service alterations and changes to safety and comfort in the home	Complementary relationship between carers and paid helpers strengthened the care network	

assessment and care planning tool, by a case manager would have fulfilled this requirement. It also incorporated an assessment of the carer's needs and their role, identified as a discrete area of assessment in policy guidance (Department of Health 2001c,d). Interestingly, other research has found reluctance among care managers to complete a separate carer's assessment, maintaining that carers did not wish to go through this separate process (Seddon and Robinson, 2001). The CAPRE also encompassed the older person's network of care, necessary to the practice of care management in respect of older people with dementia and their carers (Fisher, 1991 a,b; Stanley and Cantley, 2001).

Case managers held a devolved budget, permitting the occasional purchase of small items of household equipment, although the majority of service development monies funded the paid helper service, described in Chapter 6, which facilitated the provision of a needs-led response. This control over resources is in contrast to the findings of some other research studies. For example, a project undertaken shortly after implementation of the community care reforms reported dissatisfaction among staff with the lack of control over budgets and a lack of available services, despite identifying the presence of unmet needs at assessment (Hoyes et al., 1994). Furthermore, subsequent research found evidence of difficulties reported by practitioners in establishing and maintaining a needs-led approach to assessment, in distinguishing between need and unmet need, and dealing with resource restrictions (Parry-Jones and Soulsby, 2001). The LCMS paid helper service, although predating the personalisation agenda in adult social care, provides an exemplar of a domiciliary care service offering flexible and individually determined care packages in response to identified need.

Box 11.2 illustrates another feature of the scheme: the importance attached to the monitoring and review function. Interestingly, evidence from other research which gathered the views of care managers, older people and their carers has found monitoring and review procedures, which are central to a model of long-term care, to be underdeveloped and variable geographically, although users and carers were generally satisfied with these arrangements (Hardy et al., 1999). Moreover, these core tasks reflected policy guidance that promotes care planning, regular reviews and monitoring as important principles of care (Department of Health, 2002b,c; Cm 6499, 2005; Cm 6737, 2006).

Service Development

The paid helper service was developed specifically to provide more specialist assistance to older people with dementia and their carers in the experimental group in receipt of case management, and it provided one of the most significant innovations within the scheme. As described in Chapter 6, this was available at short notice and outside the normal hours available from existing services. One of its most important features was an ability to respond effectively to the idiosyncratic needs of a group of older people with dementia whom statutory services found difficult to support, and this was crucial in maintaining them at home. Paid helpers assisted with household activities and shopping, and also provided companionship and supervision, tasks generally given low priority by social services but greatly valued by some older people (Patmore, 2001). The location of the paid helper service within an integrated care setting and the nature of the service provided reflected subsequent development. It was, for example, illustrative of the 'professional integration model' for the development of home care, that valued the role of home care staff, linked them to other services, and provided users with emotional and social support, as identified by Sinclair and colleagues (2000). Their study into the role and performance of home care found that management arrangements developed to administer services were logistically very difficult due to the need to provide care for large numbers of people around the same time of day. They suggested that home care services should follow an integrated option using committed and multi-skilled staff acting as key workers who could bring together health and social care expertise. Such an approach to service development would also overcome the inherent difficulties of commissioning services for older people with mental health problems, as discussed in Chapter 2.

It is also helpful to review the service development associated with the scheme in the context of later changes in domiciliary care nationally so that the significance of the paid helper scheme can be assessed. National statistics on local authority purchased or provided home care services suggest that local authorities now provide a more intensive service for fewer service users (Department of Health, 2008c). Between 1992 and 2000, there was a 25 per cent decrease in the number of households receiving services while the number of contact hours increased by 65 per cent, largely as a result of considerable growth in the independent sector, dominated by new and small-scale organisations (Wistow and Hardy, 1999; Ware et al., 2001). The latter's share of the home care market increased from 2 per cent in 1992 to 36 per cent in 1996 (Wistow, 2000), and from 67 per cent in 2003 to 78 per cent in 2007 (Department of Health, 2008c). This change in emphasis towards larger packages of complex care for frail older people with varied needs has required care staff to not only undertake more demanding tasks, but also move towards provision of personal care such as helping people wash, dress and use the toilet, as distinct from a previously domestic cleaning service (Leece, 2003). The importance of staff development, better training and delivery of care by suitably qualified domiciliary care workers was identified in the *National Minimum Care Standards for Domiciliary Care* (Department of Health, 2003c). However, difficulties relating to a lack of training of care staff in dementia care, low pay, and high turnover were subsequently noted in respect of the quality of domiciliary care (National Audit Office, 2007; Committee of Public Accounts, 2008). It has been suggested that home care services have become too narrowly targeted and should be extended to a wider group of older people (Commission for Social Care Inspection, 2006; Wanless, 2006). Such home care packages which include low-level support may also assist older people with dementia to remain independent and at home for longer (Knapp et al., 2007). In advance of these recommendations, the development of the paid helper service demonstrated the importance of developing a specialist service for older people with dementia, rather than a generic service response (Department of Health, 2002c; 2009b). Subsequently, some schemes providing more specialist home care services for older people with dementia have indeed highlighted the importance of specialist staff training, good communication between professionals, continuity of staff and flexibility (Chilvers, 2003; Walker, 2003; Rothera et al., 2008).

Transition from Research to Mainstream Service

Once the pilot phase of the scheme had ended, local commissioners of health and social care jointly agreed to maintain the LCMS. It has continued as an example of intensive case management with the case manager co-ordinating the delivery of a wide range of services. However, there have been a number of major developments and changes made to the service since the completion of the pilot project. A return visit to the service in 2004 provided the opportunity to capture some of these. The team in which the LCMS was located became one of three multidisciplinary teams within the Lewisham Mental Health of Older Adults (MHOA) service, which provided assessment, treatment, rehabilitation and case management to people aged over 65 with a range of mental health problems and people under 65 with progressive cognitive impairment. The service met the recommendations of the National Service Framework for Older People (NSFOP) (Department of Health, 2001b) and the Audit Commission (Audit Commission, 2000; 2002) in terms of its composition and was recognised as providing good practice in terms of its integration and co-location of staff (Rendell and Haw, 2001). Over the years, care management arrangements within the service and commitment within the team to integrated service provision, including multidisciplinary working, have provided a framework conducive to the development of integrated care to the individual users referred to the MHOA service. These are discussed in more detail below.

Care Management Arrangements

In 2004 the MHOA service operated an open referral system, with general practitioners and local authority personnel being the principal referrers. There was a single integrated assessment document, used by all team members. This long established practice of specialist assessment within the multidisciplinary process constituted a specialist assessment within the SAP, with the social worker co-ordinating these to compile, in effect, a comprehensive assessment (Department of Health, 2002b). A separate carer's assessment was undertaken if applicable (Department of Health, 1999a) and older people and carers were involved in reviews. Following the pilot phase of the scheme, eligibility criteria for the case management service were subsequently widened from a primary diagnosis of dementia and at high risk of admission to a care home, to include people over 65 years of age with functional mental health problems such as severe depression, schizophrenia, or anxiety disorders and at risk of admission to a care home. The principles of case management in the research study were apparent in the core services at the time of the return visit to the service in 2004 as illustrated in Box 11.3. Several points are of note in this context: the longevity of the scheme; management arrangements; the provision of services to support vulnerable older people in their own homes; and links with the local authority. First, the longevity of the scheme is significant particularly since, with exceptions (Challis et al., 2002a), many of the early case management experiments were, in retrospect, time-limited (Challis, 1994b; Weiner et al., 2002). Within the MHOA service in 2004 responsibility for case management remained the preserve of the professionally qualified social worker although successive policy initiatives have sought to promote integrated working between health and social care by means of encouraging arrangements which permit other professional groups to act as a care manager (SSI/SSWG, 1991 a,b; Department of Health, 2002b).

Second, in reviewing the development of the role of case management within this service over time, it is important to note changes to the arrangements for the management and supervision of case managers reflecting, in part, the evolution of its multidisciplinary approach. As noted in Chapter 5, at its inception the line manager and supervisor of the case managers, whilst closely associated with the service, was not part of the multidisciplinary team, but based within a specialist older people's mental health team within the social services department. Subsequently, line management became located within the team, and was similar for all social workers within it. Within this arrangement a distinction has been made between management monitoring and clinical supervision (Ovretveit, 1997) with the former vested in the team manager and the latter in the lead social worker within the service. This approach is widely adopted within multidisciplinary teams (Ovretveit, 1997), but different to that typically adopted within local authority social services departments (Cypher, 1982).

Third, the services which are essential for care management to support vulnerable old people with mental health problems in their homes have changed considerably since the end of the research study. Those formerly available are illustrated in Table 9.2 in Chapter 9. During the study, the paid helpers provided the majority of the domiciliary care. Subsequently, the paid helper scheme became integrated into the local authority home care service, as a discrete specialist service and many of the paid helpers were recruited as home carers. The local authority then established a specialist home care team for older people with mental health problems available throughout the day and in the evening and weekends. As far as possible, people supported by the MHOA service have received care from this service. Nevertheless, a shortfall in this specialist domiciliary care service was reported, with the consequence that case managers had to purchase help often from independent providers, losing continuity of care and specialist knowledge, both of which have been recognised as important for the care of older people with mental health problems (Audit Commission, 2000). Similar difficulties in guaranteeing worker hours and training care staff have been noted elsewhere (Young and

Box 11.3   The Lewisham Case Management Scheme: transition to mainstream service

	The research study	The MHOA service 2004
Goals and objectives	Alternative to residential and nursing home care for older people with dementia	Alternative to care homes for older people with mental health problems
Case-finding	Community mental health team for older people, home care service, and hospital staff	Community mental health team for older adults, hospital staff (older adult health ward) and older adults' team in the local authority social care services
Assessment	Initial assessment by community mental health team for older people. Detailed assessment by case managers	Continuity in assessment approach within the SAP. Overview and specialist assessment undertaken by members of the multidisciplinary team and if referred for case management, social worker co-ordinated a comprehensive assessment and care package
Care plans/range of help	Predominantly local authority home care service and specialist paid helpers. Also independent sector domiciliary care and voluntary sector provision. Emphasis on care at home	Local authority domiciliary care service and within this specialist mental health domiciliary service, independent sector home care and voluntary sector provision. Emphasis on care at home
Case responsibility	Case manager (social worker by profession)	Social workers
Budgets	Budget devolved to scheme, responsibility for expenditure per client basis. Cost ceiling 2/3 cost of residential care	Local authority held budget. Cost ceiling applied equivalent to placement in long-term care. Responsibility for authorising plans to meet assessed need of user and/or carer with the MHOA service. This included care plans consequent on assessment of carer needs
Helpers	Specialist paid helper service developed by case managers for their clients	No longer exists
Monitoring and reviews	Monitoring and review integral to the case management process	Monitoring and review integral to the service. Requirement for six-monthly review but more frequent in practice as a result of significant changes to circumstances
Management	Line management arrangements for case managers within social services department	Management functions within the multidisciplinary team divided into two: operational management the responsibility of team manager who may or may not be a social worker; professional management and development undertaken by a lead social worker
Supervision and support	Case managers received peer support from the multidisciplinary team both formally in team meetings and informally	Continued the same

Wistow, 1996; Wistow and Hardy, 1999; Wistow, 2000). In comparison with services available during the research study, a shortage of specialist day care in the locality was apparent. However, it is noteworthy that a specialist day care facility was developed for Afro-Caribbean elders with mental health problems, reflecting an ethnic diversity that did not exist to the same extent during the pilot phase of the LCMS. Changes to long-term residential care have meant that most provision is provided by the independent sector, mirroring developments nationally, and continuing care for older people with serious or enduring mental health problems funded by the NHS was provided by a housing association. A need to develop more specialist provision in care homes locally was recognised, reflecting the national situation and policy recommendations (Audit Commission, 2000; Department of Health, 2001b; Bush, 2003).

Fourth, since the end of the research study links have evolved between the MHOA service and the local authority, reflecting policy guidance promoting the joint commissioning of services (Cm 4169, 1998; Cm 4818-I, 2000; Cm 6268, 2004; Cm 6499, 2005; Cm 6737, 2006). In 2004, this was reflected in the case management service in terms of management arrangements and operational practice, and associated service development. The development of a single operational policy within the MHOA service incorporating explicit standards relating to key areas of practice, such as response times to receipt of referrals, provided a framework to monitor and review the interface between the two services. Furthermore, a management agreement between the service and the local authority was established for the integrated management of health and social care staff. As noted in Box 11.3, respite care and high cost care packages were authorised within the MHOA though the budget remained within social service department control. Access to long-term care was by application to the relevant interagency panel within the borough. At practitioner level, the links remained informal with MHOA staff making joint visits with social services staff to assess clients, an arrangement which has been found to be as effective as formal arrangements for collaborative working (Kharicha et al., 2004). In the context of service development, the MHOA and local authority sought to collaborate in the further development of a specialist domiciliary care service specific to the clients of the service and be managed within it.

In terms of care management arrangements, one of the features of the MHOA service in 2004 was that it offered a structured range of responses reflecting the differing needs of those referred to it, evidence of a differentiated approach to need. This is one of the prerequisites for the successful establishment of intensive care management within a service, as described in Chapter 2. Some time ago, policy guidance identified three approaches to care management, each broadly reflecting different levels of need: administrative; co-ordinating; and intensive. A summary description of each is provided in Box 11.4, together with projections of practical application within the existing service structure. Further enhancement of the distinction between a care management service for those with needs that could be met with modest care packages comprising one or two services and for those with multiple health and social care needs requiring complex packages of care as provided by the case management service was planned. In this, case management would cease to be a role undertaken by designated social workers with the title case manager within the multidisciplinary team and become a process undertaken by all social workers as appropriate to the needs of the older person. If this course of action were to be pursued, it would be of paramount importance that case management remained focused on users with enduring and multiple needs which spanned the health and social care divide. This would avoid the pitfall characteristic of many services which regard care management as a process or approach applied to all users irrespective of the complexity or otherwise of their needs (Challis, 1994c; Challis et al., 2001a).

Box 11.4   MHOA service: Types of care management appropriate for different levels of response

Type	MHOA service 2004	Projected service delivery arrangements
Administrative	Provides information and advice. Typically not provided directly to users and carers but to colleagues in the social services department to assist them in the provision of care to older people whose mental health is of concern but does not require referral to secondary mental health care	No change
Co-ordinating	Deals with a large volume of referrals needing either a single service or a range of fairly straightforward services which should be properly planned and administered. Undertaken exclusively by social workers	Described as *care* management and undertaken by social workers and nurses specialising in short term work within the team
Intensive	A designated case manager (a social worker) combines the planning and co-ordination with a therapeutic, supportive role for a much smaller number of cases who have complex and frequently changing needs	Described as *case* management and undertaken by all social workers within the MHOA service

Adapted from: SSI (1997a)

Integrated Service Provision

The MHOA service in Lewisham in 2004 represents an example of an experimental case management project which has made a successful transition into mainstream service whilst maintaining many of its core original features of care practice. Box 11.5 summarises the evidence for this and each of the hallmarks of integrated service provision is discussed in the context of the service. Community care of older people with dementia is a challenge to health and social care services due to the complex medical needs of this group, their functional disabilities, and their precarious social support networks, which together contribute to occasional inappropriate use of services (Bergman et al., 1997; Johri et al., 2003). Johri and colleagues reviewed major demonstration programmes for frail older people and noted that cost-effective integrated systems of care were possible, although the ability of such programmes to make an impact upon national expenditure and care depended upon successful extension from demonstration phase to implementation. They concluded that, as here, successful initiatives were those which were large-scale programmes with a single entry point, employing both specialist assessment and case management. They also highlighted the importance of integrating case managers into a multidisciplinary team thereby pairing specialist assessment with long-term case management.

The longevity of case management within the service provides evidence of the incorporation of the research into the multidisciplinary team. However, for it to be construed as part of mainstream provision within the locality required that its links

Box 11.5   Features of effective integrated care for older people

Evidence from demonstration programmes	MHOA service 2004
• Extension of research to mainstream provision	• LCMS integrated into the MHOA service with links defined in a protocol for care management arrangements provided by the local authority social services
• A single point of entry system	• For those in the community requiring assessment or possible hospital admission, a single point of entry
• Incorporating both specialist assessment and case management	• Retaining specialist assessment procedures and extending the number of social workers in the multidisciplinary team undertaking this task; confirmation of continued importance of case management in multidisciplinary teams
• Integrating case managers into the multidisciplinary team	• Management of case managers within the team but budgetary responsibility outside of it

Adapted from Johri et al. (2003)

with care management arrangements for older people provided within the local authority were clarified, so that the specialist service provided for older people with mental health problems was seen as part of a continuum of care management arrangements within the locality. This has required the development of protocols which facilitated decision-making as to whether care management was provided by the specialist MHOA service or the local authority social services department. The 'trick' in this context has been to produce guidance and working arrangements which promote integrated service provision rather than lines of demarcation. Such issues are, of course, not new but policy initiatives provide an added incentive (Cm 4169, 1998; Cm 4818-I, 2000; Department of Health, 2001b; 2002b; Cm 6737, 2006). Johri and colleagues (2003) identified a single point of entry as a core feature of integrated care for older people. The establishment of this in respect of referrals for all community and most inpatient assessments within the MHOA service has been a significant further development of integrated service provision for older people with mental health problems within the locality.

Perhaps most importantly of all, in 2004 there was evidence that assessment and care management arrangements within this multidisciplinary setting were continuing to evolve in a way that reflected the two components identified as important by Johri and colleagues (2003): specialist assessment and case management. Within the MHOA there were plans to develop the assessment procedure through greater standardisation of the process, thereby ensuring greater consistency irrespective of the professional orientation of the team member undertaking it. Such an approach was consistent with the guidance of the SAP (Department of Health, 2002b). It offered the opportunity for NHS staff to undertake care management (as defined within the service) and for social workers to extend their skills and competence in the specialist assessments required by older people with mental health problems. Furthermore, the retention of a discrete case management service, as discussed previously, provided evidence of intensive care management as defined in policy guidance (SSI, 1997a; Department of Health, 2002b) and a differentiated approach to care management which enabled assistance to be targeted on certain older people with mental health problems and as a consequence, complex health and social care needs. A further development would be for the MHOA service to have the associated budgetary responsibility for support. In 2004 this was vested in the local authority but the MHOA service was able to authorise community care packages. Whilst the legislative framework exists to formalise this, it remains a matter of local negotiation to find the most appropriate way to effect it. If this was to be achieved and a means were to be found to allow social workers undertaking case management to have full devolved budgetary responsibility with appropriate accountability, then another hallmark of integrated service provision, as identified by Johri and colleagues, would have been achieved by the MHOA service in Lewisham. It would also have met the requirements for the transparent and equitable allocation of finance enshrined in the personalisation agenda (Department of Health, 2008a; 2009a).

In Retrospect

The Lewisham study offers important insights regarding three current concerns about the development of services and the implementation of policy. These relate to the sustainability of innovatory service models, personalisation and the deployment of personal budgets, and the roll out of the National Dementia Strategy.

A striking feature of the Old Age Mental Health Services in Lewisham is the coherence and logic of the organisational model within which the service operates and the staff undertake their roles (Macdonald, 1991; Murphy and Banerjee, 1993; Macdonald et al., 1994). Not only was this coherence evident but there appeared to be a strong shared vision about the logic of the services, about how and why things were done in a particular way, shared by staff from different disciplinary perspectives. The service model in short is more than the balance of commitments and beliefs negotiated between the current stakeholders. Some considerable time after the initial project was undertaken, it was evident how the case management service had been incorporated within the overall operational model of the service. The importance of such a coherent service model is that it provides the basis for innovatory approaches to be transported and employed in other settings and locations.

As part of the personalisation agenda, the strategy of providing personal budgets to those using social care services has been identified as a strategy to increase choice and maximise the responsiveness and flexibility of support (Department of Health, 2008a). Obviously the mechanisms employed for the management and use of a personal budget will themselves vary according to the capacity and willingness of different groups of people to employ that budget. The IBSEN evaluation of individual budgets in social care noted the less than positive response of older people to what was predominantly a direct payments mode of deployment of budgets (Glendinning et al., 2008). What was needed was a variety of ways of flexibly deploying and managing the personal budget for older people who did not want to take on these tasks themselves. The Lewisham scheme and its related studies (Challis and Davies, 1986; Challis et al., 1995; 2002a) provide a model whereby case managers can deploy resources equivalent to a personal budget flexibly and responsively, maximising choice for individuals for whom a personally managed payment is either not suitable or acceptable. The outcomes of these services for older people and their carers were generally positive.

The Lewisham study also has particular relevance for the implementation of the Government's National Dementia Strategy in which a number of features of a comprehensive community personal support service are described (Department of Health, 2009b, 47–8). These include specialist dementia home care; flexibility to respond to changing needs; access to personalised social activity, short breaks and day services; responsiveness to crisis; flexible and responsive respite care in a variety of settings. These were all features delivered as part of the Lewisham Case Management Scheme. Thus, the lessons from the scheme offer more than immediate positive findings from a new approach to supporting older people with dementia at home. It provides a sound evidence base for key aspects of both the roll-out of personalisation for people with dementia and their carers and for the implementation of the National Dementia Strategy.

Appendix 1
Interview Schedules: Domains of Enquiry

All the measures included in the interview schedules in this study are listed below, followed by an indication of who completed each one. In some cases the views of more than one person were sought:

OP – older person with dementia
C – carer(s)
I – key informant (person who had most hours' contact with client, either informal or paid carer)
R – researcher rating

Client Measures

Functioning and Ill-Being

i. *Organic Brain Score (OBS)* This scale comprised part of the Comprehensive Assessment and Referral Evaluation (CARE) assessment technique (Gurland et al., 1977). A number of questions were included in the client interview schedule and these provided a measure of the level of cognitive impairment. [OP]

ii. *ADL functioning* This describes the actual support provided and performance of the client (i.e. not their potential ability) on 14 activities of daily living (ADL) domains. It was based on that used for similar studies (Bebbington et al., 1986; Davies et al., 1990; Challis et al., 1995). [C / I / R]

iii. *The Behaviour Rating Scale (CAPE)* was a standardised measure that consisted of the subscales 'physical disability', 'apathy', 'communication difficulties' and 'social disturbance'. The BRS formed part of the Clifton Assessment Procedure for the Elderly (CAPE) (Pattie and Gilleard, 1979). [C / I / R]

iv. *'Signs of distress and disturbing actions'* This was based on Platt et al.'s (1980) Behaviour–Mood Disturbance Scale. This looked at a variety of signs of distress and ill-being, and disturbing actions of the client. [I]

v. *Misery/depression* was an item taken from Platt et al.'s Scale (as mentioned above). [I]

Perspectives

    i. *Care dissatisfaction* was created specifically for this research study. It comprised a number of closed questions regarding problems with care or feelings of burden. [OP]

    ii. *Activity occurrence* was also designed for use on this study and it sought to question clients about their awareness of activities and social support. [OP]

    iii. *Activity dissatisfaction* also devised for this study, and comprised a mixture of items asking for example, 'Do you feel bored?', 'Do you have enough to do to keep occupied?' [OP]

    iv. *Satisfaction with lifestyle within the home* These questions were derived from a study by Peace et al. (1982). [OP]

    v. *Depression* This used the CARE Depression Scale (Gurland et al., 1977; 1984) which was adapted from the Geriatric Mental State Schedule (Copeland et al., 1976) and further refined by Lindesay et al. (1989). [OP]

Quality of Life

    i. *Client activity score* was a summary measure of frequency of: occurrence of activities at home; visitors; and going out. It was based upon Wing (1989). [C/ I/ R]

    ii. *Client length of time spent alone* This recorded the average number of hours in the waking day (6a.m. – 6p.m.) that the client was totally alone, including weekends. [C/ I/ R]

    iii. *Carers overall perception* was a five item Semantic Differential Scale, covering the items: boring/interesting, enjoyable/miserable, useless/ worthwhile, friendly/lonely, full/empty, based on Lorr and Wunderlich (1988). [C]

    iv. *Researcher's perception of life dissatisfaction* These were rated following the interview with the client on a variety of domains, including expressed enthusiasm, dissatisfaction, and awareness of social contact. They were based on ratings used by Neugarten (1961). [R]

    v. *Perceived change in activities and company* This was an item devised for the study to code perceived change for each six-month period, 'a little/ much worse, same, a little/much better'. [C]

Quality of Care

    i. *Personal care and environment* This was based on a number of items taken from the MEAP Scale (Moos and Lemke, 1984), which rated the client's quality of personal care and environment, 'home neat and tidy'. [R]

    ii. *Satisfaction with care* was designed for this study for completion by a carer living apart from the client. It used a seven point visual analogue scale ranging from 'I feel extremely dissatisfied' to 'I feel extremely satisfied' relating to a variety of care items. [C]

iii. *Service satisfaction* was a visual analogue scale devised for this study. This was to give an overall rating of 'how satisfied are you with the help you and *<client>* receive?'. [C]

Carer Measures

Support to Client

The following measures were based on those used in other studies (Bebbington et al., 1986; Challis et al., 1995).

i. *Main carer contribution to client care* describes the number of tasks from 14 activities of daily living domains, with which the main carer provided support. [C]

ii. *Other carer's contribution to client care* This was the same as above but described support given by any other carers, to be completed by the most appropriate person. [C]

iii. *Paid services contribution to client care* describes the input of any private or statutory services and was designed for completion by a carer, preferably the same individual completing (i) and (ii) above. [C]

iv. *Main carer hours input* This information reflected the number of hours per week the main carer spent in contact with, or doing things on behalf of the client. [C]

v. *Other carer hours input* This information reflected the number of hours per week other carers spent in contact with, or doing things on behalf of the client. [C]

vi. *Hours input (cost to carer)* Carer costings were devised specifically for the study and measured the total number of family carer hours, main carer hours, and other carer hours and were based on all descriptive data collected. [R]

Burden

i. *Carer felt burden* was adapted for this study to measure the effect of caring on five life domains including finances, sleep, work, social and leisure. The item format was derived from Platt et al. (1980) and Challis et al. (1995). [C]

ii. *Carer burden (perceived change)* was designed for this study to measure perceived change in each six-month period for six domains of life burden including: finances, sleep, work, social/leisure, strain and relationship with client. [C]

iii. *Carer overall strain* This was based on a standardised measure (Morris et al., 1988) to rate carers' overall level of strain on a visual analogue scale, ranging from 'I feel no strain', to 'I feel severe strain'. [C]

iv. *Tension in relationship between client and carer* This was derived from a study by Brown and Rutter (1966). [R]

Malaise

i. *Malaise Inventory* This was a well-established measure of symptoms related to carer stress (Rutter et al., 1970). Two subscales, *Malaise Physical subscale,* and *Malaise Psychological subscale* were derived from this (Nolan et al., 1990). [C]

Client and Carer Measures

Overall Need and Related Outcomes

i. *Overall need* This scale was designed for the study and covered a variety of domains, mainly ADL tasks plus need for day care/respite/day sitting. For clients with a carer this included three additional items: night sitter, respite at home, and relatives group. [I]

ii. *ADL need shortfall* This was based on a PSSRU scale (Challis, 1981; Challis and Davies, 1986; Challis et al., 1995; 2002a) looking particularly at four domains: rising and retiring, personal care needs, daily domestic assistance, weekly domestic assistance. [R]

iii. *Special carer support* This scale was designed for the study for completion by a carer who lived with the client, to describe any special needs or support provided, for example, attendance at a relatives' group. [C]

iv. *Overall risk* This was a scale designed for the study. It assessed risk as present or absent in a variety of domains: carer distress; client's ADL; client's health; client's behaviour; and environmental factors. These were summed as an aggregate measure of risk. [R]

Appendix 2

Services: Sources of Record of Receipt and Derivation of Price

Service	Derivation of price		Record of receipt
	Local	**Standard reference**	
1. Hospital – day patients, acute and long-term care	Financial returns to SE Thames Regional Health Authority 1990, Domus: service receipt[2]	DHSS[1] (1982) Beecham et al. (1993) Kavanagh et al. (1993)	Computerised hospital admission system
2. Residential and nursing home care	Social Services Committee report on payment for private and voluntary care	Beecham et al. (1993)	SSD[3] central registry
3. SSD[3] day care	Social Services Committee report and SSD[3] finance department	Davies and Challis (1986) Netten (1994)	CAPRE[4] Case records
4. Social work	Costs of visits with overheads	Netten (1994)	SSD[3] case files
5. CMHT[5] for older people, case managers	Costs of visits with overheads	Netten (1994) von Abendorff (1994)	CMHT[5] case files
6. Home care	SSD[3] finance department	Netten (1994)	CAPRE[4] Case records
7. Paid helper service and private sector domiciliary care	Costs of visits with overheads		Service receipts Paid helper payment analysis
8. Community nursing service	Costs of visits with overheads	Netten (1994)	Computerised record system
9. Other:			CAPRE[4] Case files
a. Aids and adaptations		PSSRU Care Management studies (Challis and Davies, 1986)	
b. Incontinence services and equipment	Community nursing service		
c. Sheltered housing	Housing Department	Netten (1994)	
d. Voluntary sector groups/day care	Consultation with services	Bebbington (1993)	
e. Other professionals including chiropody and voluntary sector e.g. carer support	Local data returns SSD[3]	Netten (1994), Knapp et al. (1989)	
f. GP		Butler and Calnan (1987), Netten (1994)	
g. Adult family placement		Netten (1994)	

Note to Appendix 2:

(1993/94 prices)

1. DHSS: Department of Health and Social Security
2. Domus: specialist care facility for older people with dementia provided by the NHS
3. SSD: *S*ocial Services Department
4. CAPRE: Case Planning and Review Form
5. CMHT: Community Mental Health Team

References

Abendstern, M., Reilly, S., Hughes, J., Venables, D. and Challis, D. (2006) Levels of integration and specialisation within professional community teams for people with dementia, *International Journal of Geriatric Psychiatry*, 21, 77–85.

Abendstern, M., Hughes, J., Clarkson, P., Sutcliffe, C. and Challis, D. (2007) A Systematic Evaluation of the Development and Impact of the Single Assessment Process in England. Stage II – Impact of the SAP from the perspective of multiple stakeholders, Volume 4 – The National Survey of SAP Lead Officers, Discussion Paper M148, Personal Social Services Research Unit, University of Manchester [not publicly available].

Abrams, P. (1977) Community care: some research problems and priorities, *Policy and Politics,* 6, 125–151.

Akkerman, R. and Ostwald, S. (2004) Reducing anxiety in Alzheimer's disease family caregivers: The effectiveness of a nine-week cognitive-behavioural intervention, *American Journal of Alzheimer's Disease and Other Dementias*, 19, 117–123.

Allen, C. and Beecham, J. (1993) Costing services: ideals and reality, in Netten, A. and Beecham, J. (eds), *Costing Community Care: Theory and Practice*, Ashgate, Aldershot.

Allen, I. and Perkins, E. (1995) *The Future of Family Care for Elderly People*, HMSO, London.

Allen, I., Hogg, D. and Peace, S. (1992) *Elderly People: Choice, Participation and Satisfaction,* Policy Studies Institute, London.

Altman, D., Gore, S., Gardner, M. and Pocock, S. (2000) Statistical guidelines for contributors to medical journals, in Altman, D.G., Machin, D., Bryant, T.N. and Gardner, M.J. (eds) *Statistics With Confidence,* BMJ Books, Bristol.

American Psychiatric Association (1987) *Diagnostic and Statistical Manual, 3rd edition Revised (DSM-IIIR),* American Psychiatric Association, Washington DC.

Andresen, E., Lollar, D. and Meyers, A. (2000) Disability outcomes research: Why this supplement on this topic, at this time?, *Archives of Physical Medicine and Rehabilitation,* 81, (Suppl. 2), S1–S4.

Andrew, T., Moriarty, J., Levin, E. and Webb, S. (2000) Outcome of referral to social services department for people with cognitive impairment, *International Journal of Geriatric Psychiatry*, 15, 406–414.

Aneshensel, C., Pearlin, L., Levy-Storms, L. and Schuler, R. (2000) The transition from home to nursing home. Mortality among people with dementia, *Journal of Gerontological Social Sciences,* 55, S152–S162.

Anthony, W., Cohen, M., Farkas, M. and Cohen, B. (1988) Clinical care update, the chronically mentally ill. Case management – more than a response to a dysfunctional system, *Community Mental Health Journal*, 24, 219–228.

Applebaum, R., Seidl, F.W. and Austin, C.D. (1980) The Wisconsin Community Care Organization: preliminary findings from the Milwaukee experiment, *The Gerontologist*, 20, 3, 350 -355.

Applebaum, R. and Austin, C. (1990) *Long-term Care Case Management: Design and Evaluation,* Springer Publishing Co., New York.

Arber, S., Gilbert, N. and Evandrou, M. (1988) Gender, household composition and receipt of domiciliary services by the elderly disabled, *Journal of Social Policy*, 17, 2, 153–175.

Arksey, H., Jackson, K., Croucher, K., Weatherly, H., Golder, S., Hare, P., Newbronner, E. and Baldwin, S. (2004) Review of respite services and short-term breaks for carers for people with dementia, Report for the National Co-ordinating Centre for NHS Service Delivery and Organisation R&D (NCCSDO), Social Policy Research Unit, The University of York, York.

Askham, J. and Thompson, C. (1990) *Dementia and Home Care: A Research Report on a Home Support Scheme for Dementia Sufferers*, Age Concern, Mitcham.

Audit Commission (1985) *Managing Services for Elderly People More Effectively*, HMSO, London.

Audit Commission (1986) *Making A Reality of Community Care,* HMSO, London.

Audit Commission (1993) Taking care: progress with care in the community, *Health and Personal Social Services Bulletin No. 1*, December 1993, HMSO, London.

Audit Commission (1996) Balancing the care equation: progress with community care, *Community Care Bulletin Number 3*, March, HMSO, London.

Audit Commission (1997) *The Coming of Age: Improving Care Services for Older People*, Audit Commission, London.

Audit Commission (2000) *Forget Me Not: Mental Health Services for Older People*, Audit Commission, London.

Audit Commission (2002) *Forget Me Not 2002: Developing Mental Health Services for Older People in England*, Audit Commission, London.

Audit Commission (2004) *Older People- Independence and Well-being*, Audit Commission, London.

Audit Commission (2006) *Living Well in Later Life: A Review of Progress Against the National Service Framework for Older People*, Commission for Healthcare Audit and Inspection, London.

Baldwin, C. (2006) Reflections on ethics, dementia and technology, in Woolham, J. (ed.) *Assistive Technology in Dementia Care: Developing the Role of*

Technology in the Care and Rehabilitation of People with Dementia – Current Trends and Perspectives, Hawker Publications, London.

Ball, M., Whittington, F., Perkins, M., Patterson, V., Hollingsworth, C., King, S. and Combs, B. (2000) Quality of life in assisted living facilities: Viewpoints of residents, *Journal of Applied Gerontology*, 19, 3, 304–325.

Bamford, C. and Bruce, E. (2000) Defining the outcomes of community care: the perspectives of older people with dementia and their carers, *Ageing and Society*, 20, 543–570.

Banerjee, S. and Chan, J. (2008) Organization of old age psychiatric services, *Psychiatry,* 7, 49–53.

Banerjee, S. and Macdonald, A. (1996) Mental disorder in an elderly home care population: Associations with health and social service use, *British Journal of Psychiatry*,168, 6, 750–756.

Banerjee, S., Murray, J., Foley, B., Atkins, L., Schneider, J. and Mann, A. (2003) Predictors of institutionalisation in people with dementia, *Journal of Neurology, Neurosurgery and Psychiatry*, 74, 1315–1316.

Banerjee, S., Willis, R., Matthews, D., Contell, F., Chan, J. and Murray, J. (2007) Improving the quality of care for mild to moderate dementia: an evaluation of the Croydon Memory Service Model, *International Journal of Geriatric Psychiatry*, 22, 782–788.

Barnett, E. (1997) Listening to people with dementia and their carers, in Marshall, M. (ed.) *State of the Art in Dementia Care*, Centre for Policy on Ageing, London.

Bauld, L., Chesterman, J., Davies, B., Judge, K. and Mangalore, R. (2000a) *Caring for Older People: An Assessment of Community Care in the 1990s*, Ashgate, Aldershot.

Bauld, L., Chesterman, J. and Judge, K. (2000b) Measuring satisfaction with social care amongst older service users: issues from the literature, *Health and Social Care*, 8, 5, 316–324.

Beardshaw, V. and Towell, D. (1990) *Assessment and Care Management: Implications for the Implementation of 'Caring for People'*, Briefing Paper No. 10, King's Fund Institute, London.

Bebbington, A. (1993) Calculating unit costs of a centre for people with AIDS/HIV, in Netten, A. and Beecham, J. (eds) *Costing Community Care: Theory and Practice*, Avebury, Aldershot.

Bebbington, A., Charnley, H., Davies, B., Ferlie, E., Hughes, M. and Twigg, J. (1986) *The Domiciliary Care Project: Meeting the Needs of the Elderly. Interim Report,* Discussion Paper 456, Personal Social Services Research Unit, University of Kent at Canterbury.

Beecham, J., Cambridge, P., Hallam, A. and Knapp, M. (1993) The costs of domus care, *International Journal of Geriatric Psychiatry*, 8, 827–831.

Bergman, H., Beland, F., Lebel, P., Contandriopoulos, A. P., Tousignant, P., Brunelle, Y., Kaufman, T., Leibovich, E., Rodriguez, R. and Clarfield, M. (1997) Care for Canada's frail elderly population: Fragmentation or integration?, *Canadian Medical Association Journal*, 157, 1116–1121.

Bergmann, K., Foster, E.M., Justice, A.W. and Matthews, V. (1978) Management of the demented elderly patient in the community, *British Journal of Psychiatry*, 132, 441–449.

Bernabei, R., Landi, F., Gambassi, G., Sgadari, A., Zuccala, G., Mor, V., Rubenstein, L. and Carbonin, P. (1998) Randomised trial of impact of model of integrated care and case management for older people living in the community, *British Medical Journal*, 316, 1348–1351.

Bjorkman, T. and Hansson, L. (2000) What do case managers do? An investigation of case manager interventions and their relationship to client outcome, *Social Psychiatry and Psychiatric Epidemiology*, 35, 43–50.

Bland, R., Hudson, H. and Dobson, B. (1992) *The EPIC Evaluation: Interim Report*, University of Stirling, Scotland.

Bond, G.R. and McGrew, J.H. (1995) Assertive outreach for frequent users of psychiatric hospitals: A meta-analysis, *Journal of Mental Health Administration*, 22, 1, 4–17.

Bowes, A. (2007) Research on the costs of long-term care for older people – current and emerging issues, *Social Policy and Society*, 6, 447–459.

Briar, S. and Miller, H. (1971) *Problems and Issues in Social Casework,* Columbia University Press, New York.

Brodaty, H. and Gresham, M. (1989) Effect of a training programme to reduce stress in carers of patients with dementia, *British Medical Journal*, 299, 1375–1379.

Brodaty, H. and Gresham, M. (1992) Prescribing residential respite care for dementia – effects, side-effects, indications and dosage, *International Journal of Geriatric Psychiatry*, 7, 357–362.

Brodaty, H., Green, A. and Koschera, A. (2003) Meta-analysis of psychosocial interventions for caregivers of people with dementia, *Journal of the American Geriatric Society*, 51, 657–664.

Brown, G. and Rutter, M. (1966) The measurement of family activities and relationships, *Human Relations*, 19, 241–263.

Brown, P., Challis, D. and von Abendorff, R. (1996) The work of a community mental health team for the elderly: referrals, caseloads, contact history and outcomes, *International Journal of Geriatric Psychiatry*, 11, 29–39.

Burns, A., Guthrie, E., Marino-Francis, F., Morris, J., Russell, E., Margison, F., Lennon, S. and Byrne, J. (2005) Brief psychotherapy in Alzheimer's disease: randomised controlled trial, *British Journal of Psychiatry*, 187, 143–147.

Bush, J. (2003) Working in Partnership, *Working with Older People*, 7, 1, 26–29.

Butler, J.R. and Calnan, N. (1987) *Too Many Patients? A Study of the Economy of Time and Standards in General Practice*, Gower, Aldershot.

Byford, S., McDaid, D. and Sefton, T. (2003) *Because it's Worth It: A Practical Guide to Conducting Economic Evaluations in the Social Welfare Field*, Joseph Rowntree Foundation, York.

Bywaters, P. and Harris, A. (1998) Supporting carers: is practice still sexist?, *Health and Social Care in the Community*, 6, 6, 458–463.

Caldock, K. (1993) A preliminary study of changes in assessment: examining the relationship between recent policy and practitioner's knowledge, opinions and practice, *Health and Social Care*, 1, 139–146.

Caldock, K. (1994) The new assessment: Moving towards holism or new roads to fragmentation?, in Challis, D., Davies, B. and Traske, K. (eds) *Community Care: New Agendas and Challenges from the UK and Overseas*, Arena, Aldershot.

Campbell, D.T. and Stanley, J.C. (1966) *Experimental and Quasi-Experimental Designs for Research*, Rand McNally, Chicago, Illinois.

Cantley, C. and Smith, G. (2001) Research, policy and practice in dementia care, in Cantley, C. (ed.) *A Handbook of Dementia Care*, Open University Press, Philadelphia.

Carcagno, G.J. and Kemper, P. (1988) The evaluation of the National Long Term Care Demonstration. 1. An overview of the channeling demonstration and its evaluation, *Health Services Research*, 23, 1, 1–22.

Care and Social Services Inspectorate Wales (CSSIW) (2008a) *Chief Inspector's Overview, Care and Social Services in Wales*, CSSIW, Nantgarw.

Care and Social Services Inspectorate Wales (CSSIW) (2008b) *Social Services in Wales Annual Report 2006–2007*, CSSIW, Nantgarw.

Care Services Improvement Partnership (CSIP) (2005) *Everybody's Business. Integrated Mental Health Services for Older Adults: A Service Development Guide. Key Messages for Commissioners,* Department of Health, Leeds.

Care Services Improvement Partnership (CSIP) (2007) *Strengthening the Involvement of People with Dementia*, Department of Health, Leeds.

Carpenter, I. (2005) Aging in the United Kingdom and Europe – A snapshot of the future?, *Journal of the American Geriatrics Society*, 53, S310-S313.

Carpenter, I., Gambassi, G., Topinkova, E., Schroll, M., Finne-Soveri, H., Henrard, J.C., Garms-Homolova, V., Jonsson, P., Frijters, D., Ljunggren, G., Sørbye, L., Wagner, C., Onder, G., Pedone, C. and Bernabei, R. (2004) Community care in Europe. The Aged In Home Care project (AdHOC), *Aging Clinical and Experimental Research*, 16, 259–269.

Cash, M. (2006) Exploring the potential of existing low-key technological devices to support people with dementia to live at home, in Woolham, J. (ed.) *Assistive Technology in Dementia Care: Developing the Role of Technology in the Care and Rehabilitation of People with Dementia – Current Trends and Perspectives*, Hawker Publications, London.

Central Council for Education and Training in Social Work (1975) *Working Group Discussion Paper on Education and Training for Social Work*, Paper 10, Central Council for Education and Training in Social Work, London.

Central Statistical Office, (1994) *Family Spending: A Report on the 1993 Family Expenditure Survey,* HMSO, London.

Centre for Policy on Ageing (CPA) (1984) *Home Life: A Code of Practice for Residential Care,* Centre for Policy on Ageing, London.

Challis, D. (1981) The measurement of outcome in social care of the elderly, *Journal of Social Policy*, 10, 2, 179–208.

Challis, D. (1992a) Community care of elderly people: bringing together scarcity and choice, needs and costs, *Financial Accountability and Management*, 8, 2, 77–95.

Challis, D. (1992b) The care of the elderly in Europe. New perspectives – social care, *European Journal of Gerontology*, 1, 334–347.

Challis, D. (1993) Alternative to long-stay care, in Levy, R., Howard, R. and Burns, A. (eds) *Treatment and Care in Old Age Psychiatry*, Wrightson Biomedical Publishing Ltd, Hampshire.

Challis, D. (1994a) Care management, in Malin, N.A. (ed.) *Implementing Community Care,* Open University Press, Buckingham.

Challis, D. (1994b) Case management: A review of UK developments and issues, in Titterton, M. (ed.) *Caring for People in the Community: The New Welfare*, Jessica Kingsley Publishers, London.

Challis, D. (1994c) *Implementing Caring for People. Care Management: Factors Influencing its Development in the Implementation of Community Care*, Department of Health, London.

Challis, D. (1998) Integrating health and social care: problems, opportunities and possibilities, *Research Policy and Planning*, 16, 2, 7–12.

Challis, D. and Chesterman, J. (1985) A system for monitoring social work activity with the frail elderly, *British Journal of Social Work*, 15, 115–132.

Challis, D. and Darton, R. (1990) Evaluation research and experiment in social gerontology, in Peace, S. (ed.) *Researching Social Gerontology: Concepts, Methods, Issues*, Sage, London.

Challis, D. and Davies, B. (1986) *Case Management in Community Care: An Evaluated Experiment in the Home Care of the Elderly*, Gower, Aldershot.

Challis, D. and Ferlie, E. (1987) Changing patterns of fieldwork organization: II: The team leaders' view, *British Journal of Social Work*, 17, 2, 147–167.

Challis, D. and Hughes, J. (2000) Multidisciplinary approaches in the management of dementia – b. Social work, in O'Brien, J., Ames, D. and Burns, A. (eds) *Dementia, Second Edition*, Arnold, London.

Challis, D. and Hughes, J. (2002) Frail people at the margins of care: some recent research findings, *British Journal of Psychiatry*, 180, 126–130.

Challis, D., Knapp, M. and Davies, B. (1988) Cost effectiveness in social care, in Lishman, J. (ed.) *Research Highlights in Social Work 8: Evaluation, Second edition,* Jessica Kingsley Publishers, London.

Challis, D., Chessum, R., Chesterman, J., Luckett, R. and Traske, K. (1990) *Case Management in Social and Health Care: The Gateshead Community Care Scheme*, Personal Social Services Research Unit, University of Kent at Canterbury.

Challis, D., Chesterman, J. and Traske, K. (1993) Case management: Costing the experiments, in Netten, A. and Beecham, J. (eds) *Costing Community Care: Theory and Practice*, Ashgate, Aldershot.

Challis, D., Darton, R., Johnson, L., Stone, M. and Traske, K. (1995) *Care Management and Health Care of Older People: The Darlington Community Care Project*, Ashgate, Aldershot.

Challis, D., von Abendorff, R., Brown, P. and Chesterman, J. (1997a) Care management and dementia: an evaluation of the Lewisham Intensive Case Management Scheme, in Hunter, S. (ed.) *Dementia. Challenges and New Directions*, Jessica Kingsley Publishers, London.

Challis, D., Hughes, J., Schneider, J., Carpenter, I. and Huxley, P. (1997b) *Enabling Information and Technology Support for Community Focused Healthcare. An Evaluation of the Requirement for National Consistency in the Definition of Care Packages*, Discussion Paper 1310/M004, Personal Social Services Research Unit, University of Kent at Canterbury and University of Manchester.

Challis, D., Darton, R. and Stewart, K. (1998a) Linking community care and health care: A new role for secondary health care services, in Challis, D., Darton, R. and Stewart, K. (eds) *Community Care, Secondary Health Care and Care Management*, Ashgate, Aldershot.

Challis, D., Darton, R., Hughes, J., Huxley, P. and Stewart, K. (1998b) Emerging models of care management for older people and those with mental health problems in the United Kingdom, *Journal of Case Management*, 7, 4, 153–160.

Challis, D., Darton, R., Hughes, J., Stewart, K. and Weiner, K. (1999) *Mapping and Evaluation of Care Management Arrangements for Older People and Those With Mental Health Problems: An Overview of Care Management Arrangements*, Discussion Paper 1519/M009, Personal Social Services Research Unit, University of Kent at Canterbury and University of Manchester [not publicly available].

Challis, D., Darton, R., Hughes, J., Stewart, K. and Weiner, K. (2001a) Intensive care-management at home: an alternative to institutional care?, *Age and Ageing*, 30, 409–413.

Challis, D., Darton, R., Hughes, J., Stewart, K. and Weiner, K. (2001b) *Mapping and Evaluation of Care Management Arrangements for Older People and Those with Mental Health Problems*, Discussion Paper 1692/M029, Personal Social Services Research Unit, University of Kent at Canterbury and University of Manchester [not publicly available].

Challis, D., Chesterman, J., Luckett, R., Stewart, K. and Chessum, R. (2002a) *Care Management in Social and Primary Health Care. The Gateshead Community Care Scheme,* Ashgate, Aldershot.

Challis, D., Reilly, S., Hughes, J., Burns, A., Gilchrist H. and Wilson, K. (2002b) Policy, organisation and practice of specialist old age psychiatry in England, *International Journal of Geriatric Psychiatry,* 17, 1018–1026.

Challis, D., von Abendorff, R., Brown, P., Chesterman, J. and Hughes, J. (2002c) Care management, dementia care and specialist mental health services: an evaluation, *International Journal of Geriatric Psychiatry*, 17, 315–325.

Challis, D., Clarkson, P., Williamson, J., Hughes, J., Burns, A., Venables, D. and Weinberg, A. (2004) The value of specialist clinical assessment of older people prior to entry to care homes, *Age and Ageing,* 33, 25–34.

Challis, D., Stewart, K., Donnelly, M., Weiner, K. and Hughes, J. (2006a) Care management for older people: Does integration make a difference?, *Journal of Interprofessional Care*, 20, 335–348.

Challis, D., Clarkson, P. and Warburton, R. (2006b) *Performance Indicators in Social Care for Older People*, Ashgate, Aldershot.

Challis, D., Hughes, J., Jacobs, S., Stewart, K. and Weiner, K. (2007) Are different forms of care management for older people in England associated with variations in case-mix, service use and care managers' use of time? *Ageing and Society*, 27, 25–48.

Challis, D., Hughes, J., Clarkson, P., Tucker, S., O'Shea, S., Brand, C., Abendstern, M. and Wenborn, J. (2008) *Enhancing the Efficiency and Effectiveness of Assessment in Community Care, Volume II, Self Assessment Pilot Projects: User Needs and Outcomes*, Discussion Paper M178, Personal Social Services Research Unit, University of Manchester [not publicly available].

Chilvers, D. (2003) The case for specialist home care for people with dementia, *Journal of Dementia Care*, Jan/Feb, 20–21.

Chiu, L., Tang, K., Shyu, W., Huang, C. and Wang, S. (2000) Cost analysis of home care and nursing home services in the Southern Taiwan area, *Public Health Nursing*, 17, 325–335.

Chu, P., Edwards, J., Levin, R. and Thomson, J. (2000) The use of clinical case management for early stage Alzheimer's patients and their families, *American Journal of Alzheimer's Disease and Other Dementias*, 15, 5, 284–290.

Clarke, C.L. (1999) Family care-giving for people with dementia: some implications for policy and professional practice, *Journal of Advanced Nursing*, 29, 3, 712–720.

Cm 849 (1989) *Caring for People: Community Care in the Next Decade and Beyond*, HMSO, London.

Cm 4169 (1998) *Modernising Social Services. Promoting Independence, Improving Protection, Raising Standards*, The Stationery Office, London.

Cm 4818-I (2000) *The NHS Plan: A Plan for Investment. A Plan for Reform*, The Stationery Office, London.

Cm 6268 (2004) *The NHS Improvement Plan: Putting People at the Heart of Public Services*, The Stationery Office, London.

Cm 6499 (2005) *Independence, Well-being and Choice: Our Vision for the Future of Social Care for Adults in England*, The Stationery Office, London.

Cm 6737 (2006) *Our Health, Our Care, Our Say: A New Direction for Community Services,* The Stationery Office, London.

Cmnd 6404 (1942) *Inter-Departmental Committee on Social Insurance and Allied Services: Report by Sir William Beveridge*, HMSO, London.

Cmnd 169 (1957) *Royal Commission on the Law Relating to Mental Illness and Mental Deficiency 1954–1957: Report*, HMSO, London.

Cmnd 1973 (1963) *Health and Welfare: The Development of Community Care,* HMSO, London.

Cmnd 3703 (1968) *Report of the Committee on Local Authority and Allied Personal Social Services,* HMSO, London.

Cmnd 6233 (1975) *Better Services for the Mentally Ill,* HMSO, London.

Cmnd 8173 (1981) *Growing Older,* HMSO, London.

Cohen, C.A. and Pushkar, D. (1999) Transitions in care. Lessons learned from a longitudinal study of dementia care, *American Journal of Geriatric Psychiatry,* 7, 139–146.

Cohen-Mansfield, J., Marx, M.S., Lipson, S. and Werner, P. (1999) Predictors of mortality in nursing home residents, *Journal of Clinical Epidemiology,* 52, 273–280.

Coleman, B. (1995) European models of long-term care in the home and community, *International Journal of Health Services,* 25, 3, 455–474.

Coles, R.J., von Abendorff, R. and Herzberg, J.L. (1991) The impact of a new community mental health team in an inner city psychiatric service, *International Journal of Geriatric Psychiatry,* 6, 1, 31–39.

Collighan, G., Macdonald, A., Herzberg, J., Philpot, M. and Lindesay, J. (1993) An evaluation of the multidisciplinary approach to psychiatric diagnosis in elderly people, *British Medical Journal,* 306, 821–824.

Comas-Herrera, A., Wittenberg, R., Costa-Font, J., Gori, C., Di Maio, A., Patxo, C., Pickard, L., Possi, A. and Rothgang, H. (2006) Future long-term care expenditure in Germany, Spain, Italy and the United Kingdom, *Ageing and Society,* 26, 285–302.

Comas-Herrera, A., Wittenberg, R., Pickard, L. and Knapp, M. (2007) Cognitive impairment in older people: future demand for long-term care services and the associated costs, *International Journal of Geriatric Psychiatry,* 22, 1037–1045.

Commission for Social Care Inspection (CSCI) (2006) *Time to Care? An Overview of Home Care Services for Older People in England, 2006,* CSCI, London

Commission for Social Care Inspection (CSCI) (2008) *See Me, Not Just the Dementia,* CSCI, London.

Committee of Public Accounts (2008) *Improving Services and Support for People with Dementia. Sixth Report of Session 2007–08,* The Stationery Office, London.

Copeland, J.R.M., Kelleher, M.J., Kellet, J.M., Gourlay, A.J., Gurland, B.J., Fleiss, J.L. and Sharpe, L. (1976) A semi-structured clinical interview for the assessment of diagnosis and mental state in the elderly. The Geriatric Mental State Schedule: 1. Development and reliability, *Psychological Medicine,* 16, 89–99.

Curtis, L. (2007) *Unit Costs of Health and Social Care,* Personal Social Services Research Unit, Kent.

Cypher, J. (1982) Team leadership in the social services, in Cypher, J. (ed.) *Team Leadership in the Social Services,* BASW Publications, Birmingham.

Dant, T., Carley, M., Gearing, B. and Johnson, M. (1989) *Co-ordinating Care: Final Report of the Care for Elderly People at Home (CEPH) Project*, Open University, Milton Keynes, and Policy Studies Institute, London.

Darton, R. (2004) What types of home are closing? The characteristics of homes that closed between 1996–2001, *Health and Social Care in the Community*, 12, 254–264.

Davey, B., Levin, E., Iliffe, S. and Kharicha, K. (2005) Integrating health and social care: implications for joint working and community care outcomes for older people, *Journal of Interprofessional Care*, 19, 22–34.

Davies, B. and Challis, D. (1986) *Matching Resources to Needs in Community Care: An Evaluated Demonstration of a Long-Term Care Model*, Gower, Aldershot.

Davies, B. and Knapp, M. (1981) *Old People's Homes and the Production of Welfare,* Routledge and Kegan Paul, Henley.

Davies, B., Bebbington, A., and Charnley, H. (1990) *Resources, Needs and Outcomes in Community-based Care*, Avebury, Aldershot.

Davies, S. (2001) The care needs of older people and family caregivers in continuing care settings, in Nolan, M., Davies, S. and Grant, G. (eds) *Working With Older People and Their Families: Key Issues in Policy and Practice,* Open University Press, Buckingham.

Degenholtz, H., Kane, R.A., Kane, R.L. and Fich, M.D. (1999) Long term care case managers' out-of-home placement decisions – An application of hierarchical logistic regression, *Research On Aging*, 21, 240–74.

Delaney, S., Garavan, R., McGee, H. and Tynan, A. (2001) *Care and Case Management for Older People in Ireland. An outline of current status and a best practice model for service development,* Report No. 66, National Council on Ageing and Older People, Dublin.

Dening, T. (1992) Community psychiatry of old age. A UK perspective, *International Journal of Geriatric Psychiatry*, 7, 757–766.

Department of Health (1990a) *Health and Social Services Development: 'Caring for People'. The Care Programme Approach for People with a Mental Illness Referred to the Specialist Psychiatric Services*, HC(90)23/LASSL(90)11, Department of Health, London.

Department of Health (1990b) *Community Care in the Next Decade and Beyond: Policy Guidance,* HMSO, London.

Department of Health (1993) *Monitoring and Development: Assessment Special Study*, Department of Health, London.

Department of Health (1994a) *Monitoring and Development: Care Management Special Study,* Department of Health, London.

Department of Health (1994b) *Inspection of Assessment and Care Management Arrangements in Social Services Departments, Oct. 1993–March 1994*, Department of Health, London.

Department of Health (1995) *Building Bridges: A Guide to Arrangements for Inter-agency Working for the Care and Protection of Severely Mentally Ill People,* Department of Health, London.

Department of Health (1996a) *Carers (Recognition and Services) Act 1995 Policy Guidance and Practice Guide,* Department of Health, London.

Department of Health (1996b) *Caring for People at Home – Part II. Report of a Second Inspection of Arrangements for Assessment and Delivery of Home Care Services,* CI(96)34, Department of Health, London.

Department of Health (1997a) *At Home with Dementia: Inspection of Services for Older People with Dementia in the Community,* CI(97)03, Department of Health, London.

Department of Health (1997b) *The Cornerstone of Care: Inspection of Care Planning for Older People,* CI(97)21, Department of Health, London.

Department of Health (1997c) *Better Services for Vulnerable People,* EL(97)62, CI(97)24, Department of Health, London.

Department of Health, (1998) *Care Management Study – Care Management Arrangements,* CI(98)15, Department of Health, London.

Department of Health (1999a) *Caring About Carers. A National Strategy for Carers,* LASSL(99)2, Department of Health, London.

Department of Health (1999b) *Fit for the Future? National required standards for residential and nursing homes for older people consultation document,* Department of Health, London.

Department of Health (2000a) *Community Care (Direct Payments) Amendment Regulations,* (LAC(2000)1), Department of Health, London.

Department of Health (2000b) *A Quality Strategy for Social Care,* LASSL(2000)9, Department of Health, London.

Department of Health (2001a) *Community Care Statistics 2001; Residential Personal Social Services for Adults, England,* Department of Health, London.

Department of Health (2001b) *The National Service Framework for Older People,* Department of Health, London.

Department of Health (2001c) *Carers and Disabled Children Act 2000. Carers and people with parental responsibility for disabled children practice guidance,* Department of Health, London.

Department of Health (2001d) *A Practitioner's Guide to Carers' Assessments under the Carers and Disabled Children Act 2000,* Department of Health, London.

Department of Health (2002a) *Community Care Statistics 2001: Private Nursing Homes, Hospitals and Clinics, England,* Department of Health, London.

Department of Health (2002b) *The Single Assessment Process. Key Implications, Guidance for Local Implementation and Annexes to the Guidance,* Health Services Circular/Local Authority Circular (HSC2002/001; LAC(2002)1), Department of Health, London.

Department of Health (2002c) *Fair Access to Care Services: Guidance on Eligibility Criteria for Adult Social Care,* Local Authority Circular, (LAC(2002)13), Department of Health, London.

Department of Health (2002d) *Improving Older People's Services – Policy Into Practice*, CI(2002)14, Department of Health, London.

Department of Health (2002e) *Criminal Records Bureau, Police Checks, Protection of Children, and Protection of Vulnerable Adult*, Department of Health, London.

Department of Health (2002f) *National Service Framework for Older People: Supporting Implementation – Intermediate Care: Moving Forward*, Department of Health, London.

Department of Health (2002g) *Care Homes for Older People and Younger Adults, National Minimum Standards for Care Homes for Older People –Proposed Amended Environmental Standards*, Department of Health, London.

Department of Health (2003a) *Direct Payments Guidance Community Care, Services for Carers and Children's Services (Direct Payments) Guidance England*, Department of Health, London.

Department of Health (2003b) *Single Assessment Process for Older People: The Accreditation Process for Off-the-shelf Assessment Tools*, Department of Health, London.

Department of Health (2003c) *Domiciliary Care: National Minimum Standards*, Department of Health, London.

Department of Health (2005a) *Supporting People with Long Term Conditions. An NHS and Social Care to Support Local Innovation and Integration*, Department of Health, London.

Department of Health, (2005b) *Securing Better Mental Health for Older Adults*, Department of Health, London.

Department of Health (2006) *A New Ambition for Old Age. Next Steps in Implementing the National Service Framework for Older People*, Department of Health, London.

Department of Health (2008a) *Transforming Social Care*, LAC(DH)(2008)1, Department of Health, London.

Department of Health (2008b) *Transforming the Quality of Dementia Care: Consultation on a National Dementia Strategy*, Department of Health, London.

Department of Health (2008c) *Community Care Statistics 2007: Home Care Services for Adults, England*, Department of Health, London.

Department of Health (2009a) *Transforming Adult Social Care*, LAC(DH)(2009)1, Department of Health, London.

Department of Health (2009b) *Living Well with Dementia: A National Dementia Strategy*, Department of Health, London.

Department of Health and Children (2001) *Quality and Fairness. A Health System for You*, The Stationery Office, Dublin.

Department of Health and Children (2005) *Quality and Fairness: A Health System for You. Action Plan Progress Report 2004*, The Stationery Office, Dublin.

Department of Health and Department of Environment, Transport and Regions (1999) *Better Care, Higher Standards. A charter for long term care: Guidance for Local Housing, Health and Social Services,* Department of Health, London.

Department of Health and Social Security (1982) *Steering Group on Health Services Information. 1st Report to the Secretary of State for Social Services (the Korner Report)*, HMSO, London.

Department of Health and Social Services (1991) *People First. Care Management: Guidance on Assessment and the Provision of Community Care*, HMSO, Belfast.

Department of Health Education and Welfare (1980) Request for Proposal RFP-74-80-HEW-OS. National Long-term Care Channeling Demonstration, Division of Contract and Grant Operations, Department of Health Education and Welfare, Washington DC.

Department of Health/Social Services Inspectorate (1989) *Homes Are For Living In,* HMSO, London.

Department of Health, Social Services and Public Safety (2006) *Care Assessment and Placement Guidance*, ECCU 3/2006, DHSSPS, Belfast.

Derbyshire, M. (1987) Statistical rationale for grant related expenditure assessment (GREA) concerning personal social services, *Journal of the Royal Statistical Society,* 150, 309–333.

Diwan, S. (1999) Allocation of case management resources in long-term care: predicting high use of case management time, *Gerontologist*, 39, 580–90.

Downs, M.G. and Zarit, S.H. (1999) What works in dementia care? Research evidence for policy and practice: Part I, *International Journal of Geriatric Psychiatry*, 14, 83–85.

Droes, R., Breebaart, E., Ettma, T., van Tilburg, W. and Mellenbergh, G. (2000) Effect of integrated family support versus day care only on behaviour and mood of patients with dementia, *International Psychogeriatrics*, Mar 12,1, 99–115.

Duijnstee, M. and Ros, W. (2004) Caring together for persons with dementia, in Jones, G.M.M. and Miesen, B.M.L. (eds) *Care-giving in Dementia. Research and Applications, Volume 3*, Brunner-Routledge, East Sussex.

Eastley, R. and Wilcock, G. (2000) Assessment and differential diagnosis of dementia, in O'Brien, J., Ames, D. and Burns, A. (eds) *Dementia, second edition,* Arnold, London.

Eggert, G.M., Friedman, B. and Zimmer, J.G. (1990) Models of intensive case management, in Reif, L. and Trager, B. (eds) *Health Care of the Aged: Needs, Policies, and Services*, The Haworth Press, New York.

Eggert, G.M., Zimmer, J.G., Hall, W.J. and Friedman, B. (1991) Case management: a randomized controlled study comparing a neighborhood team and centralized individual model, *Health Services Research*, 26, 4, 471–507.

Fein, E. and Staff, I. (1991) Measuring the use of time, *Administration in Social Work*, 15, 4, 81–91.

Fernández, J., Kendall, J., Davy, V. and Knapp, M. (2007) Direct payments in England: Factors linked to variations in local provision, *Journal of Social Policy*, 36, 97–121.

Fisher, M. (1990–91) Defining the practice content of care management, *Social Work and Social Sciences Review*, 2, 3, 204–230.

Fisher, M. (1991a) Care management and social work: clients with dementia, *Practice*, 4, 239–241.

Fisher, M. (1991b) Care management and social work: working with carers, *Practice*, 4, 242–252.

Flynn, M. (1986a) Adults who are mentally handicapped as consumers: issues and guidelines for interviewing, *Journal of Mental Deficiency Research*, 30, 369–377.

Flynn, M.C. and Saleem, J.K. (1986b) Adults who are mentally handicapped and living with their parents: satisfaction and perceptions regarding their lives and circumstances, *Journal of Mental Deficiency Research*, 30, 379–387.

Förstl, H. (2000) What is Alzheimer's disease?, in O'Brien, J., Ames, D. and Burns, A. (eds) *Dementia, second edition,* Arnold, London.

Gaugler, J.E., Kane, R.L., Kane, R.A., Clay, T. and Newcomer, R. (2003a) Caregiving and institutionalization of cognitively impaired older people: utilizing dynamic predictors of change, *The Gerontologist*, 43, 219–229.

Gaugler, J.E., Zarit, S.H. and Pearlin, L. (2003b) The onset of dementia caregiving and its longitudinal implications, *Psychology and Aging,* 18, 171–180.

Gaugler, J.E., Jarrott, S.E., Zarit, S.H., Parris Stephens, M., Townsend, A. and Greene, R. (2003c) Respite for dementia caregivers: the effects of adult day service use on caregiving hours and care demands, *International Psychogeriatrics*, 15, 37–58.

Gaugler, J.E., Kane, R.L., Kane, R.A., Clay, T. and Newcomer, R. (2005a) The effects of duration of caregiving on institutionalization, *The Gerontologist,* 45, 78–89.

Gaugler, J.E., Kane, R.L., Kane, R.A. and Newcomer, R. (2005b) Early community-based service utilization and its effects on institutionalization in dementia caregiving, *The Gerontologist*, 45, 177–185.

George, L.K. and Gwyther, L.P. (1986) Care-giver well-being: A multidimensional examination of family caregivers of demented adults, *The Gerontologist,* 26, 3, 253–259.

Gilhooly, M.L.M. (1990) *Do Services Delay or Prevent Institutionalisation of People with Dementia?*, Research Paper 4, Dementia Services Development Centre, University of Stirling.

Gilhooly, M., Sweeting, H., Whittick, J. and McKee, K. (1994) Family care of the dementing elderly, *International Review of Psychiatry,* 6, 29–40.

Gilleard, C.S. (1984) *Living With Dementia: Community Care of the Elderly Mentally Infirm*, Croom Helm, London.

Gilleard, C. (1992) Community care services for the elderly mentally infirm, in Jones, G.M.M. and Miesen, B.M.L. (eds) *Care-giving in Dementia: Research and Applications*, Routledge, London.

Glendinning, C., Challis, D., Fernández, J.L., Jacobs, S., Jones, K., Knapp, M., Manthorpe, J., Moran, N., Netten, A., Stevens, M. and Wilberforce, M. (2008)

Evaluation of the Individual Budgets Pilot Programme – Final Report, Social Policy Research Unit, University of York, York.

Goering, P.N., Wasylenki, D.A., Farkas, M., Lancee, W.J. and Ballantyne, R. (1988) What difference does case management make?, *Hospital and Community Psychiatry*, 39, 3, 272–276.

Goldberg, M. and Warburton, W. (1979) *Ends and Means in Social Work,* Allen and Unwin, London.

Goldberg, E.M., Gibbons, J. and Sinclair, I. (1985) *Problems, Tasks and Outcomes: The Evaluation of Task-Centred Casework in Three Settings*, George Allen and Unwin, London.

Goldsmith, M., (1996) *Hearing The Voice of People with Dementia: Opportunities and Obstacles,* Jessica Kingsley, London.

Gostick, C., Davies, B., Lawson, R. and Salter, C. (1997) *From Vision to Reality in Community Care: Changing Direction at the Local Level*, Arena, Aldershot.

Gottlieb, B.H. and Wolfe, J. (2002) Coping with family caregiving to persons with dementia: A critical review, *Aging and Mental Health*, 6, 4, 325–342.

Government Actuary's Department (2006) *National population projections 2004– based,* The Stationery Office, London.

Greene, V.L., Ondrich, J. and Laditka, S. (1998) Can home care services achieve cost savings in long-term care for older people?, *Journal of Gerontology,* 53B, 4, S228–S238.

Griffiths, R. (1988) *Community Care: Agenda for Action*, HMSO, London.

Gurland, B., Kuriansky, J., Sharpe, L., Simon, R., Stiller, P. and Birkett, P.L. (1977) The comprehensive assessment and referral evaluation (CARE) – rationale, development and reliability, *International Journal of Ageing and Human Development*, 8, 1, 9–42.

Gurland, B., Golden, R., Teresi, J., and Challop J. (1984) The Short CARE: an efficient instrument for the assessment of depression, dementia and disability, *Journal of Gerontology,* 39, 166–169.

Hancock, G.A., Reynolds, T., Woods, B., Thornicroft, G. and Orrell, M. (2003) The needs of older people with mental health problems according to the user, the carer, and the staff, *International Journal of Geriatric Psychiatry*, 18, 803–811.

Hardy, B., Young, R. and Wistow, G. (1999) Dimensions of choice in the assessment and care management process: the views of older people, carers and care managers, *Health and Social Care in the Community*, 7, 6, 483–491.

Hedrick, S.C., Rothman, M.L., Chapko, M., Ehreth, J., Diehr, P., Inui, T.S., Connis, R.T., Grover, P.L. and Kelly, J.R. (1993) Summary and discussion of methods and results of the Adult Day Health Care Evaluation Study, *Medical Care,* 31 SS94–SS103.

Henwood, M. and Wistow, G. (1999) (eds) Evaluating the impact of caring for people, in Royal Commission on Long-Term Care, Executive Summary, Cm 4192-II/3, *With Respect to Old Age: Long Term Care – Rights and*

Responsibilities. Community Care and Informal Care. Research Volume 3, The Stationery Office London.

HM Government (2007) *Putting People First – A Shared Vision and Commitment to the Transformation of Adult Social Care,* Department of Health, London.

HM Government (2008) *Carers at the Heart of 21st Century Families and Communities: A Caring System on Your Side, A Life of Your Own*, Department of Health, London.

Hoyes, L., Lart, R., Means, R. and Taylor, M. (1994) *Community Care in Transition*, Joseph Rowntree Foundation, York.

Hudson, B. and Hardy, B. (2002) What is a 'successful' partnership and how can it be measured?, in Glendinning, C., Powell, M. and Rummery, K (eds) *Partnerships, New Labour and the Governance of Welfare*, The Policy Press, Bristol.

Hudson, B., Hardy, B., Glendinning, C. and Young, R. (2002) *National Evaluation of Notification for use of the Section 31 Partnership Flexibilities for the Health Act* 1999 *Final Project Report*, National Primary Care Research and Development Centre, University of Manchester, and the Nuffield Institute for Health, University of Leeds, Leeds.

Hughes, J. and Challis, D. (2004) Frail older people – margins of care, *Reviews in Clinical Gerontology*, 14, 155–164.

Hughes, J., Stewart, K., Challis, D., Darton, R. and Weiner, K. (2001) Care management and the care programme approach: towards integration in old age mental health services, *International Journal of Geriatric Psychiatry*, 16, 266–272.

Hughes, J., Sutcliffe, C. and Challis, D. (2005) Social Work, in Burns, A. (ed.) on behalf of the European Dementia Consensus Network (EDCON) Group, *Standards In Dementia Care*, Taylor Francis, New York.

Huxley, P., Hagan, T., Hennelly, R. and Hunt, J. (1990) *Effective Community Mental Health Services*, Gower, Aldershot.

Improvement and Development Agency (2007) *The Equality Standard for Local Government*, Improvement and Development Agency, London.

Johnston, R. and Lawrence, P.R. (1991) Beyond vertical integration – the rise of the value-adding partnership, in Thompson, G., Frances, J., Levačić, R. and Mitchell, J. (eds) *Markets, Hierarchies and Networks. The Coordination of Social Life*, Sage Publications, London.

Johri, M., Beland, F. and Bergman, H. (2003) International experiments in integrated care for the elderly: a synthesis of the evidence, *International Journal of Geriatric Psychiatry*, 18, 222–235.

Kane, R.A. (2000) Long-term case management for older adults, in Kane, R.L. and Kane, R.A. (eds) *Assessing Older Persons: Measures, Meaning, and Practical Applications,* University Press, Oxford.

Kane, R.A., Penrod, J., Davidson, G., Moscovice, I. and Rich, E. (1991) What cost case management in long term care?, *Social Services Review*, 65, 281–303.

Kanter, J. (1989) Clinical case management: definition, principles, components, *Hospital and Community Psychiatry*, 40, 361–368.

Kavanagh, S., Schneider, J., Knapp, M., Beecham, J. and Netten, A. (1993) Elderly people with cognitive impairment: costing possible changes in the balance of care, *Health and Social Care,* 1, 69–80.

Kemper, P., Applebaum, R. and Harrigan, M. (1987) Community care demonstrations: What have we learned?, *Health Care Financing Review*, 8, 87–100.

Kharicha, K., Levin, E., Iliffe, S. and Davey, B. (2004) Social work, general practice and evidence-based policy in collaborative care of older people: current problems and future possibilities, *Health and Social Care in the Community*, 12, 2, 134–141.

Kirkhart, K.E. and Ruffolo, C. (1993) Valued bases of case management evaluation, *Evaluation and Program Planning*, 16, 1, 55–65.

Kitwood, T. (1997) *Dementia Reconsidered; the person comes first*, Open University Press, Buckingham.

Knapp, M.R. (1984) *The Economics of Social Care*, Macmillan, London.

Knapp, M.R. (1993) Background theory, in Netten, A. and Beecham, J. (eds) *Costing Community Care: Theory and Practice,* Ashgate, Aldershot.

Knapp, M., Beecham, J. and Allen, C. (1989) The methodology for costing community and hospital services used by clients of the care in the community demonstration programme, Discussion paper 647, Personal Social Services Research Unit, University of Kent at Canterbury.

Knapp, M., Cambridge, P., Thomason, C., Beecham, J., Allen, C. and Darton, R. (1992*) Care in the Community: Challenge and Demonstration*, Ashgate, Aldershot.

Knapp, M., Prince, M., Albanese, E., Banerjee, S., Dhanasiri, S., Fernández JL., Ferri, C., McCrone, P., Snell, T. and Stewart, R. (2007) *Dementia UK: The Full Report,* Alzheimer's Society, London.

Knight, B.G., Lutzky, S.N. and Macofsky-Urban, F. (1993) A meta-analytic review of interventions for caregivers' distress: recommendations for future research, *The Gerontologist*, 33, 240–248.

Kraan, R., Baldock, J., Davies, B., Evers, A., Johansson, L., Knapen, M., Thorslund, M. and Tunissen, C. (1991) *Care for the Elderly: Significant Innovations in Three European Countries,* Campus/Westview, Boulder, Colorado.

Lacey, D. (1999) The evolution of care: A 100-year history of institutionalization of people with Alzheimer's Disease, *Journal of Gerontological Social Work*, 31, 3/4, 101–131.

Leece, J. (2003) The development of domiciliary care: What does the future hold?, *Practice*, 15, 3 17–30.

Levin, E. and Moriarty, J. (1996) Evaluating respite services, in Bland, R. (ed.) *Developing Services for Older People and Their Families*, Jessica Kingsley, London.

Levin, E., Sinclair, I. and Gorbach, P. (1989) *Families, Services and Confusion in Old Age*, Gower, Aldershot.

Levin, E., Moriarty, J. and Gorbach, P. (1994) *Better for the Break*, HMSO, London.

Lewis, J.E. and Glennerster, H. (1996) *Implementing the New Community Care*, Open University Press, Buckingham.

Lewis, J. with Bernstock, P., Bovell, V. and Wookey, F. (1997) Implementing care management: issues in relation to the new community care, *British Journal of Social Work*, 27, 1, 5–24.

Lieberman, M. and Kramer, J. (1991) Factors affecting decisions to institutionalise demented elderly, *The Gerontologist*, 31, 371–374.

Lindesay, J. (ed.) (1991) *Working Out. Setting up and Running Community Psychogeriatric Teams*, Research and Development for Psychiatry, London.

Lindesay, J. and Murphy, E. (1989) Dementia, depression and subsequent institutionalisation – the effect of home support, *International Journal of Geriatric Psychiatry*, 4, 3–9.

Lindesay, J., Briggs, L. and Murphy, E. (1989) The Guy's/Age Concern Survey. Prevalence rates of cognitive impairment, depression and anxiety in an urban elderly community, *British Journal of Psychiatry*, 155, 317–329.

Lindesay, J., Herzberg, J., Collighan, G., Macdonald, A. and Philpot, M. (1996) Treatment decisions following assessment by multidisciplinary psychogeriatric teams, *Psychiatric Bulletin*, 20, 78–81.

Lorr, M. and Wunderlich, R.A. (1988) A semantic differential mood scale, *Journal of Clinical Psychology*, 44, 1, 33–36.

Lowin, A., Knapp, M. and McCrone, P. (2001) Alzheimer's disease in the UK: comparative evidence on cost of illness and volume of health services research funding, *International Journal of Geriatric Psychiatry*, 16, 1143–1148.

Lyons, K. and Zarit, S.H. (1999) Formal and informal support: The great divide, *International Journal of Geriatric Psychiatry*, 14, 183–196.

Macdonald, A. (1991) Running a Team, in Lindesay, J. (ed.) *Working Out: Setting up and Running Community Psychogeriatric Teams,* Research and Development for Psychiatry, London.

Macdonald, A., Mann, A.H., Jenkins, R., Richard, R., Godlove, C. and Rodwell, G. (1982) An attempt to determine the impact of four types of care upon the elderly in London by the study of matched groups, *Psychological Medicine*, 12, 193–200.

Macdonald, A., Goddard, C. and Poynton, A. (1994) Impact of 'open access' to specialist services – the case of community psychogeriatricians, *International Journal of Geriatric Psychiatry*, 9, 709–712.

Manthorpe, J. (2004) Risk Taking, in Innes, A., Arcibald, C. and Murphy, C. (eds) *Dementia and Social Inclusion*, Jessica Kingsley, London.

Manthorpe, J. and Moriarty, J. (2007) Models from other countries: Social work with people with dementia and their caregivers, in Cox, C. (ed.) *Dementia and*

Social Work Practice: Research and Interventions, Springer Publishing, New York.

Marks, D.F. and Sykes, C. (2000) *Dealing with Dementia. Recent European Research*, Middlesex University Press, London.

Marriott, A., Donaldson, C., Tarrier, N. and Burns, A. (2000) Effectiveness of cognitive-behavioural family intervention in reducing the burden of care in carers of patients with Alzheimer's disease, *British Journal of Psychiatry,* 176, 557–562.

Marshall, M. (1990) *Working with Dementia: Guidelines for Professionals*, British Association of Social Work, Venture, Kent.

Marshall, M. (1999) What do service planners and policy-makers need from research?, *International Journal of Geriatric Psychiatry*, 14, 86–96.

Marshall, M. (2000) (ed.) *ASTRID: A Social and Technological Response to Meeting the Needs of Individuals With Dementia and Their Carers: A Guide to Using Technology within Dementia Care*, Hawker, London.

Marshall, M. and Tibbs, M. (2006) *Social Work and People with Dementia*, The Policy Press, Bristol.

McCrone, P., Dhanasiri, S., Patel, A., Knapp, M. and Lawton-Smith, S. (2008) *Paying the Price: The cost of mental health care in England to 2026*, King's Fund, London.

McKee, K.J. (1999) This is your life: Research paradigms in dementia care in Adams, T. and Clarke, C.L. (eds) *Dementia Care, Developing Partnerships in Practice*, Bailliere Tindall, London.

Means, R. and Smith, R. (1998) *Community Care Policy and Practice, Second edition*, Macmillan, Basingstoke.

Meiland, F.J., Danse, J.A., Gunning-Schepers, L.J. and Klazinga, N.S. (2001) Burden of delayed admission to psychogeriatric nursing homes on patients and their informal caregivers, *Quality in Health Care,* 10, 218–228.

Melzer, D., Ely, M. and Brayne, C. (1997) Cognitive impairment in elderly people: population based estimate of the future in England, Scotland, and Wales, *British Medical Journal*, 315, 462.

Melzer, D., McWilliams, B., Brayne, C., Johnson, T. and Bond, J. (1999) Profile of disability in elderly people: estimates from a longitudinal study, *British Medical Journal*, 318, 1108–1111.

Miller, R., Newcomer, R. and Fox, P. (1999) Effects of the Medicare Alzheimer's Disease Demonstration on nursing home entry. (The Medicare Alzheimer's Disease Demonstration Program), *Health Services Research*, 34, 691–700.

Mittelman, M., Roth, D., Coon, D. and Haley, W. (2004) Sustained benefit of supportive intervention for depressive symptoms in caregivers of patients with Alzheimer's Disease, *American Journal of Psychiatry*, 161, 850–856.

Mittelman, M., Haley, W., Clay, O. and Roth, D. (2006) Improving caregiver well-being delays nursing home placement of patients with Alzheimer disease, *Neurology,* 67, 1592–1599.

Mittelman, M., Roth, D., Clay, O. and Haley, W. (2007) Preserving health of Alzheimer caregivers: Impact of a spouse caregiver intervention, *American Journal of Geriatric Psychiatry*, 15, 9, 780–789.

Mohide, E.A., Pringle, D.M., Streiner, D.L., Gilbert, J.R., Muir, G. and Tew, M. (1990) A randomised trial of family caregiver support in the home management of dementia, *Journal of the American Geriatrics Society*, 38, 4, 446–454.

Moniz-Cook, E., Elston, C., Gardiner, E., Agar, S., Silver, M., Win, T. and Wang, M. (2008) Can training community mental health nurses to support family carers reduce behavioural problems in dementia? An exploratory pragmatic randomised controlled trial, *International Journal of Geriatric Psychiatry*, 23, 185–191.

Montgomery, R. and Rowe, J. (2007) Respite, in Cox, C. (ed.) *Dementia and Social Work Practice: Research and Interventions*, Springer Publishing, New York.

Mooney, G.H. (1978) Planning for the balance of care of the elderly, *Scottish Journal of Political Economy*, 25, 2, 149–64.

Moore, M., Zhu, C. and Clipp, E. (2001) Informal costs of dementia care: estimates from the National Longitudinal Caregiver study, *Journal of Gerontology: Series B Psycholocical Sciences and Social Sciences,* 56(B), S219–S228.

Moos, R.H. and Lemke, S. (1984) *Multiphasic Environmental Assessment Procedure (MEAP)*, Stanford University Medical Centre, United States.

Moriarty, J. and Levin, E. (1998) Respite care in homes and hospitals, in Jack, R. (ed.) *Residential versus Community Care*, Macmillan, Basingstoke.

Moriarty, J., and Webb, S. (1997a) How do older people feel about assessment?, *Journal of Dementia Care Sep/Oct* 20–22.

Moriarty, J. and Webb, S. (1997b) Carers experiences of community care, *Alzheimer's Disease Society Newsletter*, October, 7.

Moriarty, J. and Webb, S. (2000) *Part of their Lives: Community Care for Older People with Dementia,* The Policy Press, Bristol.

Morris, L., Morris, R., and Britton, P. (1988) The relationship between marital intimacy, perceived strain and depression in spouse caregivers of dementia sufferers, *British Journal of Medical Psychology,* 61, 231 – 236.

Moxley, D.P. (1989) *The Practice of Case Management,* Sage Publications Inc, California.

Mozley, C., Huxley, P., Sutcliffe, C., Bagley, H., Burns, A., Challis, D., and Cordingley, L., (1999) 'Not knowing where I am doesn't mean I don't know what I like': Cognitive impairment and quality of life responses in elderly people. *International Journal of Geriatric Psychiatry*, 14, 776–783.

Mozley, C., Sutcliffe, C., Bagley, H., Cordingley, L., Huxley, P., Challis, D., and Burns, A. (2004) *Towards Quality Care: Outcomes for Older People in Care Homes*, Ashgate, Aldershot.

Mueser, K.T., Bond, G.R., Drake, R.E. and Resnick, S.G. (1998) Models of Community Care for severe mental illness: A review of research on case management, *Schizophrenia Bulletin,* 24, 1, 37–74.

Murphy, E. and Banerjee, S. (1993) The organisation of old-age psychiatry services, *Reviews in Clinical Gerontology,* 3, 367–78.

Myers, F. and MacDonald, C (1996) Power to the people? Involving users and carers in needs assessments and care planning – views from the practitioner, *Health and Social Care in the Community*, 4, 2, 86–95.

Myllykangas, M., Ryynänen, O.P., Lammintakanen, J., Isomäki, V., Kinnunen, J. and Halonen, P. (2003) Clinical management and prioritisation criteria: Finnish experiences, *Journal of Health Organization and Management*, 17, 338–348.

National Assembly for Wales (2002) *Health and Social Care for Adults: Creating a Unified and Fair System for Assessing and Managing Care. Guidance for Local Authorities and Health Services*, National Assembly for Wales, Cardiff.

National Audit Office (2007) *Improving Services and Support for People with Dementia*, The Stationery Office, London.

National Institute for Health and Clinical Excellence (NICE) and Social Care Institute for Excellence (SCIE) (2006) *Dementia – Supporting people with dementia and their carers in health and social care*, www.nice.org.uk/CG042

National Statistics (2007) *Community Care Statistics 2007 Supported Residents (Adults), England,* The Information Centre, Leeds.

Netten, A. (1994) *Unit Costs of Community Care,* Personal Social Services Research Unit, Canterbury.

Netten, A. and Beecham, J. (eds) (1993) *Costing Community Care: Theory and Practice,* Ashgate, Aldershot.

Netten, A., Darton, R. and Williams, J. (2003) Nursing home closures: effects on capacity and reasons for closure, *Age and Ageing*, 32, 332–337.

Netten, A., Williams, J. and Darton, R. (2005) Care home closure in England: Causes and implication, *Ageing and Society*, 25, 319–338.

Neugarten, B.L., Havighurst, R.J. and Tobin, S.S. (1961) The measurement of life satisfaction, *Journal of Gerontology*, 16, 134–143.

Newcomer, R., Yordi, C., DuNah, R., Fox, P. and Wilkinson, A. (1999) Effects of the Medicare Alzheimer's Disease Demonstration on caregiver burden and depression. (The Medicare Alzheimer's Disease Demonstration Program), *Health Services Research,* 34, 669–680.

Nolan, M. and Keady, J. (2001) Working with carers, in Cantley, C. (ed.) *A Handbook of Dementia Care*, Open University Press, Buckingham.

Nolan, M.R., Grant, G. and Ellis, N.C. (1990) Stress is in the eye of the beholder: reconceptualising the measurement of carers burden, *Journal of Advanced Nursing*, 15, 544–555.

Nolan, M., Grant, G. and Keady, J. (1996) *Understanding Family Care*, Open University Press, Buckingham.

Nuffield Provincial Hospital Trust (1946) *The Hospital Surveys: The Domesday Book of the Hospital Services*, Oxford University Press, Oxford.

O'Connor, D.W., Pollitt, P.A., Brook, C.P.B., Reiss, B.B. and Roth, M. (1991) Does early intervention reduce the number of elderly people with dementia admitted to institutions for long-term care?, *British Medical Journal*, 302, 871–875.

O'Reilly, S. and O'Shea, E. (1999) *An Action Plan for Dementia*, Report No. 54, National Council on Ageing and Older People, Dublin.

O'Rourke, N. and Tuokko, H. (2000) The psychological and physical costs of caregiving: the Canadian study of health and aging, *Journal of Applied Gerontology*, 19, 4, 389–405.

O'Shea, E. and O'Reilly, S. (2000) The economic and social cost of dementia in Ireland, *International Journal of Geriatric Psychiatry*, 15, 208–218.

Onor, M., Trevisiol, M., Negro, C., Alessandra, S., Saina, M. and Aguglia, E. (2007) Impact of a multimodal rehabilitative intervention on demented patients and their caregivers, *American Journal of Alzheimer's Disease and Other Dementias*, 22, 261–272.

Øvretveit, J. (1997) How to describe interprofessional working, in Øvretveit, J., Mathias, P. and Thompson, T. (eds) *Interprofessional Working for Health and Social Care*, Palgrave Macmillan, Basingstoke.

Parker, G. (1990) *With Due Care and Attention: A Review of Research on Informal Care*, Family Policy Studies Centre, London.

Parry-Jones, B. and Soulsby, J. (2001) Needs-led assessment: The challenges and the reality, *Health and Social Care in the Community*, 9, 6, 414–428.

Patmore, C. (2001) Improving homecare quality: An individual-centred approach, *Quality in Ageing-Policy Practice and Research*, 2, 3, 15–24.

Patterson, T.L. and Grant, I. (2003) Interventions for caregiving in dementia: physical outcomes, *Current Opinion in Psychiatry*, 16, 6, 629–633.

Pattie, A.H. and Gilleard, C.J. (1979) *Manual of the Clifton Assessment Procedures for the Elderly*, Hodder and Stoughton, Kent.

Payne, K., Wilson, C., Caro, J. and O'Brien, J. (1999) Resource use by dementia patients and caregivers: An international survey of medical and social services and processes of long-term care, *Annals of Long-Term Care*, 7, 7, 263–276.

Payne, M. (1995) *Social Work and Community Care*, MacMillan, Basingstoke.

Peace, S., Kellaher, L. and Willcocks, D. (1982) *A Balanced Life? A Consumer Study of Residential Life in 100 Local Authority Old People's Homes*, Polytechnic of North London, London.

Phillipson, C., Bernard, M., Phillips, J. and Ogg, J. (2001) *The Family and Community Life of Older People: Social Networks and Social Support in Three Urban Areas*, Routledge, London.

Philp, I. and Appleby, L. (2005) *Securing Better Mental Health for Older Adults*, Department of Health, London.

Philpot, M.P. (1990) *A Short Report on Prioritization*, unpublished report – Lewisham and North Southwark Health Authority.

Philpot, M. and Banerjee, S. (1997) Mental health services for older people in London, in Johnson, S., Ramsay, R., Thorneycroft, G., Brooks, L., Lelliot, P., Peck, E., Smith, H., Chisholm, D., Audini, B., Knapp, M. and Goldberg, D. (eds) *London's Mental Health*, King's Fund Publishing, London.

Pickard, L. (1999) Policy options for informal carers of elderly people, in Royal Commission on Long Term Care, Cm 4192-II/3, *With Respect to Old Age: Long Term Care – Rights and Responsibilities. Community Care and Informal Care, Research Volume 3,* The Stationery Office, London.

Pickard, L. (2004) *The Effectiveness and Cost-effectiveness of Support and Services to Informal Carers of Older People. A Review of the Literature Prepared for The Audit Commission*, Audit Commission, London.

Pickard, L., Wittenberg, R., Comas-Herrera, A., King, D. and Malley, J. (2007) Care by spouses, care by children: Projections of informal care for older people in England to 2031, *Social Policy and Society*, 6, 353–366.

Pincus, A. and Minahan, A. (1973) *Social Work Practice: Model and Method,* Peacock Publishers, Illinois.

Pincus, A. and Minahan, A. (1977) A model for social work practice, in Sprecht, H. and Vickery, A. (eds) *Integrating Social Work Methods*, George Allen and Unwin Ltd, London.

Platt, S.D., Weyman, A.J., Hirsch, S.R. and Hewitt, S. (1980) The Social Behaviour Assessment Schedule (SBAS): rationale, contents, scoring and reliability of a new interview schedule, *Social Psychiatry*, 15, 43–55.

Pot, A. (2004) The care-giving stress process, in Jones, G.M.M. and Miesen, B.M.L. (eds) *Care-giving in Dementia. Research and Applications Volume 3,* Brunner-Routledge, East Sussex.

Pushkar Gold, D., Feldman Reis, M., Markiewicz, D. and Andres, D. (1995) When home caregiving ends: a longitudinal study of outcomes for caregivers of relatives with dementia, *Journal of the American Geriatric Society*, 43, 10–16.

Quill, S. (2002) (ed.) *Conference Proceedings Towards Care Management in Ireland*, Report No. 71, National Council on Ageing and Older People, Dublin.

Qureshi, H. and Walker, A. (1989) *The Caring Relationship*, Macmillan Education Ltd, Basingstoke.

Qureshi, H., Challis, D. and Davies, B. (1989) *Helpers in Case-managed Community Care*, Gower, Aldershot.

Raiff, N.R. and Shore, B.K. (1993) *Advanced Case Management. New Strategies for the Nineties*, Sage, London.

Reed, J. (1998) Gerontological nursing research – future directions. Paper given to the Agenet/Royal College of Nursing gerontological nursing research seminar, Regents College, London, December.

Reid, W.J. and Shyne, A.W. (1969) *Brief and Extended Casework*, Columbia University Press, New York.

Reilly, S., Challis, D., Burns, A. and Hughes, J. (2004) The use of assessment scales in old age psychiatry services in England and Northern Ireland, *Aging and Mental Health,* 8, 3, 249–255.

Reilly, S., Abendstern, M., Hughes, J., Challis, D., Venables, D. and Pedersen, I. (2006) Quality in long-term care homes for people with dementia: an assessment of specialist provision, *Ageing and Society,* 26, 649–668.

Rendell, C. and Haw, D. (2001) Mental Health Services for Older People, Lambeth, Southwark and Lewisham Health Authority, South London and the Maudsley NHS Trust, London Borough of Lewisham, Audit 1999/2000, District Audit [not publicly available].

Robb, B. (1967) *Sans Everything*, Nelson and Sons Ltd, London.

Roth, M., Huppert, F.A., Tym, E. and Mountjoy, C.Q. (1988) *CAMDEX: The Cambridge Examination for Mental Disorders of the Elderly*, Cambridge University Press, Cambridge.

Rothera, I., Jones, R., Harwood, R., Avery, A., Fisher, K., James, V., Shaw, I. and Waite, J. (2008) An evaluation of a specialist multiagency home support service for older people with dementia using qualitative methods, *International Journal of Geriatric Psychiatry*, 23, 65–72.

Rutter, M., Tizard, J. and Whitmore, I.C. (1970) *Education, Health and Behaviour*, Longman, London.

Ryan, T., Nolan, M., Enderby, P. and Reid, D. (2004) 'Part of the family': sources of job satisfaction amongst a group of community-based dementia care workers, *Health and Social Care in the Community*, 12, 111–118.

Ryynänen, O.P., Myllykangas, M., Kinnunen, J., Halonen, P., and Takala J. (2000) Prioritization attitudes among doctors and nurses examined by a scenario method, *International Journal of Technology Assessment in Health Care*, 16, 1, 92–99.

Schneider, J., Hallam, A., Kamul Islam, M., Murray, J., Foley, B., Atkins, L., Banerjee, S. and Mann, A. (2003) Formal and informal care for people with dementia: variations in cost over time, *Ageing and Society*, 23, 303–326.

Scottish Executive (2000) *Community Care: A Joint Future. Report by the Joint Future Group,* The Stationery Office, Edinburgh.

Scottish Executive Joint Future Unit (2004) *Guidance on Care Management in Community Care,* Circular No. CCD 8.2004, Scottish Executive, Edinburgh.

Scottish Office (1998) *Modernising Community Care: An Action Plan,* The Stationery Office, Edinburgh.

Seddon, D. and Robinson, C. (2001) Carers of older people with dementia: assessment and the Carers Act, *Health and Social Care in the Community,* 9, 3, 151–158.

Seddon, D., Robinson, C. and Perry, J. (2008) Unified Assessment: Policy, implementation and practice, *British Journal of Social Work,* Advance Access published June 19, 2008; doi:10.1093/bjsw/bcn097.

Seebohm Rowntree Committee (1947) *Old People: Report of a Survey Committee on the Problems of Ageing and the Care of Old People*, The Nuffield Foundation, Oxford University Press, London.

Sinclair, I., Gibbs, I. and Hicks, L. (2000) *The Management and Effectiveness of the Home Care Service*, Social Work Research and Development Unit, The University of York.

Slade, M. (1994) Needs assessment: involvement of staff and users will help to meet needs, *British Journal of Psychiatry*, 165, 293–296.

Sloane, P., Zimmerman, S., Gruber-Baldini, A., Hebel, J., Magaziner, J. and Konrad, T. (2005) Health and functional outcomes and health care utilization of persons with dementia in residential care and assisted living facilities: comparison with nursing homes, *Gerontologist,* 45, Special Issue 1, 124–132.

Smale, G., Tuson, G., with Biehal, N. and Marsh, P. (1993) *Empowerment, Assessment, Care Management and The Skilled Worker,* National Institute for Social Work, HMSO, London.

Social Services Inspectorate (SSI) (1987) *From Home Help to Home Care: An Analysis of Policy Resourcing and Service Management,* SSI, London.

Social Services Inspectorate (SSI) (1993) *Inspection of Assessment and Care Management Arrangements in Social Services Departments. Interim Overview Report,* Department of Health, London.

Social Services Inspectorate (SSI) (1995) *Partners in Caring – The Fourth Annual Report of the Chief Inspector Social Services Inspectorate 1994/95,* HMSO, London.

Social Services Inspectorate (SSI) (1997a) *Better Management, Better Care, The Sixth Annual Report of the Chief Inspector Social Services Inspectorate 1996/7,* HMSO, London.

Social Services Inspectorate (SSI) (1997b) *Older People with Mental Health Problems Living Alone: Anybody's Priority?,* Department of Health, London.

Social Services Inspectorate (SSI) (1998a) *They Look After their Own Don't They? Inspection of Community Care Services for Black and Ethnic Minority People,* CI(98)2, Social Services Inspectorate, Department of Health, London.

Social Services Inspectorate (SSI) (1998b) *Social Services Facing the Future, The Seventh Annual Report of the Chief Inspector Social Services Inspectorate 1997/98,* HMSO, London.

Social Services Inspectorate (SSI) (2003) *Modern Social Services – A Commitment to the Future, The 12th Annual Report of the Chief Inspector of Social Services 2002–2003,* Department of Health, London.

Social Services Inspectorate and Social Work Services Group (SSI/SWSG) (1991a) *Care Management and Assessment: Managers' Guide,* HMSO, London.

Social Services Inspectorate and Social Work Services Group (SSI/SWSG) (1991b) *Care Management and Assessment: Practitioners' Guide,* HMSO, London.

Spruytte, N., Van Audenhove, C. and Lammertyn, F. (2001) Predictors of institutionalization of cognitively-impaired elderly cared for by their relatives, *International Journal of Geriatric Psychiatry,* 16, 1119–1128.

Stalker, K. and Campbell, I. (2002) *Review of Care Management in Scotland,* Scottish Executive Central Research Unit, Edinburgh.

Stanley, D. and Cantley, C. (2001) Assessment, care planning and care management, in Cantley, C. (ed.) *A Handbook of Dementia Care,* Open University Press, Buckingham.

Stein, L.I. and Test, M.A. (1980) An alternative to mental hospital treatment: I. Conceptual model, treatment program, and clinical evaluation, *Archives of General Psychiatry,* 37, 392–397.

Stein, L.I. and Test, M.A. (1985) The evolution of the Training in Community Living Model, in Stein, L.I. and Test, M.A. (eds) *The Training in Community Living Model: A Decade of Experience*, New Directions for Mental Health Services, No. 26, Jossey-Bass, San Francisco, California.

Stewart, K., Challis, D., Carpenter, I. and Dickinson, E. (1999) Assessment approaches for older people receiving social care: content and coverage, *International Journal of Geriatric Psychiatry*, 14, 147–156.

Stewart, K., Hughes, J., Challis, D. and Weiner, K. (2003) Care management for older people: Access, targeting and the balance between assessment, monitoring and review, *Research Policy and Planning*, 21, 13–22.

Sutcliffe, C., Hughes, J., Abendstern, M., Clarkson, P. and Challis, D. (2008) Developing multidisciplinary assessment – exploring the evidence from a social care perspective, *International Journal of Geriatric Psychiatry*, 23, 1297–1305.

Teague, G.B., Bond, G.R. and Drake, R.E. (1998) Program fidelity in assertive community treatment: Development and use of a measure, *American Journal of Orthopsychiatry*, 68, 2, 216–232.

Teri, L., McCurry, S., Logsdon, R. and Gibbons, L. (2005) Training community consultants to help family members improve dementia care: A randomized controlled trial, *Gerontologist*, 45, 802–811.

Test, M. (1992) Training in community living, in Liberman, R. (ed.) *Handbook of Psychiatric Rehabilitation*, Macmillan, New York.

Thompson, R., Lewis, S., Murphy, M., Hale, J., Blackwell, P., Acton, G., Clough, D., Patrick, G. and Bonner, P. (2004) Are there sex differences in emotional and biological responses in spousal caregivers of patients with Alzheimer's disease?, *Biological Research for Nursing*, 5, 319–330.

Tibbitt, J. and Martin, P. (1991) *Where the Time Goes: The Allocation of 'Administration' and 'Casework' Between Client Groups in Scottish Departments of Social Work*, Central Research Unit, Scottish Office, Edinburgh.

Tilki, M. (1999) Reminiscence, in Corley, G. (ed.) *Older People and Their Needs*, Athenaeum Press, Tyne and Wear.

Tornatore, J.B. and Grant, L.A. (2002) Burden among family caregivers of persons with Alzheimer's disease in nursing homes, *The Gerontologist*, 42, 497–506.

Townsend, A., Noelker, L., Deimling, G. and Bass, D. (1989) Longitudinal impact of interhousehold caregiving on adult children's mental health, *Psychology and Aging*, 4, 393–401.

Townsend, P. (1957) *The Family Life of Old People; An Enquiry in East London*, Routledge and Keegan Paul, London.

Townsend, P. (1962) *The Last Refuge*, Routledge and Kegan Paul, London.

Trevillion, S. (1992) *Caring in the Community: A Networking Approach to Community Partnership*, Longman, Harlow.

Tucker, S., Baldwin, R., Hughes, J., Benbow, S., Barker, A., Burns, A. and Challis, D. (2007) Old age mental health services in England: implementing the National Service Framework for Older People, *International Journal of Geriatric Psychiatry*, 22, 211–217.

Tucker, S., Baldwin, R., Hughes, J., Benbow, S., Barker, A., Burns, A. and Challis, D. (2009) Integrated services for older people with mental health problems – From rhetoric to reality, *Journal of Interprofessional Care*, 23, 4, 341–354.

Tunstall, J. (1966) *Old and Alone: A Sociological Study of Old People*, Routledge and Keegan Paul, London.

Twigg, J. (1992) Carers in the service system, in Twigg, J. (ed.) *Carers: Research and Practice*, HMSO, London.

Twigg, J. (1998) Informal care of older people, in Bernard, M. and Phillips, J. (eds) *The Social Policy of Old Age,* Centre for Policy on Ageing, London.

Twigg, J. and Atkin, K. (1994) *Carers Perceived: policy and practice in informal care*, Open University Press, Buckingham.

Ulstein, I., Sadvik, L., Wyller, T. and Engedal, K. (2007) A one-year randomized controlled psychosocial intervention study among family carers of dementia patients – effects on patients and carers, D*ementia and Geriatric Cognitive Disorders*, 24, 469–475.

Venables, D., Clarkson, P., Hughes, J., Burns, A. and Challis, D. (2006) Specialist clinical assessment of vulnerable older people: outcomes for carers from a randomised controlled trial, *Ageing and Society*, 26, 867–882.

Victor, C., Scambler, S., Bowling, A. and Bond, J. (2005) The prevalence of, and risk factors for, loneliness in later life: A survey of older people in Great Britain, *Ageing and Society,* 25, 357–275.

von Abendorff, R., Challis, D. and Netten, A. (1994) Staff activity patterns in a community mental health team for older people, *International Journal of Geriatric Psychiatry*, 9, 897–906.

Walker, B. (2003) Key factors that can make specialist homecare work, *Journal of Dementia Care*, May/June, 25–27.

Wanless, D. (2006) *Securing Good Care for Older People. Taking a Long-term View,* King's Fund, London.

Warburton, R. and McCracken, J. (1999) An evidence-based perspective from the Department of Health on the impact of the 1993 reforms on the care of frail, elderly people, in Henwood, M. and Wistow, G. (1999) (eds) Evaluating the impact of caring for people in Royal Commission on Long Term Care, Cm 4192-II/3, *With Respect to Old Age: Long Term Care – Rights and Responsibilities. Community Care and Informal Care. Research Volume 3*, The Stationery Office London.

Ware, P., Matosevic, T., Forder, J., Hardy, B., Kendall, J. and Knapp, M. (2001) Movement and change: independent sector domiciliary care providers between 1995 and 1999, *Health and Social Care in the Community*, 9, 6, 334–340.

Ware, T., Matosevic, T., Hardy, B., Knapp, M., Kendall, J. and Forder, J. (2003) Commissioning care services for older people in England: The view from care managers, users and carers, *Ageing and Society*, 23, 411–428.

Watt, H.M. (2001) Community-based case management: A model for outcome-based research for non-institutionalized elderly, *Home Health Care Services Quarterly*, 20, 1, 39– 65.

Weinberg, A., Williamson, J., Challis, D. and Hughes, J. (2003) What do care managers do? A study of working practice in older people's services, *British Journal of Social Work*, 33, 901–919.

Weiner, K., Stewart, K., Hughes, J., Challis, D. and Darton, R. (2002) Care management arrangements for older people in England: key areas of variation in a national study, *Ageing and Society*, 22, 419–439.

Weiner, K., Hughes, J., Challis, D. and Pederson, I. (2003) Integrating health and social care at the micro level: Health care professionals as care managers for older people, *Social Policy and Administration*, 37, 5, 498–515.

Weissert, W. G. and Hedrick, S.C. (1994), Lessons learned from research on effects of community-based long-term care, *Journal of the American Geriatrics Society*, 42, 348–353.

Weissert, W., Chernew, M. and Hirth, R. (2003) Titrating versus targeting home care services to frail elderly clients, *Journal of Aging and Health*, 15, 99–123.

Wells, Y.D. and Jorm, A.E. (1987) Evaluation of a special nursing home unit for dementia sufferers, *Australian and New Zealand Journal of Psychiatry*, 21, 524–531.

Whitlach, C.J., Feinberg, L.F. and Stevens, E.J. (1999) Predictors of institutionalization for persons with Alzheimer's Disease and the impact on family caregivers, *Journal of Mental Health and Aging*, 5, 3, 275–288.

Willcocks, D., Peace, S. and Kellaher, L. (1987) *Private Lives in Public Places*. Tavistock, London.

Wing, L. (1989) *Hospital Closure and the Resettlement of Residents: The Case of Darenth Park Mental Handicap Hospital*, Avebury, Aldershot.

Wistow, G. (1995) Aspirations and realities: community care at the crossroads. *Health and Social Care in the Community*, 3, 4, 227–40.

Wistow, G. (2000) Home care and the reshaping of acute hospitals in England, *Journal of Management in Medicine*, 14, 1, 7–24.

Wistow, G. and Hardy, B. (1999) The development of domiciliary care: mission accomplished?, *Policy and Politics,* 27, 2, 173–186.

Wistow, G., Knapp, M., Hardy, B. and Allen, C. (1994) *Social Care in a Mixed Economy*, Open University Press, Buckingham.

Wittenberg, R., Pickard, L., Comas-Herrera, A., Davies, B. and Darton, R. (2001) Demand for long-term care for older people in England to 2031, *Health Statistics Quarterly*, 12, 5–17.

Wood, S. (1999) Informal carers of people with dementia: the new national carers framework, *Nursing Standard,* 14, 41–43.

Woods, B. (2008) Residential care, in Woods, B. and Clare, L. (eds) *Handbook of the Clinical Psychology of Ageing, 2nd Edition,* John Wiley and Sons, Chichester.

Woods, B. and Clare, L. (2008) Psychological interventions with people with dementia, in Woods, B. and Clare, L. (eds), *Handbook of the Clinical Psychology of Ageing, 2nd Edition,* John Wiley and Sons, Chichester.

Woolham, J. (2006) Introduction, in Woolham, J. (ed.) *Assistive Technology in Dementia Care: Developing the Role of Technology in the Care and Rehabilitation of People with Dementia – Current Trends and Perspectives,* Hawker Publications, London.

Wright, R., Skelbar, H. and Heiman, J. (1987) Patterns of case management activity in an intensive community support program: the first year, *Community Mental Health Journal,* 23, 1, 53–59.

Yee, J. and Schulz, R. (2000) Gender differences in psychiatric morbidity among family caregivers: A review and analysis, *Gerontologist,* 40, 147–164.

Young, R. and Wistow, G. (1996) *Domiciliary Care Markets: Growth and Stability?* Charhalton Beeches: United Kingdom Home Care Association and Leeds Nuffield Institute for Health, Community Care Division.

Zarit, S. and Edwards, A. (2008) Family caregiving: research and clinical intervention, in Woods, B. and Clare, L. (eds), *Handbook of the Clinical Psychology of Ageing, 2nd Edition*, John Wiley and Sons, Chichester.

Zarit, S. and Femia, E. (2008) A future for family care and dementia intervention research? Challenges and strategies, *Aging and Mental Health,* 12, 5–13.

Zarit S. and Leitsch, S.A. (2001) Developing and evaluating community based intervention programs for Alzheimer's patients and their caregivers, *Aging and Mental Health,* 5, 1, S84–S98.

Zarit, S. and Whitlach, C. (1992) Institutional placement: phases of the transition, *Gerontologist,* 32, 665–672.

Zarit, S. and Zarit, J. (2006) *Mental Disorders in Older Adults: Fundamentals of Assessment and Treatment, Second Edition*, Guildford Press, New York.

Zarit, S., Stephens, M., Townsend, A. and Greene, R. (1998) Stress reduction for family caregivers: Effects of adult day care use, *Journal of Gerontological Social Science,* 53B, S267–S277.

Zarit, S., Gaugler, J. and Jarrott, S. (1999) Useful services for families: research findings and directions, *International Journal of Geriatric Psychiatry,* 14, 3, 165–177.

Zimmerman, S., Sloane, P., Heck, E., Maslow, K. and Schulz, R. (2005) Introduction: Dementia care and quality of life in assisted living and nursing homes, *Gerontologist,* 45, Special Issue 1, 5–7.

Name Index

Subject Index